Inheritance and Wealth
in America

Inheritance and Wealth in America

Edited by

ROBERT K. MILLER, JR.
AND
STEPHEN J. MCNAMEE
University of North Carolina at Wilmington
Wilmington, North Carolina

PLENUM PRESS • NEW YORK AND LONDON

Library of Congress Cataloging-in-Publication Data

Inheritance and wealth in America / edited by Robert K. Miller, Jr.
and Stephen J. McNamee.
        p.   cm.
    Includes bibliographical references and index.
    ISBN 0-306-45652-4
    1. Inheritance and·succession--United States. 2. Wealth--United
States.   I. Miller, Robert K., 1948-   . II. McNamee, Stephen J.,
1950-   .
HB715.I54   1997
330.1'6'0973--dc21   97-35298
                                                                CIP

ISBN 0-306-45652-4

© 1998 Plenum Press, New York
A Division of Plenum Publishing Corporation
233 Spring Street, New York, N.Y. 10013

http://www.plenum.com

Printed in the United States of America

Contributors

RONALD CHESTER • Professor of Law, New England School of Law, 154 Stuart Street, Boston, Massachusetts 02116

REMI P. CLIGNET • ORSTOM, Institut Français de Recherche Scientifique pour le Developpment en Cooperation, 213 Rue La Fayette, 75480 Paris, France

MARTHA BRITTON ELLER • Internal Revenue Service, P.O. Box 2608, Washington, D.C. 20013

JOAN R. GUNDERSEN • Dean of Social Science Division, Elon College, Elon College, North Carolina 27244

PETER DOBKIN HALL • Program on Non-Profit Organizations, Yale University, 88 Trumbull Street, P.O. Box 208253, New Haven, Connecticut 06520

NANCY A. JIANAKOPLOS • Department of Economics, Colorado State University, Fort Collins, Colorado 80525

BARRY W. JOHNSON • Internal Revenue Service, P.O. Box 2608, Washington, D. C. 20013

GEORGE E. MARCUS • Department of Anthropology, Rice University, Houston, Texas 77251

PAUL L. MENCHIK • Department of Economics, Michigan State University, East Lansing, Michigan 48824

ROBERT K. MILLER, JR. • Department of Sociology and Anthropology, University of North Carolina at Wilmington, North Carolina 28403

STEPHEN J. MCNAMEE • Department of Sociology and Anthropology, University of North Carolina at Wilmington, North Carolina 28403

JEFFREY P. ROSENFELD • Department of Sociology, Nassau Community College, Garden City, New York 11530

Preface

The transfer of wealth from one generation to the next is a basic fact of social life that involves key issues that strike at the core of social science — who gets what and how much under what conditions, producing what effects. Inheritance is an integral component of family, economic, and legal institutions, and a basic mechanism of class stratification. It is widely believed that most modern industrial societies, including American society, operate as meritocracies. Much is known about the processes of individual attainment and social mobility within these systems. However, relatively little is known about inheritance as the other different, yet fundamentally important, way that valued resources are distributed. What information on inheritance that is available is scattered among several academic disciplines and is largely inaccessible across their boundaries. This collection of original essays is intended as a general, multidisciplinary, and nontechnical resource that brings together summaries of the most recent work on the small but growing body of literature on inheritance from a variety of disciplinary perspectives, including economics, sociology, history, law, and anthropology.

In the first chapter, we provide an overview of relevant issues related to inheritance and extended summaries of the remaining chapters. In Chapter 2, Ronald Chester — author of the award-winning *Inheritance, Wealth, and Society* — presents an interpretive history of inheritance in American legal thought. Next economists Paul L. Menchik and Nancy A. Jianakoplos critically review the literature on the economics of inheritance at the household and societal levels. In Chapter 4, Barry Johnson and Martha Britton Eller of the Internal Revenue Service present a detailed and interpretive history of federal taxation of inheritance and wealth transfers in the United States. In Chapter 5, an historical case study, Joan R. Gundersen provides a detailed comparison of the place of women in inheritance in Virginia and New York from 1700 to 1860. In Chapter 6, sociologist Remi P. Clignet reviews the literature on the impact of ethnicity on inheritance practices. His work illustrates the continuing difficulties of conceptualization and measurement of ethnicity, of separating the effects of ethnicity from other variables, and, most important, how little we actually know about the effects of ethnicity on inheritance practices. In Chapter 7, Peter Dobkin Hall and George E. Marcus examine the emergence of dynastic wealth and philanthropy in Boston, arguing that these practices have formed the basis of the American pattern in which philanthropy legitmates dynastic wealth holding. In Chapter 8, sociologist Jeffrey P. Rosenfeld takes a look at will contests, examining the conditions under which they are likely to occur and why they remain so infrequent despite major demographic, socioeconomic, and familial structural changes. In the final chapter, we return to a more general discussion of inheritance and its implications for stratification.

This book is intended as a resource volume for anyone interested in the topic of wealth and inheritance. The book may also be useful as a supplemental text for courses in stratification, kinship, macroeconomics, and other related areas that in some way deal with the process of the transmission of wealth and privilege across generations.

We have numerous intellectual debts, most of which cannot possibly be acknowledged here. Most generally, the University of North Carolina at Wilmington provided institutional support for the completion of this project. We also acknowledge the generous support and patience of our collegues in the Department of Sociology and Anthropology, who listened as we "thought aloud" while we worked our way through our first experience as editors. We thank the contributors for their fine chapters and their cooperation in meeting our deadlines. We especially thank Jeffrey Rosenfeld for his positive spirit, unwavering support, and sound advice on the project as a whole. We also would like to acknowledge the excellent work of Eliot Werner and the editorial staff at Plenum, who have made putting this work together as painless as possible. We would like to thank our wives, Mary Susan Miller and Christine McNamee, for their ongoing support of our professional endeavors. Finally, we would like to dedicate our efforts on this project to our respective children — Emory Miller, Gregory McNamee, and Catherine McNamee — who, unfortunately, stand to inherit little wealth from us. Each, however, has inherited from us a full measure of parental love which, in the end, is all that most of us can hope to receive and bequeath.

Contents

1. The Inheritance of Wealth in America 1

Robert K. Miller, Jr. and Stephen J. McNamee

2. Inheritance in American Legal Thought 23

Ronald Chester

3.   Economics of Inheritance   45

Paul L. Menchik and Nancy J. Jianakoplos

4.   Federal Taxation of Inheritance and Wealth Transfers   61

Barry W. Johnson and Martha Britton Eller

5.   Women and Inheritance in America: Virginia and New York as a Case Study, 1700–1860   91

Joan R. Gundersen

6.   Ethnicity and Inheritance   119

Remi P. Clignet

7. Why Should Men Leave Great Fortunes to Their Children? Dynasty and Inheritance in America   139

Peter Dobkin Hall and George E. Marcus

8. Will Contests: Legacies of Aging and Social Change   173

Jeffrey P. Rosenfeld

9. Inheritance and Stratification 193

Stephen J. McNamee and Robert K. Miller, Jr.

1

The Inheritance of Wealth in America

ROBERT K. MILLER, JR. AND STEPHEN J. MCNAMEE

Introduction

A central fact of social life is that when people die, whatever personal property they have managed to accumulate over their lifetimes is left behind. Since death is inevitable and since "you can't take it with you," societies establish rules for the disposition of property at death. This book is about how such property transfers occur in American society.

Americans are ambivalent about inheritance. On the one hand, they seem to enthusiastically embrace an ideology of individual opportunity based upon merit (Huber and Form, 1973; Kluegel and Smith, 1986; Ryan, 1981). According to this dominant ideology, getting ahead in America is a matter of individual achievement—people get out of the system what they put into it. The system is fair and opportunity is limited only by the extent of one's ability.

On the other hand, Americans simultaneously endorse the right of individuals to bequeath estates to designated heirs. According to the principle of testamentary freedom, individuals should be able to dispose of their accumulated property at death as they see fit. Inheritance and merit, however, are incompatible ways to distribute valued resources in society. To the extent that resources are distributed on the basis of inheritance, they are not distributed

ROBERT K. MILLER, JR. AND STEPHEN J. MCNAMEE • Department of Sociology and Anthropology, University of North Carolina at Wilmington, Wilmington, North Carolina 28403-3297.

Inheritance and Wealth in America, edited by Robert K. Miller, Jr., and Stephen J. McNamee. Plenum Press, New York, 1998.

on the basis of merit. These contradictory ways to distribute valued resources pose a fundamental dilemma between freedom of choice at the individual level and equality of opportunity at the societal level.

For the most part, American stratification research has focused on income over wealth and occupational attainment over inheritance (McNamee and Miller, 1989). Relatively little attention has been paid to the transfer of wealth across generations. Recently, however, there has been a flurry of interest in this area of investigation (McCubbin and Rosenfeld, 1989; Rossi and Rossi, 1990; Clignet, 1992; Oliver and Shapiro, 1995; Burkhauser and Gertler, 1995). This volume is intended to bring together summaries of some of the most recent work on the small but growing body of literature on inheritance from a variety of disciplinary perspectives, including economics, sociology, history, law, and anthropology.

Inheritance is an integral component of family, economic, and legal institutions, and a basic mechanism of class stratification. A complex phenomenon, its study calls for an interdisciplinary approach. Economists are most interested in how inheritance affects savings, consumption, investment, and employment decisions at the individual level and how inheritance affects the distribution of wealth at the societal level. Legal scholars are interested in fundamental justifications and location of the "rights" of inheritance and in its regulation through state and federal taxation. Historians have traced the development of inheritance practices, as well as how and why these have changed over time and have varied from place to place. Sociologists are primarily interested in how inheritance affects the internal dynamics of families and how inheritance practices impact the class system. Like sociologists, anthropologists are interested in how inheritance affects families, and in its connections with systems of kinship and more general patterns of social organization. As an introduction to this body of work, we will present an overview of some of the central issues that have emerged from these investigations, then present a brief summary of each chapter.

The total cumulative effect of inheritance on stratification outcomes takes three forms. The first form of inheritance is the inheritance of cultural capital. Cultural capital is generally defined as proficiency in and familiarity with dominant cultural codes, outlooks, predispositions, and practices, including linguistic styles, aesthetic preferences, and styles of interaction (Bourdieu, 1973; Bourdieu and Passeron, 1977). While cultural capital is not simply supplied or purchased by parents for their children, the motivation and ability of parents to assist their children in its acquisition vary by social class. Thus, their social class standing constitutes a strong base of differential opportunities for access to cultural capital. As children mature within the class-based social worlds of their parents, the cultural capital to which they are exposed expands to include the type of formal education received, informal and supplementary educational experiences, and class-based friendships. In short, cultural capital is an important resource, and individuals inherit differential opportunities for its acquisition. Since cultural capital is required for entry and acceptance into higher status social circles, lack of cultural capital for individuals from modest social backgrounds poses a significant impediment to their prospects for upward social mobility. In this way, barriers of entry are created and existing forms of inequality are reinforced.

A second way in which advantages are passed on from one generation to the next is through familial interventions in the form of *inter vivos* transfers (gifts between the living) especially at crucial junctures in the life course, or what Oliver and Shapiro (1995) refer to as "milestone life events." Broadly conceived, *inter vivos* gifts can include parental care and support (advice, comfort, help during illness), domestic help (fixing things, making things, home chores, child care), or instrumental help (special gifts, job leads, money) (Rossi and Rossi, 1990). Although *inter vivos* gifts are given to children thoughout the life course, those given to children at "milestone" stages—going to college, getting a job, getting married, purchasing a first home, establishing a business, having children of their own—have an especially critical impact on children's life circumstances.

In the modern era, financing education has become an increasingly important form of *inter vivos* giving. In preindustrial societies, most children worked on family farms or for family businesses and learned what occupational skills they would need as adults primarily from their parents. In the modern era, parental investment in enhancing the human capital of children through formal education has replaced the inheritance of the family farm or the family business as the major form of intergenerational wealth transfer (Langbein, 1991). Because access to educational opportunities is stratified, so is the ability of parents to provide this access (Collins, 1979; Bowles and Gintis, 1976). Parents also often provide help to adult children during crisis periods and catastrophic life events such as injury, illness, unemployment, or other setbacks that would otherwise result in downward mobility. This type of familial assistance provides a powerful yet largely hidden means of transmitting privilege across generations. The family "safety net" thus insulates its members from the vicissitudes of market forces and erodes the effect of strictly individual merit factors on life chances and life circumstances.

The third form of inheritance is the transfer of bulk estates at the time of death of the testators. This type of inheritance is the type most people think of when they think about inheritance and is the primary subject of this volume. While we recognize the importance of the other forms of inheritance, we have focused on estate inheritance as a first step in understanding the full effect of the inheritance factor on stratification outcomes.

With an average life expectancy currently in the midseventies, this form of inheritance is now not typically received by adult children until they are themselves in their fifties and sixties. Nevertheless, this form of inheritance can result in significant economic advantage accruing to adult children, especially in the case of large estates. Recent studies (Oliver and Shapiro, 1995; Smith, 1995) estimate that about 30 percent of the population receives some form of estate inheritance. These estates, however, are highly skewed in terms of size, with large amounts received by a relatively small percentage of the population.

Clearly, there is considerable cultural and historical variation in the specific patterns of inheritance related to (1) the timing of transfers (*inter vivos* vs. testamentary transfers), (2) the size or amount of wealth transferred, (3) the form/kind of property transferred, and (4) the proportionality of distribution among siblings (equal vs. unequal). Numerous other important issues have emerged in the study of estate inheritance, many of which remain unresolved. For example, is inheritance a natural right (which the state should not abridge) or a civil right (not existing in nature but a privilege granted by the state and subject to its regulation)? To whom do testators bequeath their estates, and what are their motivations for doing so? What are the specific mechanisms of transfer, and what factors affect allocation decisions? In what ways are heirs affected by the receipt of estates? How do inheritance practices differ between men and women, among different ethnic groups, and by social class? How does estate inheritance affect family dynamics? Under what conditions are estates likely to be contested or are family members likely to be disinherited? What are the economic impacts of inheritance for individuals and for society as a whole? How has inheritance law developed and changed over time, and what are the causes of these changes? How are inheritance taxes levied (and avoided), and how does this affect testamentary behavior? These and related questions reflect the variety and scope of the questions addressed in the chapters in this book, each of which is briefly summarized below.

Inheritance in American Legal Thought

In Chapter 2, Ronald Chester outlines inheritance in American legal thought. He notes that from the time of the Revolution, American legal thinkers have viewed both the rights to transmit and to receive property at the death of its owner as *civil* or *positivistic*—rights created and regulated by the state—not as *natural* rights. Laws of succession to property were simply formalizations of customs that were pragmatic ways to avoid the "endless disturbances" that might otherwise develop. This utilitarian view saw inheritance law as a tool useful to civil society in reallocating the rights of an individual no longer alive. Thus, the views of Thomas Jefferson and others of the revolutionary generation, grounded in the work of British utilitarians, argued that letting the dead control property was a danger to be strictly controlled by society, that the earth belongs to the living, and that the dead have neither powers nor rights over it. By the midnineteenth century, America courts were consistent in applying this Jeffersonian, positivistic view, and the declaration of the civil as opposed to natural origin of these rights became the mainstay in the power of the states to tax inheritance.

Chester next presents a nuanced outline of the evolution of legal rationalism from the late eighteenth to midnineteenth century. What emerged was a separation of inheritance rights from property rights, such that lifetime property rights were strongly defended as deeper and more fundamental, based upon a combination of natural, positive, and common law. Inheritance rights were separate, quite different from property rights, and more limited by government (civil) power. He implies that this position represents a compromise of sorts—the outcome of conflict between interests of the propertied classes represented by a judicial elite and those of a more egalitarian (and less propertied) majority represented by (Jacksonian) democratic legislatures.

Chester next discusses legislative control of interitance through regulation and taxation, and judicial responses to such legislation. He argues that from midnineteenth century, Supreme Court decisions consistently separated the civil institution of inheritance from property itself. Heirs did not possess a natural right to inherit; the right to take property by devise or descent is the creature of the law, and not a natural right, and taxes on inheritance were not direct taxes on people's property, but indirect duties on the process of transferring that property from the dead to the living. By the end of the nineteenth century, the natural right to property had been reduced to its specific enumeration in the Constitution and Bill of Rights, and bequest and succession were specifically guaranteed neither in the Fifth or Fourteenth amendment nor in the Constitution as a whole.

Chester suggests that growth of social and economic inequality during the latter part of the nineteenth century provided increasing popular support for the limitation of inheritance through taxation. He argues that while ultimately resulting in little actual control of inheritance other than by taxation, the positivist view of inheritance continued to dominate the natural rights view well into the twentieth century. He presents *Irving Trust v. Day* (1942) as the most influential statement that both the rights to transmit and to succeed to property at death were not natural or constitutionally protected rights, but rights freely alterable at the whim of Congress or legislature.

Historically, the positivist view has been dominant, but the natural rights view has persisted in our legal and political thought in a subordinate role. Recently, the positivist view has been challenged by the decision handed down in *Hodel v. Irving* (1987), which appears to reverse the long-dominant positivist view. Chester presents an outline of the facts of this watershed case, reaction to it, and a reading of the decision that limits its radical potential.

At issue in *Irving* was the excessive fragmentation of Indian lands, which had occurred since the Dawes Act of 1887. To rectify the division of parcels into tiny noneconomic units, Congress passed the Indian Land Consolidation Act of 1983, which provided for escheat (forfeit) to the tribe of units below a certain size and value at the death of the property holder. The Court unanimously declared that the right to pass on property at death is a significant, constitutionally protected property right. On the facts of the case, the Court decided that the Act totally abrogated this right to pass on property, was a regulatory "taking" of property, and since the statute failed to provide compensation for this "taking," it was unconstitutional as written. Chester argues that the Court's constitutional protection of the right of disposition in *Hodel v. Irving* is akin to declaring "dead-hand control" of property a natural right, and that *Irving* is thus potentially revolutionary.

He argues that the conservative revolution of the 1980s produced *Irving*, and that a nostalgic desire for a return to an unrestrained individualism happily producing wealth in a context of a laissez-faire state was the hallmark of the Reagan years. Chester points out what he regards as fundamental flaws in this vision, but more important, attempts to draw the connections between the legal institutional change represented by *Irving* and larger changes occurring in the political economy. In short, in the legal field, *Hodel v. Irving* is the logical outgrowth of this conservative revolution, itself the product of larger political-economic change.

Chester further points out that *Hodel v. Irving* implies that *devise*, the less established of the two rights of descent and devise, may be the only right finally protected. Furthermore, the opinion seems to suggest that it is the practical unfeasibility in this case of *inter vivos* transfers that renders the statute unconstitutional. In short, abolition of both descent and devise of a particular class of property may be taking in circumstances where alternative means of passing property at death were not realistically available. Thus, as long as Congress or legislatures leave open the route of *inter vivos* will substitutes, the opinion appears to allow continued regulation of the right to devise by will.

For Chester, the case of *Hodel v. Irving* symbolizes American inheritance law at a crossroads. The positivist tradition is certainly threatened by the case, and the long-subordinate natural rights view of inheritance is potentially greatly strengthened. But coming near the end of the "Reagan Revolution," the case may have stated the extreme individualistic view of inheritance just at the time such ideas had begun to fade. Chester concludes that for those interested in the long and fascinating attempt of America to square elite interests in inheritance with the nation's egalitarianism, what happens to this case as precedent over the next few years should be carefully watched.

The Economics of Inheritance

In Chapter 3, Paul L. Menchik and Nancy A. Jianakoplos outline basic issues in the economics of inheritance. Economists have been concerned with inheritance at both economywide and household levels. At the economywide level, the main focus has been attempts to determine the proportion of total wealth in the economy that is received as an inheritance or accumulated with the intent to bequeath. At the household level, the main focus is on determining the motivation for making bequests.

Menchik and Jianakoplos first discuss several distinctions that are important in the conceptualization of inheritance: *inter vivos* transfers versus bequests, human (capital) versus nonhuman wealth, and intended versus unintended bequests. Lack of data has hindered attempts to quantify the relative importance of bequests and *inter vivos* transfers. Economists tend to limit their studies of inheritance to transmission of tangible financial assets, but there is disagreement about whether parental financing of college education, which enhances "human capital" and provides returns in the form of higher earnings, should be treated as an intergenerational transfer. Finally, unintended bequests result from precautionary motives rather than bequest motives. Those who die earlier than anticipated leave some accumulated wealth to heirs that otherwise would have been consumed if life had continued as expected.

Economic wealth arises from two sources: inherited wealth—accumulated by previous generations and transferred to the current generation—and life-cycle wealth—accumulated by saving out of current income. Menchik and Jianakoplos discuss the two basic methods—direct and indirect—used to estimate the proportion of total wealth that is inherited. They outline the problems inherent in each and note the ongoing controversy over the proportion of accumulated wealth that was inherited. Different methods tend to produce different estimates. The "law of 20/80" refers to the fact that current best estimates suggest that inherited wealth could represent as little as 20 percent or as much as 80 percent of total wealth.

Government policy to influence the amount of saving and thus the potential for future economic growth will vary depending on whether saving is done to bequeath wealth or to finance retirement. Government programs that have an impact on resources available during retirement, such as Social Security, will have a significant impact on economic growth if most saving is done to finance retirement. Finally, policies designed to affect the degree of economic equality will vary in effectiveness depending on whether most wealth is inherited or the result of self-acculmulation. For example, estate taxes would have a much larger equalizing impact if most wealth is the result of intergenerational transfers rather than self-accumulation.

Economists have also been concerned with inheritance at the individual household level. Although the total dollar amount of inheritances is substantial, only a small percentage of all households are involved. Of course, the very wealthy are much more likely to report having received a bequest and to have made or received *inter vivos* transfers, many of which are quite substantial.

A number of theories have been advanced to explain household motivation to leave a bequest. With respect to planned bequests, *altruistic, exchange*, and *strategic* models have been developed. Altruistic models hypothesize that individuals care about the well-being of future generations and that leaving bequests provides satisfaction. Exchange models suggest that bequests are in fact payments made in order to motivate the behavior of the recipients. In exchange models, parents "purchase" annuities from their children, with the price being a bequest paid in return for support during the old age of the parent. Parents thus use bequests as a way to pay their children for care received late in life. Finally, strategic models of bequest assume that parents are indifferent to the welfare of children and suggest that they use bequests as a way to control their children's behavior using the threat of disinheritance. In addition to theory testing, research has also provided a body of factual information concerning the size and distribution of inheritance.

Although considerable research has focused on the motivation of the *givers* of bequests, there has been less research on the impact of the *receipt* of an inheritance. Receipt of an inheritance tends to reduce the hours worked by the recipient, but amount of work-effort reduction remains unresolved.

Although these theories are not mutually exclusive and people may be acting on a combination of motives, the predominance of one or the other type of motivation for making bequests does have a number of important policy implications. For example, bequests are more likely to be wealth equalizing if they are made for altruistic purposes rather than for the purpose of exchange. At a more basic level, the very existence of a bequest motive is central to resolving whether the government's budget deficit has an impact on economic activity.

Federal Taxation of Inheritance and Wealth Transfers

In Chapter 4, Barry W. Johnson and Martha Britton Eller present a history of Federal inheritance and estate taxation. They review the origins of the continuing controversy over transfer taxation—whether inheritance should be considered a "right" or a "privilege," which in turn is rooted in arguments concerning the source and limits of property rights. Following the British utilitarians, the prevailing legal opinion in America has been that inheritance is a state-granted privilege subject to regulation by the state; that is, property ownership ends at death, and the government has the right to regulate the transfer of property at death. This view has provided the fundamental legal justification for estate taxation until the *Hodel v. Irving* (1987) case in which the U.S. Supreme Court seemed to reverse this long-standing view of inheritance as a civil right by proclaiming that inheritance is a constitutionally protected natural right that the state cannot abridge.

In reviewing the early history of federal estate taxation, Johnson and Eller note that Federal death taxes were invoked primarily as means to raise needed revenue to finance war efforts. Federal death taxes were first established through the Stamp Tax of 1797. These taxes were levied in order to help finance the undeclared naval war with France. Following the end of this conflict, the taxes were repealed. Resurrection of the death tax was proposed again in 1815 to provide revenue for the war with England, but the Treaty of Ghent ended the war while the tax was still under consideration and it was subsequently dropped. Federal inheritance tax was again enacted in the Tax Act of 1862 to raise funds to finance the costs of the Civil War. The discharge of postwar debts gradually eliminated the need for this extra revenue, and the tax was repealed in 1870.

In the latter part of the nineteenth century, changes brought about by the industrial revolution, including the concentration of wealth and the perpetuation of wealth through bequests, led to renewed discussion of inheritance and the role of government in its regulation. Populists, some economists, and even the wealthy industrialist Andrew Carnegie, urged limits on rights of individuals to bequeath property to heirs, including tax on inheritances as a proper limiting mechanism. Defenders of material accumulation and the right to bequeath wealth to successive generations found refuge in social Darwinism. Reforms achieved the passage of the Income Tax Act of 1894, which called for a graduated tax on personal property acquired by gift or inheritance. This Act, however, was quickly appealed to the Supreme Court and declared unconstitutional as an unapportioned direct tax.

In response to the need for additional state revenue with the onset of World War I, Congress reintroduced a federal estate tax in 1916. This tax was applied to net estates, defined as the total property owned by a decedent— the gross estate—less deductions. The basic structure of this modern federal estate tax, as well as the law from which it is derived, has remained largely unchanged. However, since then, Congress has enacted several important additions to, and revisions of, this structure; there have also been occasional adjustments to the filing thresholds, tax brackets, and marginal tax rates. The most significant change in the basic estate tax structure was adopted through the Tax Reform Act of 1976. This Act created a unified estate and gift tax framework that consisted of a single, graduated rate of tax imposed on both lifetime gift and testamentary dispositions, thereby eliminating the cost differential that had existed between the two types of giving. Prior to the Act, it cost substantially more to leave property at death than to give it away during life, due to the lower tax rate applied to *inter vivos* gifts. The act also introduced a tax on generation-skipping transfers by adding a set of rules designed to treat the termination of the intervening beneficiaries' interests as a taxable event, ensuring that the transmission of hereditary wealth is taxed at each generation level. With various subsequent refinements and subtle adjustments to basic estate tax structure, the federal tax system became increasingly complex.

As the federal transfer tax system has become more complex, individuals have increasingly turned to estate planners for tax-minimization strategies. Estate planners, in turn, keep their clients apprised of tax-law changes that may have an adverse effect on testamentary arrangements already in place. Thus, estate planning has become more of a process than a one-time event. Federal estate taxes encourage individuals to begin transferring wealth well before death in order to minimize the size of estates. Lifetime giving may be an important component of an individual's overall bequest strategy, and children are usually the primary recipients of these transfers.

The current transfer tax system, including estate, gift and generation-skipping transfer taxes, preserved in a form that differs little from its origins, continues to generate debate and criticism. There is resentment over the use of transfer taxes as a source of revenue and as a tool for influencing the distribution of personal wealth. Some economists argue that by reducing the incentive that people have to save and invest, transfer taxation reduces capital formation which, in turn, reduces wages and job creation from what they would otherwise be. Transfer taxes also often are cited as impediments to the livelihood of small businesses and farms. Furthermore, it is clear that the scope of the transfer tax system is quite narrow: It neither provides a significant portion of federal budget inlays nor subjects a significant portion of the population to federal taxation. Finally, the estate tax is "voluntary" in the sense that far from imposing an unavoidable tax, estate tax law actually provides numerous methods for tax avoidance. One critic concludes that because estate-tax avoidance is such a successful and yet wasteful process, the present estate and gift tax serves no purpose other than to give reassurance to the millions of unwealthy that entrenched wealth is being attacked. The annual costs of estate-tax avoidance represent a large percentage of the annual receipts from estate and gift taxes.

Chester's review of the historical conflict in American legal thought between those who regard inheritance as a component of *natural* property rights, and therefore protected from government regulation, and those who regard inheritance as a *civil* right, and thus a "privilege" that can be regulated by the state, revealed that although historically the positivist position has been dominant, the struggle has not been resolved. Johnson and Eller agree, suggesting that the lack of consensus concerning government regulation and taxation of wealth transfers and the role such transfer taxes should play in the federal revenue system is due in part to these larger differences in political-economic philosophy. They conclude that these differences over the economic effects and propriety of transfer taxes, and over government's part in promoting the welfare of its citizens through their use, are not likely to be resolved soon.

Women and Inheritance

In Chapter 5, historian Joan R. Gundersen's case study of women and inheritance compares Virginia and New York from 1700 to 1860. She contends that study of the rights of women to hold, control, inherit, and alienate property in Virginia and New York can illuminate the ways that community values, formal law, and socioeconomic conditions affected such rights. Although no two states can be taken as "representative" of American society, New York and Virginia provide good case studies: Both were large, populous, economically and politically important, with functioning traditions of equity and common law. Gundersen emphasizes that families chose their inheritance strategies in response to the legal options available to them, but manipulated formal legal inheritance provisions to reach desired social outcomes. Only when they could no longer adequately manipulate existing forms were new legal forms affecting inheritance introduced.

Gundersen argues that the 1540 Statute of Wills and the English common law doctrines of heir-at-law, coverture, and dower lie at the heart of the inheritance systems of New York and Virginia by the mideighteenth century. These limited women's inheritance rights and control of property. She then outlines how women were affected by colonial inheritance law. During this period, the death of a married woman without a separate estate had little effect on property transfers because her husband already owned all personal property. The only sure way for a woman to benefit from an inheritance was to be single. Notwithstanding, the increasing, albeit informal, use of equity law during the colonial period provided women rights to retain control of their inheritances, including rights to create and control a separate estate, and to devise property in trust.

Gundersen notes that many individuals died without making wills because they legally had no status to transfer property: women without a separate estate, the poor, slaves, and children. Others, who were content with the distribution of property under the intestate laws, did not need to write wills. Of the small minority who could write wills, a large proportion chose to do so. Although women generally received the equivalent or more than what they would have received under intestate measures, their control over, and share in, estates declined during the colonial period. The changing pattern of bequests to widows in the eighteenth century reveals a growing assumption that woman's proper role was as a dependent within a family, as exemplified by bequests that stipulated provision for maintenance rather than control of property.

During the Revolutionary era, changes occurred, including the elimination of primogeniture, that made property more fluid and put sons and daughters on a more equal footing. Other changes, however, including the erosion of dower rights and the redefinition of slaves as personal property (thus becoming the husband's at marriage), placed even greater limitations on married women's inheritances. Also during this period there were changes in inheritance rights for illegitimate children, and these affected women more than men.

In the nineteenth century, Virginia and New York families chose very different strategies to achieve the same end—protection of women's inheritances from bad management by a husband. Their concern was protecting a family inheritance passed to a daughter rather than assuring equity for widows as contributors to a marriage. In Virginia, changes in inheritance law to give daughters and younger sons a greater share came at the expense of widows. Families concerned about protection of daughters turned to equity law. There was a rise in the use of antenuptial and postnuptial agreements in equity, which reserved rights to property for married women. In an agricultural society with much wealth held in the form of human capital, these provisions worked reasonably well.

In New York, the growing commercial economy led the legislature first to give males more control over assets held in a marriage, and then to eliminate most equity protections for women. However, under the economically volatile conditions of the period, families worried that their daughter's inheritance might quickly be lost to claims of her husband's creditors. Given that women also were making more independent marriage choices, and thus fathers had less say in the selection of sons-in-law, concern rose about the ability of sons-in-law to manage wisely. Under such conditions, coverture seemed a dangerous tradition to families concerned about their daughters' financial security. As a result, New York became a pioneer in developing women's separate estates through statute. The Married Women's Property Act of 1848 gave a married woman the right to inherit real and personal property directly from persons other than her husband; such property was not subject to disposal by her husband, and she was not liable for his debts. Virginia did not pass a similar measure until after the Civil War. With slavery gone and a cash-based, commercial economy growing, equity and entail no longer were equal to the task of protecting women's inheritances. By the end of the century, most states had passed Married Women's Property Acts. Further pressure to change the legal structures of inheritance dissipated. Not until the feminist movement, reorganized in the 1960s, would serious agitation for more equal laws result in legal change.

In conclusion, Gundersen notes that both Virginia and New York adopted much of English traditional law on inheritance. Colonists turned to the law of wills to modify inheritance practices that favored sons over daughters, and older sons over younger ones. They also adopted practices of equity law, which provided some opportunity to mitigate the disabilities of coverture for married women. Although these decisions set the parameters for women's inheritance in the late colonial period in the two colonies, even more important were familial definitions of desirable outcomes. Late-colonial families were more interested in seeing their children well settled with property than they were in recognizing a wife's contribution to the family estate. Thus, families increasingly chose to limit widows' inheritances and control of estates in favor of their children. Changes during the revolution further reduced women's inheritances.

Despite the differences in legal strategies chosen in the antebellum period, Gundersen concludes that the reality of women's inheritance was quite similar in Virginia and New York. In both states, conservative male courts and legislatures ensured that law reinforced the assumptions of women's dependence by reducing women's control of estates, and in both states widows continued to receive reduced inheritances in order to give children more. Thus, although the tools used were different, the outcomes were the same, because New York and Virginia men shared common ideas about who within their families should own and control different kinds of property. Having eliminated legal preferences for sons over daughters in inheritance and secured the rights of married women to control inheritances they received as daughters, the states had no incentive to recognize the wife as her husband's equal in inheritance. In a brief Afterword, Gundersen notes some important changes in inheritance law since the Civil War that have affected women. For example, most states, even community property states, eventually adopted Married Women's Property Acts. More recently, in response to the feminist movement, many states revised inheritance laws to comply with the Equal Rights Amendment, assuming its evenual passage.

Ethnicity and Inheritance

In Chapter 6, sociologist Remi P. Clignet assesses the influence of ethnicity on the acquisition and transfer of wealth in contemporary America. His review of the literature reveals continuing problems with respect to the conceptualization and measurement of ethnicity and the dangers of generalizing from a few case studies, based as they are on comparisons of pairs of groups, single occupations (farmers), and specific locations (ecological and economic conditions) and time periods. Problems of separating the effects of ethnicity from class, historical period, economic, and other variables illustrate the dangers of using case studies for explanatory rather than simply descriptive purposes.

Clignet points out that whereas some sociologists focus on material and objective factors governing the acquisition and transfer of wealth and others emphasize symbolic and subjective forces, both sets of factors must be considered. He then discusses the conditions under which ethnicity or national origin remains likely to influence the formation of individual wealth and its transfer to heirs. The impact of ethnicity varies by socioeconomic status; it is strongest among ethnics of low socioeconomic status and weakest among wealthy ethnic testators, whose inheritance practices should be more "rational." He argues that ethnic effects are a function of time (maximal for newly arrived immigrants and eroding for subsequent generations), residential and occupational concentration, and frequency and form of exogamic marriages.

In a brief section on ethnicity and ownership, Clignet notes ethnic group variation in preference for forms of assets and recipes for their acquisition, using home ownership and life insurance as examples. These are a function of variation in practices transplanted from the Old World, the impacts of which attenuate as groups gain less restricted access to the full spectrum of economic opportunities. Clignet next reviews studies, including his own (1992), that reveal ethnic differences in testamentary behavior, including variation in proportion of estates filed testate, equal versus unequal distribution among heirs, the effect of family size on equality of distribution, and the use of *inter vivos* gifts.

Clignet presents a detailed discussion of the relations between ethnicity and the treatment of heirs. He states that the concept of heritage embodies a set of norms that governs the manner in which decedents split the assets that form their estate as a function of their value and their functions, the birth order and gender of all the eligible heirs, and the needs, capabilities or responsibilities of these heirs. Although the sociological evidence is scanty, a review of several studies suggests ethnic variation in terms of a number of factors, including (1) differentiation of shares and criteria used for such differentiation (income vs. nonincome producing), (2) unigeniture or equality of shares, (3) birth order and gender of heirs, (4) kind and value of bequests to children born to successive marriages, (5) rationales invoked for rewarding or punishing particular heirs, (6) reliance on efficiency or altruism as a factor in heir selection, (7) role of marital status of sons and daughters in bequest decisions, and (8) role of reciprocal service in bequest decisions.

Clignet concludes that ethnic identities continue to affect instruments of transfer used to bequeath estates, selection of heirs, and the nature as well as the amount of shares distributed. He maintains that the causes of the persisting influence of ethnicity are twofold. First, it results from competition among immigrant groups and resulting differences in their socioeconomic success and status ranking. Second, American forms of political decentralization encourage cultural diversity. According to Clignet, the persisting impact of ethnicity on the creation and transfer of domestic wealth in America suggests two additional theoretical points. First, the reproduction at work in processes of intergenerational transfers has become less mechanical and increasingly interpretative. In short, the logic underlying transfers is independent of their specific material nature. Second, given that the impact of ethnicity on inheritance declines with the passage of time, it remains necessary to explain the pace of the process and to ascertain whether it follows linear or nonlinear patterns.

For Clignet, the perpetuation of ethnic identity lies at the very juncture of a sociological time, which is made of the repetition of cycles, and an historical time, which is made of unpredictable discontinuities. This juncture is not necessarily the same for the three aspects of inheritance considered; that is, technological, legal, or economic innovations do not strike simultaneously and/or with the same intensity the models that govern the acquisition of wealth, the use of pertinent instruments of transfer, and the nature of the transfers themselves.

Dynasty, Philanthropy, and Inheritance

In Chapter 7, "Why Should Men Leave Great Fortunes to Their Children? Class Dynasty and Inheritance in America," Peter Dobkin Hall and George E. Marcus discuss shifts in ethos and practice of wealth transmission in America. They agree with Langbein (1991) that three important changes have occurred (1) in *timing*, from testamentary to *inter vivos* transfers, (2) in *form* of inheritance, from tangible property (family farm or firm) to provision of financial means (stocks, bonds, bank deposits, mutual fund shares, insurance contracts) to accumulate human capital (educational training and credentials), and (3) *ethos* among the wealthy, from aristocratic forms to token inheritances that emphasize that children should "make it on their own."

Hall and Marcus argue that although this overall assessment of changing patterns in American wealth transmission is substantially correct, the shift from transfer of assets to investment in human capital and the "new ethos of inheritance" are not particularly new. They argue that the fundamental elements of this "revolution" actually emerged over the course of the past century and a half as strategies in the formation of Boston's elite were elaborated by the managers of dynastic family fortunes in the late nineteenth and early twentieth centuries, and in our own time became models for the population as a whole.

Family founders in the early Republic appear to have viewed trusts as a promising solution to the challenges of passing wealth intact between generations while also ensuring that the capital it represented remained undivided and available for investment. A trust estate could be left in the care of a trustee who would manage and invest it for the benefit of a testator's descendants. The property itself would remain undivided—but the descendants would receive, in more or less equal portions, shares in parental estate that they had reason to expect.

The creation of a legal environment favorable to trusts was the achievement of Boston's emerging Brahminate. They did not want to create an aristocracy along European lines; despite their growing wealth, they continued to see themselves as working merchants. Largely self-made men, they recognized that their continuing vitality depended on the ability to recruit talented outsiders. Only Boston's emergent elite were successful at striking a balance between desire for exclusivity (the need to define themselves as a group and to pool their resources) and the need for inclusivity (the need to recruit talented outsiders and to ensure that only the most competent of their own progeny assumed positions of responsibility). Although New York and Philadelphia were both larger and richer, enjoying greater access to natural resources and interior markets, their religious divisions and imperfect legal architecture hampered the capacity of their elites to pool their resources for either economic or institutional purposes.

Still very much engaged in making their money, the early Boston families had not yet acquired a distinct class identity. They were civically active, but to the extent that they conceived of themselves as a group at all, they appear to have framed their common purposes in public rather than private terms. The scope, scale, and unremitting growth of their wealth, however, made it increasingly difficult to sustain the fiction that they were merely the "better off" portion of an unstratified community. They were not only rich, but also their wealth—thanks to trusts, to its increasingly corporate character, and to the growing extent to which its competent management was becoming distinguished from its use—seemed to become more permanent with each succeeding generation. As this occurred, spokesmen for the group became increasingly preoccupied with the problem of selecting and training competent leaders and managers, and justifying the fact of possession in terms of the dominant egalitarian and democratic values of American society.

Boston's elite responded to these challenges by further increasing its commitment to the city's charitable and educational institutions. In part, this commitment represented an elaboration of the need to maintain and extend its public influence. Also, as more sons chose professional careers in preference to business, elite support of education helped to enhance the status of professions and itself became a form of wealth transmission. As young businessmen and professionals built their careers, service on corporate and charitable boards became regarded as important indicators of leadership ability as well as testing grounds for advancement to greater responsibilities in the worlds of commerce and charity. Brahmin wealth not only transformed and elevated Harvard and a constellation of other Boston institutions to national significance and set the pattern for elite philanthropy that would profoundly affect other aspiring metropolitan ruling classes, but also facilitated the creation of a class based on educational credentials—the new middle class of professionals and managers.

The industrial fortunes built up after the Civil War dwarfed the accumulations of those that preceded them. The fortune founders of the Gilded Age, like their predecessors, attempted to justify themselves in terms of a role of service to the public. But rather than seeking legitimacy at the *metropolitan* level and in the *past*, they sought it at the *national* level and in the *future*.

Hall and Marcus argue that the most fully developed model for the institutionalization of the great new fortunes was framed by John D. Rockefeller, who pioneered the mechanisms which, while nominally allowing wealth to remain under the control of the family, placed it increasingly under the management of experts who coordinated the family's investments, philanthropy, and public relations. Like the fiduciary management of their money, management of the collective identity of dynastic families has also come to exceed the capacity and competence of their own members, necessitating the involvement of expert outsiders. The study of dynasties and dynastic inheritance practices thus becomes an investigation of interfaces of public and private power—and of the ways in which public and private dimensions of family mission and identity inevitably overlap. Hall and Marcus conclude that great fortunes have both a public and private character, mixing the management of great private wealth with stewardship of the philanthropic institutions that justified the families' existence in terms of public purpose.

In a Reprise, Hall and Marcus remind us that a new generation of fortunes has come into being since World War II. They are perplexed by what they see as a lack of vision of this "new money," claiming that it has distinguished itself, not by a *new* ethos of inheritance, but by its *lack* of an ethos—its lack of commitment to anything beyond maximizing returns on investment over the short term.

Will Contests

In Chapter 8, Jeffrey P. Rosenfeld examines the incidence and changing causes of will contests in contemporary America. He argues that disinheritance and will contests are deviant components of the inheritance system—violations of inheritance norms that respresent breakdown in family solidarity. Disinheritance is an intentional departure from the norm of intergenerational continuity and is deviant behavior of the *benefactor*, whereas a will contest is deviant behavior of *beneficiaries*. He focuses on will contests because disinheritance has become increasingly rare.

Rosenfeld emphasizes that from judicial, economic, and social perspectives, estate litigation is deviant behavior. Beneficiaries are under enormous pressure not to litigate over trusts and estate plans. The clear judicial message is that proponents' claims are upheld. In the vast majority of will contests, probate courts throughout the United States favor the proponent and not the contestants. What is more, will contests are expensive. In addition to having a reputation as risky and expensive litigation, will contests are viewed as socially unacceptable: Powerful norms of familial solidarity work to maintain consensus or, at very least, to prevent legal action.

That estate litigation occurs at all is significant because will contests are rare, occurring in fewer than 3 percent of probated estates. Nevertheless, they are socially and economically significant events, because "they can rupture and realign the social fabric of families" and often involve large estates keeping millions of dollars tied up in litigation for years.

The data for Rosenfeld's study consist of telephone interviews of a snowball sample of 28 attorneys who specialize in estate litigation. Interviews with these estate litigators indicated that the causes of will contests have changed. Most generally, will contests are linked with changes in family structure and the inability of families to control bequests to outsiders such as charities, friends, or organizations. Changes in family structure, including divorce and remarriage, are the major cause of will contests. But social and demographic changes have produced new sources of litigation.

One such change involves the impact of illness and long-term care of the elderly. The U.S. population is aging, and many of the elderly need some kind of assistance with everyday activities. At the same time, the percent of elderly living with an adult child has actually declined. This has spawned the home health care industry, and increasing numbers of the elderly reciprocate for home health care with bequests to the caregiver. Such bequests are sometimes contested by the surviving children.

On the other hand, a growing number of the elderly lead vital and dynamic lives, becoming members of a wide array of service, religious, and other voluntary organizations, and entering into nontraditional relationships. These involvements with friends, neighbors, and organizations can become the basis for bequests outside the family and another source of will contests.

Another change involves cross-generational arrangements for child care. An estimated 5 percent of American families now consist of grandparents raising grandchildren. Such "unplanned parenthood" means assuming full-time responsibility for grandchildren and commonly leads to the formation of custodial and caretaker trusts. Such trusts can lead to will contests if they thwart the inheritance expectations of siblings of the parent of the children for whom the trusts are established.

The unclear legal status of gay and lesbian relationships has also recently evoked new legal challenges to traditional patterns of inheritance. Gay beneficiaries have become targets in will contests initiated by homophobic siblings, and litigation over the estates of AIDS victims who die relatively young has become more common.

It is commonly held, even among the lawyers in Rosenfeld's sample, that estate litigation is on the rise in the United States. But the evidence suggests that although the *absolute number* of will contests may be rising, the *proportion* of contested probated wills has not increased. And although most of the lawyers in Rosenfeld's sample assumed that estate litigation is a maneuver of the very rich, typically involving large—often the largest—estates, available evidence suggests that smaller estates generate about as much litigation as larger estates.

Will contests are often, but not always, simply calculated struggles for money and may be driven by nonpecuniary considerations. Historically, the vast majority of will contestants have been members of decedents' immediate families. Although this remains true, Rosenfeld notes that estate litigation increasingly involves people from nontraditional families—either the step-families formed when an older person remarries, or the ones resulting from remarriage by divorced sons or daughters of an older person. Not only are such reconstituted families becoming more common, but also the "structural ambiguity" of relationships in such families weakens the applicability and hence strength of traditional inheritance norms. Finally, nonprofit organizations have come to display a greater willingness to litigate when decedents renege on the promise to make a charitable bequest.

It may well be that the same demographic and familial changes that Rosenfeld suggests have produced these new sources of will contests are also responsible for a new and growing openness on the part of will writers, a small but growing number of whom now divulge their trust and estate plans while they are still alive.

Inheritance and Stratification

In the final chapter, McNamee and Miller first discuss the impact of economic inheritance on stratification outcomes. We review how major sociological theories of stratification have treated economic inheritance and propose a theory that more explicitly takes economic inheritance into account. Finally, we summarize the major trends in inheritance patterns and discuss both future areas of research and the policy implications associated with these trends.

Economically, inheritance provides individuals with higher standards of living and enhances opportunities to accrue additional wealth. At the societal level, inheritance reinforces and extends existing wealth inequality across generations. Those who inherit wealth also inherit the *political* advantages of wealth, including the differential ability to create social arrangements that minimize confiscation and permit the transfer of privilege across generations. Culturally, inheritance poses a challenge to those who inherit great fortunes to convince those who stand to inherit little or nothing that inheritance itself is right and just. Whatever the individual-level justifications, inheritance ultimately conflicts with equality of opportunity at the societal level. Although apparently inconsistent with the dominant ideology of meritocracy and equality of opportunity, a peculiar social Darwinist cultural logic justifies inheritance.

For the most part, inheritance is not addressed by sociological theories of stratification. Instead, stratification theory and research have focused mostly on individual occupational attainment and *income* inequality. Relatively little attention has been paid to *wealth* inequality and the transfer of assets across generations. We propose a conflict theory of stratification that directly incorporates the inheritance factor. It is inheritance in its various forms that transforms mere inequalities into durable, stratified systems through the differential, intergenerational transfer of economic privilege. Inheritance is the institutionalized process by which existing inequalities are perpetuated. To the extent that inheritance occurs, class systems are reproduced, but they are not reproduced completely, because inheritance and meritocracy coexist. For the most part, however, meritocracy is superimposed on inheritance rather than the other way around—effects produced by merit or luck occur within the context of effects produced by differential inheritance.

We offer a set of more than 50 theoretical propositions regarding inheritance that deal with numerous aspects of inheritance and its connections to other social phenomena: *inter vivos* gifts, intestacy, family, class, race and ethnicity, gender, and the state. They are not intended to be exhaustive or conclusive, but are offered as an initial way to frame the issues related to inheritance, and as a guide to future research.

We also discuss a number of historical trends during this century that have drastically altered patterns of inheritance. These include major changes in the occupational structure, the rapid decline in birthrates, strengthening of the relationship between educational achievement and access to occupations (and earnings), increasing life expectancy, increase in the divorce rate since World War II, and the unprecedented accumulation of wealth by the Depression era cohort. Finally, we note that political-economic changes over the past 30 years, including rapid deindustrialization, have led to increasing income and wealth inequality. The latter may be expected to contribute to increasing inequalities in economic inheritance, which should further increase class stratification.

In the final section on policy implications, we point out that the government's role in inheritance is both direct and indirect. The direct role of government is taxation—federal estate taxes on the transfer of property at death and state taxes of inheritances. Taxes on estates could be imposed as a means of generating state revenue or to redistribute wealth through government policy, or both. As estate taxation in the United States is currently constituted, however, the government's role in wealth redistribution is minimal, and revenues generated by estate taxation are small. The government's role in inheritance practices can also be indirect, because government policy in other arenas can impact testamentary behavior. For example, to the extent that government can provide for individuals in retirement through nonmeans-tested programs such as Social Security and Medicare, or encourage private pension programs, individuals might be less inclined to "stockpile" resources as a hedge against illness or unexpectedly long retirements. In this way, government policy could encourage greater spending prior to death, increase *inter vivos* giving, and reduce the size of estates at death.

While not interfering with the inheritance of wealth directly, the state could decide to offset the *effects* of inequality caused by inheritance by decommodification of critical resources, in essence providing collective access to essential resources and services regardless of the ability to pay. However, any change from the current "fair play" system to a "fair shares" system first requires recognition that genuine equality of opportunity is not possible to the extent that inheritance of wealth constitutes an important nonmerit factor in determining who gets what and how much. Unequal inheritances not only create unequal starting points but also provide further advantages that accumulate over the life course in the forms of differential provision of cultural capital and receipt of *inter vivos* gifts at critical junctures of the life course. Effective government policies to reduce the effects of inheritance would need to offset *wealth* inequality, not merely income inequality, by providing opportunity for asset accumulation to disadvantaged segments of the population and increasing taxation of existing wealth holdings.

We conclude that laws of succession to property are formalizations of customs, themselves based upon structures of power and privilege. Whatever policy changes that might occur should be interpreted in this context. Meanwhile, Americans largely continue to subscribe to a "fair play" ideology of meritocracy, which is ultimately in contradiction with the reality of "unequal shares" of inherited wealth.

References

Bourdieu, P. (1973). Cultural reproduction and social reproduction. In R. Brown (Ed.), *Knowledge, education, and cultural change* (pp. 71-112). London: Collier Macmillan.

Bourdieu, P., & Passeron, C. (1977). *Reproduction in education, society, culture*. Beverly Hills, CA: Sage.

Bowles, S. & Gintis, H. (1976). *Schooling in capitalist America*. New York: Basic Books.

Burkhauser, R. V., & Gertler, P. J. (Eds.). (1995). The health and retirement study: Data quality and early results. *Journal of Human Resources, 30*, S1-S318.

Clignet, R. (1992). *Death, deeds, and descendants: Inheritance in modern America*. New York: Aldine de Gruyter.

Collins, R. (1979). *The credential society*. New York: Academic Press.

Hodel v. Irving, 481 U.S. 704 (1987).

Huber, J., & Form, W. H. (1973). *Income and ideology*. New York: Free Press.

Irving Trust v. Day, 314 U.S. 556, 562 (1942).

Kluegel, J. R., & Smith, E. R. (1986). *Beliefs about inequality: Americans' vieews of what is and what ought to be*. New York: Aldine de Gruyter.

Langbein, J. H. (1991). The inheritance revolution. *The Public Interest, 102*, 15-31.

McCubbin, J., & Rosenfeld, J. P. (1989, March). Introducing an IRS data base for estate tax research. *Trusts and Estates*, pp. 62-69.

McNamee, S. J., & Miller, R. K., Jr. (1989). Estate inheritance: A sociological lacuna. *Sociological Inquiry, 38*. 7-29.

Oliver, M. L., & Shapiro, T. M. (1995). *Black wealth/white wealth: A new perspective on racial inequality*. New York: Routledge.

Rossi, A. S., & Rossi, P. H. (1990). *Of human bonding: Parent-child relations across the life course*. New York: Aldine de Gruyter.

Ryan, H. (1981). *Equality*. New York: Vintage.

Smith, J. P. (1995). Racial and ethnic differences in wealth in the health and retirement study. *Journal of Human Resources, 30*, S158-S183.

2

Inheritance in American Legal Thought

Ronald Chester

Inheritance in America: A Civil, Not a Natural Right

From the time of the Revolution, American legal thinkers viewed both the rights to transmit and to receive property at the death of its owner as positivistic, not natural rights: rights created and regulated by the state, rather than fundamental rights. In this, they were heavily influenced by William Blackstone (Ascher, 1990) who argued in his *Commentaries on the Law of England* that inheritance was "no *natural*, but merely a *civil* right":

> For naturally speaking, the instant a man ceases to be, he ceases to have any dominion; else if he had a right to dispose of his acquisitions one moment beyond his life, he would also have a right to direct their disposal for ... ages after him; which would be highly absurd and inconvenient. (Blackstone, 1803, pp. 10–11).

Blackstone thought inheritance was simply a custom that society ultimately turned into law. Because children and other near relations were usually

Portions of this chapter appeared in the author's book, *Inheritance, Wealth, and Society* (1982) and his article "Is the Right to Devise Property Constitutionally Protected?—The Strange Case of *Hodel v. Irving, Southwestern University Law Review* 24(4), 1995, pp. 1195–1213.

RONALD CHESTER • Professor of Law, New England School of Law, 154 Stuart Street, Boston, Massachusetts 02116.

Inheritance and Wealth in America, edited by Robert K. Miller, Jr., and Stephen J. McNamee. Plenum Press, New York, 1998.

around the decedent at death and generally became the next occupants of his or her property, society delineated from this a clear rule of succession to property to avoid the "endless disturbances" that might otherwise develop. (p. 10).

Since John Locke, an earlier Briton who greatly influenced American thought, had generally favored the natural rights view of inheritance (see Chester 1982a, esp. pp. 13-17), why did Americans so clearly prefer Blackstone's positivistic position (Ascher, 1990)?

To the leaders of a new nation casting off the shackles of a hereditary monarchy, the notion of inheritance rights as a creation of civil society, subject to its regulation, must have seemed both logically and politically sensible. Any society that respects lifetime property rights must find a suitable way of reallocating those rights at the property owner's death. Rather than viewing inheritance as one of the varied facets of property (such as the right to exclude), the American revolutionary generation saw inheritance law in a utilitarian way: as a tool useful to civil society in reallocating the rights of an individual no longer alive (see Ascher, 1990). Had it considered inheritance rights fundamental, this generation would have limited its freedom to alter the establishment of dynastic rule such as the one against which it had rebelled.

Among the revolutionary generation, Thomas Jefferson and his circle best exemplified American legal and political theory on the subject (Chester, 1982a). Their view was in turn grounded in the works of British utilitarians such as Jeremy Bentham and John Stuart Mill (Chester 1982a) and thus had a distinctively pragmatic bent. The Jeffersonians argued that any rights to transmit or to receive property at an owner's death were "civil" not "natural rights": rights created by our society for its own convenience.[1] Jefferson himself addressed the subject in 1789 in a letter to James Madison: "Earth belongs in usufruct to the living; the dead have neither powers nor rights over it. The portion occupied by an individual ceases to be and reverts to society" (Ford, 1895, pp. 115-116).

Thomas Paine emphasized that letting the dead control property was a danger, to be strictly controlled by society. He wrote: "[No] generation [has] a property in the generations which are to follow.... It is the living and not the dead that are to be accommodated.... When man ceases to be, his power ceases with him" (Foner, 1945, p. 251). Likewise, Jefferson's personal physician, the influential Dr. Gem, concluded that "the dead and those who are unborn can have no [natural] rights of property" (Koch, 1964, p. 64).

American courts, beginning with the Virginia case of *Eyre v. Jacob*, 55 Va. 526 (1858), were quite consistent in applying the Jeffersonian, positivistic view of the right to transmit and receive property at death (Chester, 1982a). The Virginia court's declaration of the civil as opposed to natural origin of these rights became a mainstay in the power of the states to tax inheritance (Chester, 1982a). The opinion states:

The right to take property by devise or descent is the creature of the law and secured and protected by its authority. The legislature might if it saw proper, restrict succession to a decedent's estate ... or it may tomorrow, if it pleases, absolutely repeal the statute of wills and that of descents and distributions and declare that upon the death of a party, his property shall be applied to payment of his debts and the residue appropriated to public uses. (p. 530)

Stated thus boldly was the power of legislatures to confiscate inheritances— a power affirmed by the United States Supreme Court and good law until its apparent retraction by the Court well over a century later (Chester, 1982a).

Legal Rationalism and the Jeffersonians, 1775-1860

The Jeffersonians argued that every human possessed natural reason and when properly cultivated, this capability would manifest itself in logical, commonsense decisions. In the early nineteenth century, however, they found themselves countered by a new legal elite that believed in the power of reason, but was less sure that this power generally resided in the common man (Chester, 1982a).

Typical of this group of rational jurists were prominent lawyers such as James Kent, John Marshall, and Joseph Story. In their quest to make law and lawyers autonomous from politics and politicians, they took bits and pieces from both the positivist and natural law traditions (Miller, 1965; Chester 1982a). Although they staunchly defended property rights during life, their conclusions on property rights after death differed only in emphasis from those of the Jeffersonian judge in *Eyre v. Jacob supra* (Chester, 1982a).

This prominent group tended to take its viewpoints from William Blackstone's *Commentaries on the Law of England*, which synthesized positivistic (largely legislative), natural, and common law (Chester, 1982a). Blackstone based his view largely upon that of two British political philosophers—John Locke and Thomas Hobbes. He seems to have used strands of thought from both of these sources in concluding that lifetime property rights are natural, while inheritance rights are positivistic.

Locke's core idea was that an individual possessed certain natural rights, including a right to own property once his labor was added to it. Locke thought society was created solely for the protection of these natural rights. However, he also believed that man surrendered the inheritance rights over this property to civil control as part of his "social contract" with government. Hobbes, on the other hand, asserted that the sovereign was the sole source of power and had itself created society, ordering the submission of society to its will. This was the positivist position and more directly asserted the government's control over property (and inheritance; Chester, 1982a).

William Blackstone's American counterpart, law teacher and treatise writer James Kent, was the chief architect and lawyer for the new American jurisprudence. The cornerstone of this jurisprudence was the right to property as seen through Blackstone's natural law, positivism, and common law. Kent staunchly protected the concept that property rights existed before society was created. In direct contradiction with Jeffersonianism, Kent's view would not authorize the most minute violation of property rights, even if the sacrifice meant great benefits for the community (Chester, 1982a). To Kent, the natural right to property ownership existed prior to the U.S. Constitution, state constitutions, enumerated bills of rights, and above all, prior to the demagoguery of the Jacksonian Democrats, who he felt threatened that right through the power of popular legislation (Kent, 1971).

Kent diverged somewhat from natural property rights analysis when it came to inheritance. For example, Kent admitted that title to property ceased upon the death of the occupant. However, in contrast with Blackstone (who believed that upon death the property should revert back to society for the common good), Kent referred to inheritance as derived not from the law of nature, but the voice of nature. This "voice of nature" dictated that the property owner's children "by their association and labor" in relation to the property should have better title to it than "the passing stranger" (p. 263); however, Kent still believed that "the right of succession should be attached [and] undoubtedly depend essentially upon positive [civil] institution[s]" (pp. 263-264). In essence, he was arguing that although it was "natural" for the decedent's children who had lived on and worked the land to succeed to it, it was for society to dictate the details of how and under what circumstances this succession would occur.

Supreme Court Justices John Marshall and Joseph Story were more cautious in their defense of lifetime property rights than was Kent. Like Kent, Marshall believed that man brought certain inalienable rights to society. However, Marshall parted from Kent in the idea that the right to hold and enjoy property was an absolute right. On certain occasions, he thought it could be interfered with, depending on whether this promoted natural rights in the aggregate (White, 1976).

Marshall thought that the English, upon setting foot in America, brought certain natural rights with them. These rights were subsequently codified in the U.S. Constitution, but other rights were not sacrificed in the process.[2] Hence, property rights were "vested" and protected from state interference not only by the Constitution, but also by the permissibility of such rights within the state of nature (White, 1976). These property rights were to be specifically protected if they made use of one's acquisitive skills, but if they merely represented the fruits of inheritance, they were afforded less protection; thus, institutions such as primogeniture could be abolished summarily by the new nation, whereas the right to make use of the fruits of one's labor could not be so easily curtailed (White, 1976; Chester, 1982a). Unlike Kent, Marshall appeared to have little trouble with the government's power to modify and adapt inheritance beyond what was customary or "natural" (Chester, 1982a).

Story, an advocate of autonomous, judge-made law, developed the theoretical basis Kent had constructed for natural rights. Kent had thought that the law should proceed from an occupancy-derived basis for natural rights to a more historical view of these rights. Judicial power would lead this development as society itself changed. By the time Story had completed a treatise on the Constitution, his theoretical basis for property rights had changed from a social compact between man and government to a fluctuating concept of rights that had evolved historically and was solidly backed by a written Constitution (Pound, 1938).

Still, once property rights were *vested* in an individual, Story was their staunch advocate:

> [N]o state government can be presumed to possess the transcendal sovereignty, to take away vested rights of property; to take away the property of A and transfer it to B by mere legislative act. That government can scarcely be deemed to be free, where the rights of property are left solely dependent upon a legislative body, without any restraint. The fundamental maxims of a free government seem to require that the right ... of ... private property be held sacred. (Story, 1851, § 399).

However, like most thinkers of his day, Story viewed descent and devise as privileges quite different from property rights vested in an individual. After all, after an individual's death, he or she in no sense owned the property being transferred. With respect to property rights then,

> the legislative power, except in the few cases of constitutional prohibition [e.g., a taking of vested property rights without compensation] is unlimited.... Look but at the exercise of two or three branches of its powers. It levies all taxes; ... it gives the rules for the descent, distribution, and devises of all property held by individuals. It controls the sources and resources of wealth. (§ 374).

Given this concept of the sweeping regulatory power of the state, Story had less trouble than Kent extricating the civil or positive right of inheritance from property rights. To Story, it was simply a given that "the states ... regulate, the descent, devise and distribution of estates" (§ 534). "In fact, his son, William Story, added to the above quotation in the second edition of his father's *Commentaries on the Constitution* that this power to regulate inheritance was "most indispensable in its right exercise to republicanism" (Story, § 513).

Recognition of civil authority over inheritance did not mean that the rational jurists were willing to step aside and let the prerogatives of the propertied classes be trampled. Story and Kent both viewed the elite lawyers as rightfully attempting to diffuse the Jacksonian threat to destroy both public liberty and private property (Miller, 1965). As Story wrote himself in *Providence Bank v. Billings & Pittman*, 29 U.S. 537 (4 Peters 514) (1837), "[t]hat government can scarcely be deemed free where the rights of property are left solely to depend on the will of a legislative body, without any restraint." The restraint needed was to be provided by judicial authority.

A commentator in the *American Law Magazine* in 1843 put frankly the issue bothering the rational jurists: "The real concern of society is the protection of property," which "stands in need of every paper barrier.... Democracy is incurably hostile to the possessions of a few; and the Constitution gave property 'insufficient protection' " (Miller, 1965, p. 227). As Maine Probate Judge David Bronson declared in 1857, "If the legislature can take the property of A and transfer it to B," then "they can take A himself and either shut him up in prison or put him to death" (p. 228).

Such defenses of property rights by the "elite" judiciary became even fiercer as great concentrations of family wealth were created in the late nineteenth century. Many of these jurists, like others from the upper classes, tended to believe that inequality could be explained by dividing mankind into those who diligently labored and those who were inherently idle (Miller, 1965).

Given their strong defense of property rights and their somewhat grudging recognition of the civil, positivistic control of inheritance, it is hardly suprising that the "rational jurists" were not the first to announce the possibility of confiscating inheritance in a Supreme Court opinion. Instead, this task fell to Jackson's appointee, Chief Justice Roger Taney. The case was *Mager v. Grima*, 49 U.S. 490 (1850), decided without dissent (Chester, 1982a).

Perhaps out of caution, Taney chose the case of an alien, not a citizen, to announce the doctrine Europe had developed, Jefferson had adapted, and even Story had accepted. The inheritance tax in question was, wrote Taney:

> [N]othing more than an exercise of the power which every state and sovereignty possesses of regulating the manner and term upon which property real or personal within its dominion may be transmitted by last will and testament; and of prescribing who shall and shall not be capable of taking it.... We can see no [constitutional] objection to such a tax, whether imposed on citizens [or] aliens ... (p. 493)

By the time of *Mager* the more conservative jurists who had established an autonomous legal profession were in political retreat before the democratic tide; thus, they often acquiesced in the numerous state and federal decisions that supported the constitutionality of inheritance taxation during the next half-century. Although admitting legislative power over inheritance, they continued to hope that judicial review would save the wealthy if democratic legislators became too extreme in their demands for the redistribution of property (Chester, 1982a).

Legislative Control of Inheritance through Regulation and Taxation, 1860–1984

From 1860 until 1900, the United States levied a number of inheritance taxes, due in large part to wartime revenue needs; however, Utilitarian concern for social progress also played a role (Chester, 1982a). In *Scholey v. Rew*, 90 U.S. 331 (1874), the Supreme Court held inheritance taxes constitutional, concentrating its analysis not on whether inheritance was a natural or positivist right, but on the traditional constitutionality of excise taxes.

By the 1890s, the Supreme Court majority combined a hostile attitude toward government infringements of what they considered "natural" economic rights with a conception of the appellate judiciary as an active check on the legislature. Ignoring the distinctions between natural rights and constitutional principles acknowledged even by Kent and Story, they merged the two traditions into a governing concept. By allying a constitution written by men with rights declared by nature and interpreted by the Court, the majority strengthened the autonomous role posited for the judiciary by the rational jurists. The essence of this role was to act as a buffer between the people and their government (White, 1976).

Given the Court's strong identification of natural rights with the Constitution and the use of this weapon to protect private property, one might have expected inheritance rights to be greatly strengthened. However, clearly separating the civil institution of inheritance from property itself, the Court instead affirmed that the institution was still subject to governmental control. In the Court's view, taxes on inheritance were not direct taxes on people's property, but indirect duties on the process of transferring that property from the dead to the living (Chester, 1982a).

In *Magoun v. Illinois Trust & Savings Bank*, 170 U.S. 283, 288 (1897), the Court considered the validity of an Illinois inheritance tax. Justice McKenna, writing for the Court, put the matter directly: "[t]he right to take property by devise or descent is the creature of the law, and not a natural right—a privilege, and therefore the authority which confers it may impose conditions upon it." Choosing between this widely accepted principle and the appellant's claim that children have a natural right to inherit property, McKenna accepted appellant's own admission "that [both] testamentary disposition and inheritance [by heirs] were subject to regulation." McKenna continued by citing *Mager v. Grima* (1850) as authority that both rights were civil in nature and *United States v. Fox*, 170 U.S. 291 (1897), in which the Court had acknowledged the State's power to regulate real property and the rules of its descent.

If any doubt remained as to whether heirs possessed a natural right to inherit, the Court's next major case on the subject, *Knowlton v. Moore*, 178 U.S. 41, 55 (1900), which upheld the War Revenue Act of 1898, declared that "[t]he right to take property by devise or descent is the creature of the law, and not a natural right." Citing not only *Magoun*, but *Mager* and *Eyre v. Jacob*, *Knowlton* thus announced for the twentieth century principles originally established in the eighteenth.

With the question of civilian control decided, *Knowlton* next turned to the theoretical basis for inheritance taxation itself:

> The thing forming the universal subject of taxation, upon which inheritance and legacy taxes rest is the transmission or receipt [of property]....
> Although different modes of assessing such duties prevail ... tax laws of this nature in all countries rest in their essence upon the principle that death is the generating source from which the particular taxing power takes its being, and that it is the power to transmit, or the transmission from the dead to the living, on which such taxes [are based]. (p. 56)

By the time of *Knowlton v. Moore*, growing inequities in American social and economic conditions were providing the basis for a serious discussion of the institution of inheritance. The natural right to property was no longer the vague weapon of the rational jurists, but had been reduced to its specific enumeration in the Constitution and Bill of Rights. The Fifth and Fourteenth Amendments, for example, guaranteed that property could not be taken without due process of law, including compensation. Bequest and succession, however, were specifically guaranteed neither in these amendments nor in the Constitution as a whole. America thus entered the Progressive Era with most of the philosophical barriers removed to the imposition of post-mortem redistributive measures by Congress and the legislatures without interference of the courts (Chester, 1982a).

Indicative of this situation was an editorial appearing in August 1915 in the *Chicago Tribune*—then, as now, no radical sheet. The *Tribune* declared that a sharp limitation on inheritance would be salutary and intimated its approval of the recommendation of the Federal Commission on Industrial Relations that a million dollars should be that limit.

In September 1915, John R. Montgomery of the Chicago Bar Association referred to the *Tribune* editorial in presenting a paper to the Law Club of Chicago. Montgomery was chiefly concerned with the state's power to confiscate a portion or all of inheritances. Although the federal government held a right to levy excise taxes on privileges, the state held not only a right to tax, but also a right to regulate the entire process as well (Montgomery, 1916). Montgomery pointed out that an inheritance limitation bill had been introduced in the Illinois legislature by a special commission of the Illinois Bar Association as early as 1887. If passed, the bill would have limited inheritances by individuals in a direct line to $500,000 and among collateral heirs to $100,000. He noted that this was in accord with the ideals of the philanthropist, Alfred Noble: "Experience has taught me that great fortunes acquired by inheritance never bring happiness, they only dull the faculties. Any man possessing a large fortune ought not to leave more than a small part of it to his heirs, not even his direct heirs—just enough to make their way in the world" (p. 641).

Mississippi joined the inheritance limitation debate in 1919, when its State Tax Commission openly approved an inheritance tax for the purpose of equalizing wealth and suggested an estate duty absorbing the amount by which any estate exceeded $5,000,000:

> There are many millionaires in the Union with but few heirs at law. Such estates have been accumulated out of the pockets of the citizens of the several states.... Where profits are so enormous, they cease to be profits simply, but they are nothing other than a tax. The citizenship, that has paid them, is more entitled to the benefits than the heirs at law. (p. 32)

While ultimately resulting in little actual control of inheritance other than by taxation, the positivist view of inheritance continued to dominate the natural rights view well into the 20th century. In *Irving Trust v. Day*, 314 U.S. 556, 562 (1942), the United States Supreme Court declared: "Rights of succession to property of a decedent whether by will or intestacy, are of statutory creation and the dead hand rules succession only by sufferance." This opinion stood until very recently as the most influential statement that both the rights to transmit and to succeed to property at death were not natural or constitutionally protected rights, but rights freely alterable at the whim of Congress or legislature. As to the right to transmit itself, Justice Jackson clearly stated in *Irving Trust*: "Nothing in the Federal Constitution forbids ... abolish[ing] the power of testamentary disposition."

Although the view expressed by *Irving Trust* continued to dominate the debate, an American natural rights view of inheritance coexisted with it. This underlying ambivalence about the institution may have originated in Kent's own ambivalence about whether inheritance, either in its transmission, receipt, or both, is a natural property right (Kornstein, 1984). In any event, inheritance retained the potential for elevation to a fundamental attribute of propertyhood, such as alienability or the right to exclude. Once political changes caused inheritance, either in its transmission or receipt, to be considered a fundamental or natural property right, it would be but a short step for the Supreme Court to protect this right constitutionally under the Fifth and Fourteenth Amendments.

Writing in the 1984 *Rutgers Law Review*, Daniel J. Kornstein exhaustively examined the question of whether the competing natural rights view of inheritance is logically coherent: Can inheritance be considered a natural, and thus constitutional right? As to the argument that "permitting a person to own property, but not to transmit it at death" constitutes an unconstitutional "taking" of that property, Kornstein argued:

> This approach breaks down ... because of flaws in the triple premise that there is *property* belonging to *someone* that is being *taken*.... If inheritance is not "property" then the takings clause is irrelevant.... Related to the abstract definition of property is the presupposition that there is someone whose property is being affected by [e.g., the abolition of inheritance]. Once death occurs, however, ownership of property is the very question at issue: the decedent no longer exists, and the heir never owned the property claimed to have been "taken." To assume that the "just compensation" rights of either heir or decedent exist is to assume the very question at stake.... Finally there is the issue of whether there is a "taking" [at all]. Abolishing inheritance need not reduce the market value of the property to its owner, and therefore, need not be considered a "taking." (pp. 745–746).

Kornstein concluded that "the value of the takings clause in supporting a [constitutional] right of inheritance [is "unpromising" and] "more elusive than real." Given the dominance of the positivist treatment of inheritance in American law, this conclusion is hardly surprising; thus, Kornstein and others can hardly be faulted for failing to foresee the strange U.S. Supreme Court case of *Hodel v. Irving*, 481 U.S. 704 (1987).

Hodel v. Irving: Natural Rights Triumphant?

At issue in *Irving* was the excessive fragmentation of Indian lands that had occurred since the Dawes Act of 1887 had imposed "Anglo" ideas of individual property ownership on the members of various tribes. To rectify the accelerating division of parcels into tiny, noneconomic units, Congress passed the Indian Land Consolidation Act of 1983 (the "Act") that provided for escheat (forfeit) to the tribe of units below a certain size and value at the death of the property holder. Writing for a unanimous court, Justice O'Connor declared, without reference to the dominant American political and legal theory to the contrary, and in direct defiance of *Irving Trust v. Day* (1942), that the right to pass on property at death (like to right to exclude) is a significant, constitutionally protected property right.

On the facts of the *Irving* (1987) case, the Court decided that this right to pass on property was "total[ly] abrogat[ed]" by §207 of the Act. This amounted to a regulatory "taking" under the Fifth Amendment. Because the statute failed to provide compensation for this "taking" of property, the statute was unconstitutional as written. At the same time, the Court apparently left untouched the power of Congress or the legislature to regulate the *receipt of property* not willed away by its owner.[3]

It should be understood that the Supreme Court's constitutional protection of the right of disposition in *Hodel v. Irving* is akin to declaring "dead-hand control"[4] of property a natural right (Kornstein, 1984). Thus, *Irving* is potentially revolutionary. Does it fundamentally change the way inheritance— at least its transmission component—will be treated by our legal institutions? I hope to answer this and related questions in the examination of *Hodel v. Irving* that follows.

Politically, the apparent "sea-change" in the Supreme Court's view of inheritance represented by *Irving* is not really as surprising as it might first appear. As mentioned earlier, the natural rights view of the institution has always been present in our legal and political thought, albeit in a subordinate role (Kornstein, 1984). Thus, a significant change in political climate might well be accompanied by a shift making the natural-rights view of inheritance predominate over the positivistic one. After all, the status of inheritance as a property right, including the constitutional protection of that status, will ultimately be resolved, not by doctrine, but by the dominant social and political forces of the time (Kornstein, 1984). Thus, *Hodel v. Irving* may simply be symbolic of a relatively recent and "dramatic shift in American attitudes toward inherited wealth" (Kornstein, 1984), which occurred because, as Holmes wrote, of a shift in the "felt necessities of the time" (Holmes, 1923).

The conservative revolution that produced *Irving* was associated with the rise of Presidents Nixon and Reagan in politics. This new conservatism was largely a reaction to political events of the late 1960s and early 1970s. The "Great Society" of Lyndon Johnson and the perceived excesses of the Left during the Vietnam War led a voting majority of Americans to believe that the nation had lost its way, and that a return to what "made us great" was essential. In large part, what was perceived to have "made us great" was the power of the individual, unfettered by the state.

The nostalgic desire for a return to an individualist "Garden of Eden" was particularly the hallmark of the Reagan years. If pressed, its proponents would probably date the initial rise to prominence of this philosophy as occurring during the Gilded Age of the late nineteenth century.

Of course, this vision of unrestrained individualism happily producing wealth is fundamentally flawed. First, there was never a time in American history when the government was not involved in defining property rights (Cohen, 1927). Second, governments at all levels were heavily involved in partnerships with entrepreneurs during the building of America's infrastructure during the nineteenth century.[5] Third, those very individuals who accumulated massive wealth though this partnership conveniently forgot who had helped them achieve it, and, during the Gilded Age of the late nineteenth century, led the cry to keep government out of private affairs (Gilmore, 1977).

Although individual property rights during life were bolstered by the social myths mentioned earlier, by 1980, there had been no significant inroads made on legislative ability to control or even abolish inheritance (Chester, 1982a). Nor had the philosophical, legal and political basis of inheritance and estate taxes been seriously challenged (Kornstein, 1984). In general, these taxes were accepted as regulators of "the perceived tension between the sanctity of property and equality of opportunity" (Kornstein, 1984).

Still, the warning signs of a shift were present for those who dared look. Senator George McGovern's proposal of a confiscatory inheritance tax during the presidential campaign of 1972 caused "a national cry of outrage" (Brittain, 1977, p. 30). In the ten years that followed this campaign, Congress, with popular support, eliminated all federal taxes on property inherited from a spouse and raised the individual federal estate tax exemption tenfold (Kornstein, 1984).

The philosophical underpinnings for this change are not hard to find. Libertarian thinkers such as Robert Nozick used natural law principles, submerged since the time of Chancellor Kent, to justify inheritance. In 1974, for example, Nozick focused on inheritance in *Anarchy, the State and Utopia*. Emphasizing the rights of the property owner, not its ultimate recipient, Nozick (1974, p. 160) defended a "system of natural liberty," in which inheritance is an essential aspect of the absolute liberty owed each individual. Joining Nozick in opposing interference with inheritance on the grounds of individual liberty were two winners of the Nobel Prize in economics, Milton Friedman and Fredrich Hayek (Kornstein, 1984).

In the legal field, *Hodel v. Irving* stands as the logical outgrowth of this change of view. Penned by a conservative Supreme Court fiercely protective of traditional property interests, this case appears to announce the victory of the long-dormant natural-rights tradition in inheritance.

The Reaction to *Irving*

A search of the cases and commentaries following *Irving*, however, does little to cement this triumph. Subsequent cases tend only to cite *Irving* as

representative of recent Supreme Court takings jurisprudence, without critical assessment.[6] Articles that mention the case focus on the court's "takings"
analysis. Of this they are, for the most part, highly critical.[7] In neither the
cases, nor in the general literature does an appreciation appear of the case's
potential implications for inheritance law (Chused, 1988; Kurtz and Hovenkamp, 1993; Rabin and Kwall, 1992).

Although Professors Dukeminier and Johanson complain in their casebook on trusts and estates of the Court's peculiar use of land regulation
"taking" cases to reach a conclusion about inheritance (Dukeminier and
Johanson, 1990a), this obvious point seems to have escaped most judges and
commentators. The implicit assumption of the opinion that the issues surrounding restriction of the right to transmit property at death are no different
than those germane to the transmission of property during life has gone
largely unchallenged. The lack of reaction to this assumption is surprising,
given its contradiction of generations of learning on the subject, including
the voluminous literature concerning the problem of inadequately restricted
"dead-hand control" of property (Chester, 1982b; Dukeminier and Johanson,
1990a).

Of course, it could be argued that there is a lack of reaction to the
potential of *Irving* precisely *because* of its peculiar reasoning, not to mention
its unusual facts; thus, the question remains just how important the case will
prove to be.

* * * *

According to a number of commentators, *Irving* does not withstand
scrutiny as a regulatory "takings" case in the land-use area. For our purposes
however, the central question is whether the case meant to stand the dominant positivist conception of inheritance regulation on its head, reversing
both two centuries of American case law and its philosophical underpinnings.[8]

Two prominent authorities in the inheritance field find the *Irving* court's
conceptual severance of the right to pass property at death from other
property rights, and its constitutional protection of that right, "simplistic" in
dealing with inheritance and other donative transfers (Dukeminier and Johanson, 1990b, p. 4). Regulation of such transfers

> by taxation or otherwise, raises very tricky problems of regulating con-
> sumption; serving capital formation and transmission; providing incen-
> tives to work or to care for the aged; strengthening the family structure;
> providing equality of opportunity—all problems best left to the legisla-
> ture unless there is no rational basis for what the legislature does. (p. 4)

They conclude that this decision "reversing the traditional wisdom that inheritance can be abolished if the legislature wants," is likely to prove "mischievous" (Dukeminier and Johanson, 1990b, p. 4).

Although I agree with these sentiments, so far such mischievous results have largely failed to materialize. For example, Steven Munzer's exhaustive book, *A Theory of Property*, appearing in 1990, does not seem to notice *Irving* at all. This omission seems all the more remarkable in light of Munzer's long section on "Gratuitous Transfers," in which he argues for a steeply progressive tax on inheritance and other gratuitous transfers, a section followed very closely by one on "Takings and the Constitution," in which he analyzes important takings decisions of the Rehnquist Court, *other than Irving* (Munzer, 1990). Again, we are left wondering whether a writer was oblivious to the decision's potential ramifications or merely ignored the case as anomalous.

An Analysis of *Irving* Limiting Its Radical Potential

It may be that the question of whether *Hodel* has enshrined the natural-rights view of inheritance will not need to be answered in the short run. The apparent political shift that replaced George Bush with Bill Clinton has already allowed the latter to make two new appointees to the Court.[9] A reading of the case, such as I now plan to detail, could give a less conservative Court in a post-Republican era sufficient legal grounds to limit this decision's importance in the field of inheritance law.

The first step in this analysis is to define *precisely* what the right is that Justice O'Connor's opinion views as having been taken. This is made more difficult by a certain sloppiness in the opinion, which talks in terms of the "right to transmit" but really means the "right to transmit at death by will." Although the Court discusses the "right to transmit" as the right of "*descent* [italics mine] or devise" (*Hodel v. Irving*, 1987, pp. 717–718), it admits that abolishing "the descent of such interests" may be appropriate (p. 718). Thus, all of the Court's references to the "right to pass property by descent and devise" in this analysis must be understood to comprehend this admission that *devise alone* may be the only right finally protected.

This admission leaves the Court in the position of constitutionally protecting a right which is much less established than that of the decedent without a will to have his property devolve by intestate succession, or looked at the other way, of his descendants to succeed his estate. As Dukeminier and Johanson (1990a) point out:

> In many societies wills are not permitted. With respect to Indian tribal lands, for example, wills were unknown until Congress forced individual allotments on the Indians. Even then, before 1910, Indian allottees were not permitted to devise their lands.... In Anglo–American history, the right to devise property has always been in uneasy tension with forced succession.... [F]orced succession means succession within the family.... [converting] private property at death to family property. In early feudal

times forced succession had the upper hand. Prior to 1540 when the Statute of Wills was enacted, a will of land was not permitted at law in England.... In the United States, married women could not devise land without the consent of their husbands until ... the late nineteenth century. (pp. 13-14).

In addition to ultimately protecting the right to devise alone, given her admission that succession can still be regulated, Justice O'Connor virtually ignores the route left open to the affected Indians under the Act—that of will substitutes. "The Court does not seem to recognize that far more property passes by will substitutes in this country than by will" (Dukeminier and Johanson, 1990b, p. 2). Thus, depending on local law, property holders can transfer a remainder away, reserving a life estate and general power of appointment; transfer into a joint tenancy (with the property passing automatically to the survivor); establish a revocable trust; or put a payable-on-death beneficiary on a deed or a contract (Dukeminier and Johanson, 1990a, p. 13).

Although Justice O'Connor did note that the Act allowed owners "to effectively control disposition upon death through complex *inter vivos* transactions such as the revocable trust," this was not, "given the nature of the property," an "adequate substitute" for the right to pass property by descent and devise. This right was completely abolished by the Act, and, given the tiny interests at stake, will substitutes were unfeasible alternatives (*Hodel v. Irving*, 1987, pp. 716-717).

As a commentator noted:

Justice O'Connor seemed to be saying that the right of descent and devise was essentially all that remained of the fundamental right to dispose of these interests [at death]. Taking the ability to pass property by descent and devise therefore effectively took all of the [owner's] right to dispose of property [at death]—one of the Court's fundamental property rights. (p. 624).

Although I have had to clarify the above quotation by adding "at death" to define precisely the property right being discussed, the commentator is otherwise correct. Analysis of the opinion indicates that it is the practical unfeasibility in this case of *inter vivos* transfers (that becomes *fully effective at death*) that renders the statute unconstitutional. Thus, *Hodel v. Irving* is not technically saying that the complete abrogation of the rights of descent and devise is in itself unconstitutional. What the Court *is* saying is that "complete abolition of both descent and devise of a particular class of property *may* be taking [italics mine]" (*Hodel v. Irving*, 1987, p. 717) in circumstances such as those in *Irving* where, the Court felt, alternative means of passing property at death were not realistically available.

One may question the Court's assertion on the *Irving* facts that *inter vivos* transactions would necessarily be so complex as to render them unfeasible. In fact, the revocable trust, which requires no witnessing, is probably simpler than a will; likewise, revocable deeds, where permitted, would be widely understood. By giving "talismatic importance" (Dukeminier and Johanson, 1990, p. 3) only to the right to devise *by will*, Justice O'Connor has severely limited the overall right she would no doubt have wished to strengthen—the right to pass property at death either by will or functionally equivalent instrument. Thus, the apparent damage that *Hodel v. Irving* does to the centuries-old positivist position expressed in *Irving Trust v. Day* may, upon further reflection, be minor. As long as Congress or legislature leaves open the route of effective *inter vivos* will *substitutes*, the opinion can be read to allow continued regulation of the right to devise by will.

The passing of property at death by will or by descent traditionally involved the state. In modern society, this is due chiefly to the necessity for some neutral entity to intercede after the death of the property holder. Particularly in estates of any size or complexity, this entity—the modern state—supervises administration of the property, payment of taxes due, and equitable distribution of that property that remains. Thus, the probate of a testate's or intestate's estate under state supervision has come to be seen as a largely inevitable transition stage shifting control of property from the original property owner (who has ceased to exist) to the heirs. Society has, in general, viewed this state-supervised administration as preferable, in an estate of any size or complexity, to one in which potential heirs are left to their own devices to contend over what is due to each. This state-supervised probate system would, like any state institution, naturally be established and regulated by the legislature.

In contrast, *inter vivos* transfers designed to pass property at death, were long considered private matters, regulated and protected by the common law. Therefore, such devices as the revocable *inter vivos* trust were not considered necessary subjects for legislative control and oversight.

The essential feature of such instruments is that the property owner passes a defined interest during life to another—an interest that will pass out of all control of the original owner at his or her death. Because the property owner exercises control over the transfer of the property during his or her life, state involvement at that time is generally not necessary. Although interpretation of such instruments by the courts may be sought by some interested party, traditionally these devices have been treated as acting *automatically* to transfer to or complete in another property rights without the *necessity* of government involvement.

The role of courts in such interpretation that does arise is greatly limited by several factors. First, the procedures for establishing these instruments were generally not enacted by the legislative arm of the state—a circumstance that would necessarily implicate the "legislative interpretation" function of the courts. Second, whatever interpretation is *voluntarily* sought by an interested party is made relatively straightforward by the fact that such devices often have been in operation for many years at the time of the property holder's death. Obviously this is *not* true in the case of wills, where (1) interpretive questions at some level are always necessary to effectuate transfers, no part of which has yet been made by the property owner at the time of death; and (2) the lack of prior experience with the transfer makes judicial interpretation much more difficult.

If the necessity of state involvement in the question of descent and devise led to America's positivist view that the legislation (as construed by the courts) should control these procedures, *Hodel v. Irving* can be read to continue this view so long as the common law "escape hatch" of *inter vivos* transfer (effective at death) remains open. Seen in this light, *Irving* might be viewing *Irving Trust* and its precursors merely as stating the obvious in an era where effective will substitutes were rare: that the government, not the individual, then, necessarily controlled wealth transmission at death. By 1987, however, with will substitutes quite common, the situation facing the *Irving* court had radically changed.

Because *Irving Trust* did not consider legislative regulation of will substitutes, that opinion does not exclude the possibility that a constitutional or natural right to pass on property at death *might* exist, so long as this right is exercised *during life* in ways not traditionally subject to legislative control. Thus, conceptually speaking, *Irving* could be made consistent with the earlier case of *Irving Trust v. Day* by focusing on the lifetime will substitute, not the will, as the true bearer of any constitutional right to transmit property at death. After all, *inter vivos* will substitutes are conceptually linked to individual control of property during life, the period when natural-right and constitutional protection of property has traditionally occurred; it is only after death when, in reality, the individual is unable to exercise such control.

Clearly, Justice O'Connor did not intend to place the constitutional right to transmit solely, or even primarily, on lifetime will substitutes; in fact, as we have mentioned, her primary emphasis is on the will itself. Still, there is a possible reading of *Hodel v. Irving* that contradicts *Irving Trust's* positivistic thrust only in the extremely rare case (such as Justice O'Connor felt existed in *Irving*) where the modern will substitute "escape hatch" is not practical. If the case is so limited, legislatures (or Congress) will continue to have the ability constitutionally to regulate transfers made at death in any way they like, *so long as* inter vivos *will substitutes are not foreclosed on the facts*. Thus, arguably, a 100 percent tax on transfers by will or descent would be constitutional, but not one that also tried to impose the same 100 percent tax on *inter vivos* will substitutes, unconstitutionally closing the "escape route."

Conclusion

Given the lack of attention afforded *Hodel v. Irving*'s potential effect on inheritance law, and the potential for construing away much of any importance it may have (not to mention its poor critical reception as a land-use takings case[10]), I believe that legislatures can, in general, continue to regulate freely *both* devise and descent. If, however, unique circumstances such as *Irving's* should recur, providing the owner in a court's view with no effective lifetime way of avoiding "complete abrogation" of his or her right to dispose of property at death, the decision might well resurface. In such a situation, the Court might again feel it necessary to limit legislative control over devise (and even descent) to measures less strong than abrogation. This is particularly likely in a conservative political climate.

Since the loose language of *Irving* is certainly open to interpretations other than my own, alternative ways may be necessary to restrict its potential impact. One would be to try to limit the case to its American Indian Law roots, so that its full implications could not be transferred to "Anglo" property relationships. This approach might be appealing if examples, such as those I've given, begin to arise, raising the problematic dimensions of the case for the "Anglo" inheritance system.[11]

Finally, the opinion could be discarded as poor takings law, which should therefore not be followed. Since its base in takings jurisprudence is weak, *Irving* should be regarded both as poor precedent there, and by extension, in any other areas in which it might prove important, such as inheritance.

In larger context, the strange case of *Hodel v. Irving*, and the weak reaction to its potential, symbolizes American inheritance law at a crossroads. The positivist tradition expressing state control of inheritance in all its guises is certainly threatened by the case. On the other hand, the long-subordinate natural-rights view of inheritance may be greatly strengthened. Coming near the end of the Reagan Revolution, however, the case may have stated the extreme individualistic view of inheritance just at the time such ideas had begun to fade. Still, Republican control of Congress since the midterm elections of 1994 signals the continuing potential for a return to the very politics that might support its resurrection.

For those interested in the long and fascinating attempt of America to square the elitist tradition of inheritance with the nation's egalitarian roots, I suggest that what happens to this case as precedent over the next few years should be carefully watched. By then, it should be clear if natural rights have really replaced positivist legislative control as the legal theory defining our approach to inheritance for the early years of the twenty-first century.

Notes

1. See letter from Thomas Jefferson to James Earle, September 24, 1823, 15 *The Writings of Thomas Jefferson*, 470–471 (A. E. Bergh, Ed., 1907), pp. 36–37. In this

essay, I shall generally refer to such rights as "positivistic," or the like, to distinguish them from popular connotations of the term *civil rights*. In general, positivists (or legal positivists) believe that law originates in the command of the sovereign, not in the individual; thus, there are no natural rights, just those promulgated by the government.

2. This differs from Hobbes's view that all rights are sacrificed to the government upon the formation of society.

3. See *Irving v. Clark*, 758 F.2d 1260, 1268 (8th Cir. 1985), followed in *Hodel v. Irving*, 481 U.S. at 711. In accepting the Eighth Circuit's distinction between the right of the heirs to receive property on the owner's death (not constitutionally protected) and the right of decedent to transmit it (protected), the Court also followed the appellate court's position on standing: The heirs were allowed to bring the suit not to protect their own interests but those of the decedents. Because the case involved individual American Indians, the personal representative of each of the decedents would otherwise have been the Secretary of the Interior, who could not be expected to press the claim that the statute he was administering was unconstitutional. Thus, a Supreme Court notoriously strict on standing allowed it here, despite the obvious point that a person's property cannot be "taken" if he or she doesn't exist!

4. This term was first coined by A. Hobhouse in *The Dead Hand* (1980). In their modern casebook, Dukeminier and Johanson (1990a) make it a recurrent theme.

5. See, for example, the varying degrees of government involvement in bridge building and operation at issue in the famous case of *Charles River Bridge v. Warren Bridge*, 36 U.S. (11 Peters 420) 537 (1837).

6. See *Pollard v. Sullivan*, 824 F.Supp 130 (N.D. Ill. 1992); *Amato v. Wilentz*, 952 F.2d 742 (3rd cir. 1991); and *Samaad v. City of Dallas*, 940 F.2d 925 (5th Cir. 1991).

7. See, for example, Douglas W. Kmiec, *The Original Understanding of the Takings Clause is Neither Weak nor Obtuse*, 88 Col. L. Rev. 1630, 1662-1665; Note: *Hodel v. Irving: The Supreme Court's Emerging Takings Analysis....* 18 Environ. Law 597 (1988); Jeb Rubenfeld, *Usings*, 102 Yale L.J. 1077, 1103; and Laura S. Underkuffler, *On Property: An Essay*, 100 Yale L.J. 127, 143 (1990). A major focus of this criticism has been *Irving's* isolation of the right to pass on property at death as a stick important enough in the bundle of property rights that its legislative "abrogation" is unconstitutional, despite the survival of all other such "sticks."

8. A possible reason that the Court unanimously committed this apparent gaffe is the weak argument made for the positivist position made by Edwin Kneedler, Assistant to the Solicitor General under President Reagan. I offer for study, a selected portion of the transcript of the argument before the Court (there are others of similar purport):

QUESTION [BY JUSTICE SANDRA DAY O'CONNOR]: [D]o you take the position that it [the right to pass property and to receive it by descent] can be abolished?
MR. KNEEDLER: ... no.
QUESTION: May I follow up on the question asked by Justice O'Connor?... [Doesn't] page 17 of your opening brief [state] ["Every sovereign possesses the power to regulate the manner and terms upon which property may be trans-

mitted at death as well as the authority to prescribe who shall and who shall not be capable of taking it"] say that the government may disinherit anyone it wishes to disinherit?...

MR. KNEEDLER: ... we did not intend for that language to be taken to its full implications ... we are not suggesting here that Congress could simrly [*sic*] pass a statute providing for all property to escheat to the government after one generation.

9. Ruth Bader Ginsburg (1993) and Stephen Breyer (1994). While some of this momentum seemed to shift back to the Republicans after their victories in the 1994 midterm congressional elections, Clinton's presidential victory in 1996 will continue to give him the power to appoint liberals or moderates to the Court.

10. See, for example, the articles cited in note 7 above.

11. Regardless of how conceptually attractive different treatments of American Indian and "Anglo" property regimes may appear to be, one is forced to admit that a powerful strain of American thought, perfectly exemplified by the *Irving* Court, demands that the "Anglo" view be adoped by both groups.

References

Ascher, Mark L. (1990). Curtailing inherited wealth. 89 *Michigan Law Review* 69.

Blackstone, W. (1803). *Commentaries on the laws of England*. Oxford, UK: Clarendon Press.

Brittain, J. A. (1977). *The inheritance of economic status*. Washington, DC: Brookings Institution.

Chester, R. (1976). Inheritance and wealth taxation in a just society. 30 *Rutgers Law Review* 62.

Chester, R. (1982). *Inheritance, wealth, and society*. Bloomington: Indiana University Press.

Chester, R. (1995). Is the right to devise property constitutionally protected? — the strange case of *Hodel v. Irving*, 24 *Southwestern University Law Review* 1195.

Chicago Tribune, August 24, 1915 (editorial).

Chused, R. H. (1988). *Cases, materials, and problems in property*. St. Paul MN: West.

Cohen, M. R. (1927). Property and sovereignty. 13 *Cornell Law Quarterly* 8.

Dukeminier, J., & Johanson, S. (1990a). *Wills, trusts, and estates* (4th ed.). Boston: Little, Brown.

Dukeminier, J., & Johanson, S. (1990b). Wills, trusts and estates (4th ed.). *Teacher's manual*. Boston: Little, Brown.

Foner, P. S. (1945). *The complete writings of Thomas Paine*. New York: Citadel Press.

Ford, P. L. (ed.). (1895). *The works of Thomas Jefferson*. New York and London: G. P. Putnam's Sons.

Gilmore, G. (1977). *The ages of American law*. New Haven: Yale University Press.

Holmes, O. W., Jr. (1923). *The common law*. Boston: Little, Brown.

Kent, J. (1971). *Commentaries on American law*. Birmingham, AL: Legal Classics Library.

Koch, A. (1964). *Jefferson and Madison: The great collaboration*. New York: Oxford University Press.

Kornstein, D. J. (1984). Inheritance: A Constitutional right? 36 *Rutgers Law Review* 741.

Kurtz, S. H., & Hovenkamp, H. (1993). *Cases and materials on American property law*. St. Paul, MN: West.

Langbein, J., & Waggoner, L. (1991). *Selected statutes on trusts and estates*. Westbury, NY: Foundation Press.

Miller, P. (1965). *The life of the mind in America from Revolution to the Civil War*. New York: Harcourt, Brace and World.

Mississippi State Tax Commission. (1919). Annual Report.

Montgomery, J. R. (1916). The inheritance tax and the Constitution, 10 *Illinois Law Review* 633.

Munzer, S. (1990). *A theory of property*. New York: Cambridge University Press.

Nozick, R. (1974). *Anarchy, the state, and utopia*. New York: Basic Books.

Peterson, A. L. (1989). The Takings Clause: In search of underlying principles. Part I-A: Critique of current takings clause doctrine. 77 *California Law Review* 1299.

Pound, R. (1938). *The formative era of American law*. Boston: Little, Brown.

Rabin, E. H., & Kwall, R. (1992). *Fundamentals on modern real property law* (3rd ed.) Westbury, NY: Foundation Press.

Story, J. (1851). *1 & 2 Commentaries on the Constitution of the United States* (2nd ed., 1851). Little, Brown.

White, G. E. (1976). *The American judicial tradition: Profiles of leading American judges*. New York: Oxford University Press.

3

Economics of Inheritance

Paul L. Menchik and Nancy A. Jianakoplos

Introduction

Economists are concerned with inheritance at two levels: the economywide level and the household level. At the economywide level, the principal focus of economic research has been to determine the proportion of total wealth in the economy that was either received as an inheritance or accumulated with the intent to bequeath. At the household level, the principal focus is on determining the behavioral motivation for making bequests. Our survey focuses on both of these aspects of inheritance by summarizing the frameworks through which economists have analyzed inheritances, assessing the empirical evidence accumulated, and highlighting the policy relevance and possible consequences of these findings. In the next section, we discuss in greater detail how economists' concept of inheritance may differ from the legal or commonly held definitions of inheritance.

Economic Concept of Inheritances

As Goody (1987) notes in his survey of inheritance for *The New Palgrave: A Dictionary of Economics*, "Inheritance, in the strict sense, is the

Paul L. Menchik • Department of Economics, Michigan State University, East Lansing, Michigan 48824.   Nancy A. Jianakoplos • Department of Economics, Colorado State University, Fort Collins, Colorado 80525.

Inheritance and Wealth in America, edited by Robert K. Miller, Jr., and Stephen J. McNamee. Plenum Press, New York, 1998.

transmission of relatively exclusive rights at death." However, economists view inheritance both more broadly and more narrowly than the strict definition.

Inter Vivos *Transfers versus Bequests*

In a broader sense, economists' interest in inheritance is a concern with the intergenerational transfer of wealth whether this transfer occurs at death in the form of a bequest or while living. *Inter vivos* transfers—transfers between the living—add to the wealth of the recipient just as do inheritances transferred at death. Because the timing of an intergenerational transfer may be affected by tax considerations among other things, economists tend to view the timing of the transfer as secondary to the transfer itself, although for some explanations of bequest behavior this is a crucial distinction.

A number of economists have attempted to quantify the relative importance of bequests to *inter vivos* transfers. This task is difficult because of the lack of data. Kurz (1984) used survey data from the 1979 President's Commission on Pension Policy. Respondents in this survey reported the amount of financial and material support received and given during the year. This included payment of rent, education tuition, gifts, inheritances, and other types of transfers. Based on these data, Kurz estimated that *inter vivos* transfers account for approximately 87 percent of intergenerational transfers; however, he believed the survey data underestimated bequests. Cox (1987), who relied on Kurz's estimate of *inter vivos* transfer, but using Kotlikoff and Summers's (1981) estimate of bequests, concluded that a smaller proportion, but still the majority (58 percent) of intergenerational transfers are *inter vivos*.

More recently, Gale and Scholz (1994), using data from the 1983–1986 Survey of Consumer Finances, concluded that 43 percent of intergenerational transfers are *inter vivos*. From these data they were also able to determine that about 75 percent of the *inter vivos* transfers were from parent to child, with an additional 12 percent from grandparent to grandchild.

Human versus Nonhuman Wealth

In a broader view, economists also recognize wealth to consist of more than tangible or financial assets. Economists recognize that "human capital," the knowledge and education embodied in individuals, is part of an individual's wealth. Although most studies of inheritance are limited to the intergenerational transmission of "nonhuman" wealth, there has been considerable controversy regarding whether the parental financing of college education should be treated as an intergenerational transfer (Modigliani, 1988a,b;

Kotlikoff and Summers, 1988). Those arguing in favor of inclusion view college funding as a discretionary transfer to adult children, little different than a gift of stocks and bonds. The returns to education in the form of higher incomes earned by the recipients in later life are perhaps even more valuable than the interest and dividends earned on financial assets. Those arguing for the exclusion of college tuition financing regard such payments as part of the normal cost of child rearing. They point out that no one is arguing to include food, shelter, clothing, and elementary and secondary education expenses as intergenerational transfers.

The controversy over whether the financing of college educations should be treated as an intergenerational transfer would be pointless if the magnitude of the transfer were very small. However, Gale and Scholz (1994) provide evidence that the magnitude of these transfers is substantial. They estimate that transfers to pay college expenses accounted for 12 percent of total wealth in the United States in 1986, whereas bequests represented 31 percent, and *inter vivos* transfer constituted 21 percent. They also estimate that approximately 13 percent of the households pay college expenses for children, but in the top 10 percent of the wealth holders, this fraction increases to 43 percent.

Intended versus Unintended Bequests

In the more limited sense, economists distinguish between intended and unintended bequests. Unintended bequests are the result of dying earlier than anticipated. In the process, one leaves some accumulated wealth to one's heirs that otherwise would have been consumed if life had continued as expected. Although the taxes owed on an inheritance will not be different if the bequest was unintended rather than intended, and the recipients' wealth will not differ after the receipt of an unintended rather than an intended bequest, the economic and policy implications of bequest intention are very different.

Hamermesh and Menchik (1987) empirically distinguish planned and unplanned bequests. They use the idea that people have subjective views of their life expectancy based on the experiences of their parents, which differ from the actuarial life expectancy. More specifically, they hypothesize that people will expect to live longer than others their own age if their parents lived longer, and likewise, will expect a shorter lifespan if their parents died at a relatively young age. They find that people who expect to live longer use the additional time to accumulate larger estates, which supports the idea of intended bequests. They also find that unexpected additional years of life lead to smaller estates, which is consistent with the concept of unintended bequests.

Inheritances at the Economywide Level

The wealth of the economy arises from two sources: wealth accumulated by previous generations and transferred to the current generation—inherited wealth; and wealth accumulated by saving out of current income—life-cycle wealth. The life-cycle model of saving (Modigliani and Brumberg, 1954) posits that households save out of earnings during their early years in order to finance their consumption during retirement. (Economists also believe that households save for "precautionary" reasons, for example to protect themselves against decreases in income when unemployed and needs increase, such as unusually high medical expenses. Sometimes precautionary motives are lumped together with life-cycle motives.) The implication of this model at the household level is that the pattern of wealth accumulation over a lifetime is hump-shaped—increasing until retirement, then decreasing to zero at death. For the economy as a whole, the quantity of wealth in existence at any time depends on the relative number of households in the accumulation stage versus the decumulation stage and the level of earnings of households in these groups.

Frameworks for Analysis

A number of frameworks have been developed to enable economists to empirically estimate the importance of inherited versus life-cycle wealth in total wealth. One approach is to obtain an estimate of inherited wealth directly. The alternative approach is to obtain a measure of life-cycle wealth and subtract this estimate from total wealth to obtain an indirect measure of inherited wealth.

DIRECT MEASURES OF INHERITED WEALTH.   To obtain direct estimates of inherited wealth, some researchers have used data obtained from household surveys in which respondents reported how much of their wealth was inherited. For the United States, such surveys include the 1962 Federal Reserve Survey of Financial Characteristics of Consumers (Projector and Weiss, 1964), the 1964 survey of the economic behavior of the affluent (Barlow, Brazer, and Morgan, 1966), and the 1983–1986 Survey of Consumer Finances (Hurd and Mundaca, 1989; Gale and Sholz, 1994).

Although these surveys would seem to be an obvious source of information on the size of inherited wealth, they suffer from a number of problems. Survey responses are criticized because they rely on the recall of the respondents, which may be flawed. In addition, households may understate the value of inherited wealth to give the impression that they "earned" their wealth. There is also a methodological issue of how to value inheritances received in the past. Should the income generated from the inherited wealth be counted as part of the inheritance or part of life-cycle wealth? Of course, in most cases, the surveys do not provide any information about the amount of income earned on the inherited wealth since the date of inheritance, so that researchers must make some assumptions in this regard.

Rather than collect data on the amount of wealth inherited by the entire living population, an alternative approach is to use information about the amount inherited (or transferred) in any *one year*. For example, Kotlikoff and Summers (1981) use the distribution of wealth by age, sex and marital status obtained from the 1962 Survey of Financial Characteristics of Consumers. Given the average amount of wealth owned in each age–sex–marital status category, they then apply 1962 mortality figures to these data to obtain an estimate of the amount of wealth bequeathed in 1962. For example, if the average wealth of 55-year-old married men in 1962 was $20,000 and one hundred 55-year-old, married men died in 1962, they estimate that bequests from this group equalled $2,000,000. They adjust these figures to eliminate interspousal transfers and to include life insurance death benefits, parental support for children enrolled in college, and wealth transferred via trusts. From this information on the amount of inheritance in one year, an estimate of the total amount of inherited wealth in all previous years for the living population is made. By making assumptions about the length of life, age at which bequests are made, age at which inheritances are received, the rate of growth of the economy, and the interest rate, they "blow up" this annual figure on intergenerational transfers to obtain an estimate of the total stock of inherited wealth. Obviously, this type of computation is sensitive to the numerous assumptions made.

An alternative to surveying the living to obtain information on the amount inherited is to survey the dead via probate records to obtain information on the amount bequeathed. One such study by Menchik (1980a) uses Connecticut probate-record data to assess the share of a person's wealth at death that is directly attributable to inheritance he or she received from their parents. The magnitude of the ratio of inheritance received from parents to the subject's wealth at death is very sensitive to assumptions concerning the rate of interest earned on any inheritance. Assuming an interest rate equal to the rate of inflation implies that about 30 percent of a typical heir's wealth at death is attributable to inheritance. Using the rate of interest obtainable on short-term government bonds raises the ratio to 50 percent. If the inheritor is assumed to earn the rate of return available in the stock market on inherited wealth, the ratio of the value of inherited wealth at death to total wealth exceeds one, implying that more than 100 percent of wealth is attributable to inheritance.

Although the use of probate records could theoretically be used to determine the total amount inherited by currently living individuals, the only practical application has been to determine the amount bequeathed in *one year* and then to "blow up" this amount based on assumptions regarding ages at which bequests are made and received. Menchik and David (1983) collected probate records of people who died in Wisconsin between 1947 and 1978 to do just this. Modigliani (1988a) used the average bequest made in the sample as an estimate of the typical bequest in 1962 and multiplied this by the number of people who died in 1962 to obtain an estimate of total bequests in 1962. He further adjusted this to exclude interspousal transfers and "blew up" the annual amount to obtain an estimate of the stock of inherited wealth. However, the data—collected for one state (Wisconsin)—were not assembled to be representative of the entire United States population.

LIFE-CYCLE RESIDUAL.   An indirect method to obtain a measure of inherited wealth is to first obtain a measure of life-cycle wealth. The difference between this estimate of life-cycle wealth and total wealth is then an estimate of inherited (or transferred) wealth.

One method of obtaining an estimate of life-cycle wealth is through simulations. White (1978) used a simulation approach to estimate life-cycle wealth for 1953, 1959, and 1964. The actual income and age distribution of the United States economy in these years forms the foundation of the simulations. For purposes of the simulation, everyone is assumed to start work at age 20, retire at age 65, and die at age 75. All individuals of the same age are assumed to have the same income. Using various assumptions regarding how income changes (or does not change) as individuals age, how desired consumption changes (or does not change) as one ages, and the interest rate, White calculates the quantity of life-cycle wealth in the economy as the sum of the difference between income and consumption across all individuals in the economy. She concluded that life-cycle wealth constitutes "at best" 42 percent of total wealth; thus, inherited wealth equals at least 58 percent of total wealth. Of course, the simulated values depend heavily on the assumptions made and, therefore, are always subject to criticism.

Kotlikoff and Summers (1981) used an aggregate longitudinal approach to estimate the amount of life-cycle wealth. First they obtained data on the total amount of labor earnings, consumption, and government transfers in each year between 1900 and 1974 for the entire United States. They then allocated total earnings, consumption, and transfers in each year among the population over 18 at that date classified by age and sex based on estimates of how earnings vary by age and gender. From this information, they were able to compute the average earnings, consumption, and transfer payments received by individuals in each age–sex category for each year. These annual average figures form earnings, consumption, and transfer histories for each age–sex cohort alive in 1974. For example, 50-year-olds in 1974 were assumed to have the average values of 40-year-olds in 1964, and 41-year-olds in 1965. The difference between the sum of earnings and transfers less consumption in each year is the estimate of annual savings in each year. Savings are then summed over the working lifetime for each age–sex group using alternative assumptions about the rate of interest earned on savings. This summation of savings is the estimate of life-cycle wealth for each age–sex group and is multiplied by the number of individuals in each age–sex group alive in 1974 to obtain an estimate to the total amount of life-cycle wealth in 1974.

Empirical Evidence

Given the various methods of computing the amount of inherited wealth and the problems inherent in each method, it is no wonder that in the United States there is an ongoing controversy among economists over the proportion of accumulated wealth that was inherited. This controversy has been referred to by some as resulting in the "law of 20/80" (Kessler and Masson, 1989).

On the one hand, a number of studies find that inherited wealth constitutes a relatively small proportion of total wealth—roughly 20 percent of total wealth. Life-cycle wealth, according to these studies, constitutes the remaining 80 percent. Modigliani (1988a, 1988b), one of the principal proponents of this view, summarizes the results of a number of direct measures of inherited wealth and at least one study employing the life-cycle residual method (Ando and Kennickell, 1987) to support his position.

On the other hand, some researchers find that life-cycle wealth represents only 20 percent of total wealth and conclude that inherited wealth equals 80 percent of total wealth. Kotlikoff and Summers (1981, 1988), principal proponents of this view, employ both direct and life-cycle residual approaches to measure the proportion of wealth that is inherited. They also summarize other evidence that is consistent with a large share of inherited wealth. They interpret findings by Bernheim (1985) and Hurd (1987) to indicate that households do not decumulate wealth in old age, which is contrary to the assumptions of life-cycle wealth. In addition, they point out that if households only accumulated wealth to finance old age, then households should purchase annuities that would provide income until they die. However, they do not find evidence that households annuitize a great deal of their wealth.

Attempts to reconcile these opposing views and to marshal additional evidence in support of, or to contradict, each view are an ongoing part of current economic research. Blinder (1988) made a very thoughtful attempt to adjudicate this dispute. In the end, he concludes that using direct methods to measure the amount of inherited wealth supports the view that only 20 to

30 percent of wealth is inherited. On the other hand, he concludes that the best estimates of life-cycle wealth place it in the 30 to 50 percent range. Consequently, at least 20 percent of total wealth cannot be explained as the result of either inheritances or life-cycle savings. The resolution of this issue involves how durable goods and spending by parents on adult children are treated.

Policy Implications

Resolution of this issue is important for a number of policy issues. One such issue is the determination of the amount of saving in the economy. Because saving provides the funds to finance capital investment, and capital investment increases the productive capacity of the economy, the amount of saving going on in the economy is a prime determinant of the future economic well-being of the economy. Government policy to effectively influence the amount of saving and thus the potential for future economic growth must vary depending on whether most saving is done in order to bequeath wealth to future generations or to finance retirement. Government programs that have an impact on resources available during retirement, such as Social Security, will have a significant impact on economic growth if most saving is done to finance retirement. If Social Security payments simply replace life-cycle saving, the system reduces the total amount of saving in the economy because Social Security in the United States is financed on a pay-as-you-go basis. On the other hand, David and Menchik (1985) provide empirical evidence that Social Security does not affect household bequests. Consequently, the impact of the Social Security program on economic growth will be very different depending on whether most wealth is accumulated to pass on to heirs or to finance retirement.

Policies designed to affect the degree of economic equality will also be more or less effective depending on whether most wealth is inherited or the result of self-accumulation. For example, estate taxes would have a much larger equalizing impact if most wealth is the result of intergenerational transfers rather than self-accumulation.

Inheritances at the Household Level

Although the dollar amount of inheritances is substantial, only a small percentage of households are involved. Gale and Scholz (1994) report that based on a survey of households in 1983–1985, slightly fewer than 4 percent reported receiving a bequest, and between 5 and 9 percent either made or received *inter vivos* transfers. However, both the giving and receiving of intergenerational transfers is more prevalent among the very wealthy. Among the top 10 percent of the households, when ranked by total wealth, 60 percent reported receiving a bequest, and between 27 and 58 percent reported making or receiving an *inter vivos* transfer. There are typically fewer who reported receiving a transfer than reporting making one—in the spirit of "It is better to give than receive."

Frameworks for Analysis

A number of competing bequest motives have been advanced and investigated by economists. Again, one of the issues researchers must confront is distinguishing between planned and unplanned bequests. With respect to planned bequests, theories of motive can be grouped into two types: altruistic and exchange.

ALTRUISTIC MODELS.   Altruistic models of bequests are based on the idea that parents care about the well-being of their children. The simplest approach posits that leaving bequests provides satisfaction to parents. Bequests can be added to a life-cycle model so that parents spend some proportion of their resources on "bequests" to their children. An alternative approach (Bevan and Stiglitz, 1979) views bequests following a type of "golden rule" (i.e., people bequeath an amount equal to that which they inherited plus or minus some amount to account for changes in fortune over their own lifetime). An important difference between these two approaches is that the life-cycle model incorporating bequests predicts that bequests will be proportional to *total* parental resources, whereas the "golden-rule" approach predicts that bequests will be proportional only to that part of parental resources that were inherited.

In a more complicated approach, Menchik and Γ (1983) suggest that parents make financial bequests to their children , after they have exhausted other ways to improve their children's quality of life. In this model, parents are concerned with their children's income, but they are careful to invest in their children in the most productive way. This means that they first feed them and clothe them, provide health care, and provide them with schooling. Eventually, they exhaust the productive types of expenditures and all future parental transfers are financial ones—gifts and bequests. This model implies that the more children in a family, the smaller the financial bequests, holding other factors constant; the higher the level of parental resources, the higher the level of financial bequests.

Other altruistic models of bequests imply that parents use bequests to equalize opportunities among their children who have differing abilities and to make sure that their children will enjoy the same *relative* status in life as the parents. The family is viewed as a multigenerational dynasty, and the current generation is concerned about the economic well-being of future generations. Bequests are instruments used to adjust economic well-being within and across generations.

Within-generation altruism posits that parents want all of their children to be equally well off. Becker and Tomes (1976) argue that as long as parents exhibit equal concern about their children's welfare, they will make educational decisions on the basis of "efficiency" (allocating funds for schooling on the basis of the children's abilities) but bequeath on the basis of "equity," leaving more to the less able child. In fact, in their article, Becker and Tomes stated that bequests and gifts would be used to perfectly equalize incomes of siblings (p. S154).

Across-generation altruism is concerned with the well-being of parents relative to their children. Becker and Tomes (1979) hypothesize that parents will consume, or refrain from consuming, and bequeath on the basis of the relative sizes of parental and child income. This model predicts that, holding parental income constant, the larger the average income of one's own children, the less will be bequeathed to them.

EXCHANGE MODELS. Kotlikoff and Spivak (1981) derive a model of bequests that arises because of deficiencies in the insurance market. According to this approach, individuals do not derive utility from bequeathing or augmenting their heirs' welfare, but only from their own consumption. These risk-averse individuals, uncertain about the date of their own deaths, have an incentive to purchase annuities to insure themselves against the risk of living "too long" and becoming penniless. Such an arrangement will allow them to consume all of their wealth instead of dying with a bequest going to heirs about whom they do not care. Evidence indicates that the annuities will be mispriced (because people who expect a long life and therefore collect much are more likely to purchase such a policy than a person with a shorter life span). Kotlikoff and Spivak argue that the family will construct its own annuity market. Parents will "purchase" annuities from their children with the price being a bequest paid in return for support during the old age of the parent. Parents use bequests as a way to pay their children for care received late in life.

Finally, the strategic model of bequests assumes that parents are completely indifferent to the welfare of heirs and suggests that parents use bequests as a way to control the behavior of their children, using the threat of disinheritance to manipulate their children's behavior. This point of view has been advanced in the "power" model of Thurow (1975), the "merit" good model of Becker (1981), with its most recent embodiment the "strategic" model of Bernheim, Shleifer, and Summers (1985), who argue that parents will use the threat of disinheritance, playing off one potential heir against another, to acquire the attention and services from beneficiaries.

Empirical Evidence

Joulfaian and Wilhelm (1994) report that approximately 20 percent of the respondents in the 1994 Panel Survey on Income Dynamics reported having ever received an inheritance. Among those who had received an inheritance, the average amount was $64,906 (in 1989 dollars). Approximately 28 percent expected to receive an inheritance in the future, and 5 percent expected to receive a large (greater than $120,000) inheritance in the future.

As Tachibanaki (1994) reports, there is almost no support of the pure altruistic motives for bequests. Wilhelm (1996), using Federal Estate Tax data, fails to find convincing evidence of altruism. Laitner and Juster (1996), using data on faculty pension choices, find, at best, weak support for behavior consistent with altruistic motives of saving and bequeathing. One piece of empirical evidence that could be used to distinguish between these competing theories is whether bequests are made equally to all children or whether bequests are unequal among children, as predicted by the altruistic models. Menchik (1980a,1988) finds that bequests are almost always made equally between children.

Although much empirical research has focused on the motivation of the *givers* of bequests, a few economists have examined the impact of the *receipt* of an inheritance. Joulfaian and Wilhelm (1994) make use of two sets of survey data to analyze the impact of inheritances on the receiver's labor-force participation. They find that receipt of an inheritance does tend to reduce the hours worked by the recipient but conclude that the reduction is relatively small. In contrast Holtz-Eakin, Joulfaian, and Rosen (1993) find a rather large reduction in work effort among those who receive an inheritance. If receipt of an inheritance does reduce hours worked among the recipients, and hence their income, this would partially offset the tendency for inheritances to increase the inequality of wealth.

Altonji, Hayashi, and Kotlikoff (1992) do not find evidence of an altruistic extended family. If there were altruism across generations, then the consumption of one generation would not depend on their resources, but on the resources of the extended family. Using the Panel Survey of Income Dynamics, which allows them to observe the behavior of parents and their children living independently, they find that consumption decisions, including level of the children's consumption, depend on the children's income, not on the income of the parents. Thus, they find that poor children of rich parents do not consume more than poor children of poor parents.

Policy Implications

Whether bequests are made equally or unequally among children has important implications for the distribution of income. If bequests are compensatory (i.e., parents leave more to their poorer children), then bequests are an equalizing factor. If bequests are unequal, but the more able child receives more, or if children have unequal abilities and bequests are made equally, then bequests contribute to widening the distribution of income.

Whether a bequest motive exists is crucial in the analysis of the impact of government budget deficits on the economy (Barro, 1974). According to the idea known as Ricardian equivalence, if successive generations are linked through bequests, then it does not matter whether a given level of government spending is financed through current taxes (i.e., a balanced budget) or through government borrowing (i.e., a budget deficit). The logic of this argument centers on the impact of the alternative methods of financing government spending on the interest rate. In a traditional analysis (non-Ricardian equivalence), if the government increases borrowing (i.e., runs a deficit) to finance spending, this increases interest rates, which in turn slow economic spending, such as spending on new houses and factories, and thus retards long-run economic growth. On the other hand, using the logic of Ricardian equivalence, taxpayers are aware that any government borrowing today will have to be paid back in the future. Even if current taxpayers believe that they themselves will be dead when taxes are increased in the future to pay off the government debt, current taxpayers realize that their children will have to pay higher taxes in the future. Current taxpayers, therefore, increase their saving in order to leave a larger bequest to their children who will be burdened with the higher future taxes. The increase in current saving offsets the impact of the increase in government borrowing so that the interest rate is unchanged and economic activity is unaffected. Of course, crucial links in this chain of events are that current taxpayers view themselves as part of a familial dynasty and take into consideration not only their own well-being, but the well-being of future generations, and that current generations must also engage in bequest giving to compensate future generations. Consequently, evidence of a substantial bequest motive plays an important role in assessing the impact of government budget deficits.

Summary and Conclusions

Inheritances are of interest to economists at both the economywide level and at the individual-household level. For the economy as a whole, a principal issue of concern to economists is the proportion of total wealth that was inherited versus the amount that was accumulated by the current generation. The magnitude of each of these quantities has not yet been satisfactorily established. Data providing direct measures of the amount of wealth inherited over a lifetime or any one year for the whole economy are rare and subject to both conceptual and measurement problems. As an alternative to the direct measurement of inherited wealth, a number of researchers have attempted to measure self-accumulated (or life-cycle) wealth. Once again, the lack of suitable data limits these estimates. Currently, the best estimates suggest that inherited wealth could represent as little as 20 percent or as much as 80 percent of total wealth. Whether wealth was accumulated to pass on to future generations or to finance one's own spending during retirement has an important impact on a number of policy issues, including how best to stimulate private saving and whether inheritance taxes have wealth-equalizing impacts.

At the individual-household level, a number of theories have been set forward to explain household motivation to leave a bequest. One set of theories hypothesizes that individuals are altruistic and care about the well-being of future generations. Other theories suggest that bequests are in fact payments made in order to motivate the behavior of the recipients. Although these theories are not mutually exclusive and people may be acting on a combination of motives, the predominance of one or the other type of motivation for making bequests does have a number of important implications. For example, bequests are more likely to be wealth equalizing if they are made for altruistic purposes rather than for the purpose of exchange. At a much more fundamental level, the very existence of a bequest motive is central to resolving whether a government's budget deficit has an impact on economic activity.

Although we have surveyed the central issues associated with inheritances from an economist's perspective, there are a number of aspects of inheritance that economists have investigated that we have not mentioned. Perhaps most important, the design and impact of inheritance taxes are analyzed by economists as well as accountants and lawyers. Economists and historians have investigated how inheritance changes over time. Finally, economists, anthropologists, and sociologists have studied cross-cultural variations in inheritance. In particular, differences in inheritance across countries, cultures, and times reflect important economic differences between agrarian and industrial economies.

References

Altonji, J. G., Hayashi, F., & Kotlikoff, L. (1992). Is the extended family altruistically linked? Direct tests using micro data. *American Economic Review, 82,* 1177–1198.

Ando, A. K., and Kennickell, A. B. (1987). How much (or little) life cycle is there in micro data? The cases of the United States and Japan. In R. Dornburgh, S. Fischer, and J. Bossons (eds.), *Macroeconomics and Finance.* Cambridge, MA: MIT Press.

Barlow, R., Brazer, H. E., & Morgan, J. N. (1966). *Economic behavior of the affluent.* Washington, DC: Brookings Institution.

Barro, R. J. (1974). Are government bonds new wealth? *Journal of Political Economy, 82*, 1095–1117.

Becker, G. (1981). *Treatise on the family*. Cambridge, MA: Harvard University Press.

Becker, G., & Tomes, N. (1976). Child endowments and the quantity and quality of children. *Journal of Political Economy, 84*, S143–S162.

Becker, G., and Tomes, N. (1979). An equilibrium theory of the distribution of income and intergenerational transfers. *Journal of Political Economy, 87*, 1153–1189.

Becker, G., & Tomes, N. (1986). Dissaving after retirement: Testing the pure life cycle hypothesis. In Zvi Bodi (ed.), *Issues in Pension Economics*. Chicago: University of Chicago Press.

Bernheim, B. D., Schleifer, A., & Summers, L. H. (1985). The strategic bequest motive. *Journal of Political Economy, 93*, 1045–1075.

Bevan, D. L., & Stiglitz, J. (1979). Intergenerational transfers and inequality. *Greek Economic Review, 1*, 8–26.

Blinder, A. S. (1988). Comments on Chapter 1 and Chapter 2. In D. Kessler & A. Masson (Eds.), *Modelling the accumulation and distribution of wealth* (pp. 68–76). Oxford: Clarendon Press.

Cox, D. (1987). Motives for private income transfers. *Journal of Political Economy, 95*, 508–546.

David, M., & Menchik, P. L. (1985). The effect of social security on lifetime wealth accumulation and bequests. *Economica, 52*, 421–434.

Gale, W. G., & Scholz, J. K. (1994). Intergenerational transfers and the accumulation of wealth. *Journal of Economic Perspectives, 8*, 145–160.

Goody, J. (1987). Inheritance. In J. Eatwell, M. Milgate, & P. Newman (Eds.), *The new Palgrave: A dictionary of economics* (pp. 851–855). New York: Stockton Press.

Hamermesh, D. S., & Menchik, P. L. (1987). Planned and unplanned bequests. *Economic Inquiry, 25*, 55–66.

Holtz-Eakin, D., Joulfaian, D., & Rosen, H. S. (1993). The Carnegie conjecture: Some empirical evidence. *Quarterly Journal of Economics, 108*, 413–435.

Hurd, M. D. (1987). Savings of the elderly and desired bequests. *American Economic Review, 77*, 298–312.

Hurd, M. D., & Mundaca, B. G. (1989). The importance of gifts and inheritances among the affluent. In R. E. Lipsey & H. S. Tice (Eds.), *The measurement of saving, investment and wealth* (pp. 737–758). Chicago: University of Chicago Press.

Joulfaian, D., & Wilhelm, M. O. (1994). Inheritance and labor supply. *Journal of Human Resources, 29*, 1205–1234.

Kessler, D., & Masson, A. (1989). Bequest and wealth accumulation: Are some pieces of the puzzle missing? *Journal of Economic Perspectives, 3*, 141–152.

Kotlikoff, L. J. (1988). Intergenerational transfers and savings. *Journal of Economic Perspectives, 2*, 41–58.

Kotlikoff, L. J., & Spivak, A. (1981). The family as an incomplete annuity market. *Journal of Political Economy, 89*, 272–291.

Kotlikoff, L. J., & Summers, L. H. (1981). The role of intergenerational transfers in aggregate capital accumulation. *Journal of Political Economy, 89*, 706–732.

Kotlikoff, L. J., & Summers, L. H. (1988). The contribution of intergenerational transfers to total wealth: A reply. In D. Kessler & A. Masson (Eds.), *Modelling the accumulation and distribution of wealth* (pp. 53–67). Oxford, UK: Clarendon Press.

Kurz, M. (1984). Capital accumulation and the characteristics of private intergenerational transfers. *Economica, 51*, 1–22.

Laitner, J., & Juster, F. T. (1996). New evidence on altruism: A study of TIAA-CREF retirees. *American Economic Review, 86*, 893–908.

Menchik, P. L. (1980a). The importance of material inheritance: The financial link between generations. In J. D. Smith (Ed.), *Modeling the distribution and intergenerational transmission of wealth* (pp. 159-185). Chicago: University of Chicago Press for the National Bureau of Economic Research.

Menchik, P. L. (1980b). Primogeniture, equal sharing, and the U.S. distribution of wealth. *Quarterly Journal of Economics, 94*, 299-316.

Menchik, P. L. (1988). Unequal estate division: Is it altruism, reverse bequests, or simply noise. In D. Kessler & A. Masson (Eds.), *Modelling the accumulation and distribution of wealth* (pp. 105-116). Oxford, UK: Clarendon Press.

Menchik, P. L., & David, M. (1983). Income distribution, lifetime savings and bequests. *American Economic Review, 73*, 672-689.

Modigliani, F. (1988a). Measuring the contribution of intergenerational transfers to total wealth: Conceptual issues and empirical findings. In D. Kessler & A. Masson (Eds.), *Modelling the accumulation and distribution of wealth* (pp. 21-52). Oxford, UK: Clarendon Press.

Modigliani, F. (1988b). The role of intergenerational transfers and life cycle saving in the accumulation of wealth. *Journal of Economic Perspectives, 2*, 15-40.

Modigliani, F., & Brumberg, R. (1954). Utility analysis and the consumption function: An interpretation of cross section data. In K. K. Kurihara (Ed.), *Post-Keynesian economics* (pp. 388-436). New Brunswick, NJ: Rutgers University Press.

Projector, D., & Weiss, G. S. (1964). *Survey of financial characteristics of consumers*. Washington, DC: Board of Governors of the Federal Reserve System.

Tachibanaki, T. (1994). *Savings and bequests*. Ann Arbor: University of Michigan Press.

Thurow, L. (1975). *Generating inequality*. New York: Basic Books.

Tomes, N. (1981). The family, inheritance, and the intergenerational transmission of inequality. *Journal of Political Economy, 89*, 928-958.

Tomes, N. (1988). Inheritance and inequality within the family: Equal division among unequals, or do the poor get more? In D. Kessler & A. Masson (Eds.), *Modelling the accumulation and distribution of wealth* (pp. 79-104). Oxford, UK: Clarendon Press.

White, B. B. (1978). Empirical tests of the life cycle hypothesis. *American Economic Review, 68*, 547-560.

Wilhelm, M. O. (1996). Bequest behavior and the effect of heirs' earnings: Testing the altruistic model of bequests. *American Economic Review 86*, 874-892.

4

Federal Taxation of Inheritance and Wealth Transfers

Barry W. Johnson and Martha Britton Eller

... in this world nothing is certain but death and taxes.

—Benjamin Franklin

Introduction: Inheritance and Taxation

For most of the 20th century and at key points throughout American history, the federal government has relied on estate and inheritance taxes as sources of funding. The modern transfer tax system, introduced in 1916, provides revenue to the federal government through taxes on transfers of property between living individuals—*inter vivos* transfers—as well as through a tax on transfers of property at death. Proponents of transfer taxation embrace it as both a "fair" source of revenue and an effective tool for preventing the concentration of wealth in the hands of a few powerful families. Opponents claim that transfer taxation creates a disincentive to accumulate capital and, thus, is detrimental to the growth of national productivity. Controversy over the role of inheritance in democratic society and the propriety of taxing property at death is not new but is rooted firmly in arguments that have raged

Barry W. Johnson and Martha Britton Eller • Internal Revenue Service, P.O. Box 2608, Washington, D.C. 20013.

Inheritance and Wealth in America, edited by Robert K. Miller, Jr., and Stephen J. McNamee. Plenum Press, New York, 1998.

since Western society emerged from its feudal foundations. Central to both historic and current debate is the divergent characterization of inheritance as either a "right" or a "privilege." An understanding of these arguments, and of the history surrounding the development of the modern American transfer tax system, provides a foundation for evaluating current debates and proposals for changes to that system.

Historical Overview

Taxation of property transfers at death can be traced back to ancient Egypt as early as 700 B.C. (Paul, 1954). Nearly 2,000 years ago, Roman Emperor Caesar Augustus imposed the *Vicesina Hereditatium*, a tax on successions and legacies to all but close relatives (Smith, 1913). Taxes imposed at the death of a family member were quite common in feudal Europe, often amounting to a family's annual property rent. By the 18th century, stamp duties and registration fees on wills, inventories and other documents related to property transfers at death had been adopted by many nations.

Inheritance in Early America: English Foundations

American ideas concerning the rights of individuals in the new republic can be traced to the writings of English philosopher John Locke. Writing in the last half of the 17th century, he suggested that each citizen was born with certain natural, or God-given, rights; chief among those rights was property ownership. Citizens had a right to own as much property as they could employ their labor upon, but not to own excessive amounts at the expense of the rest of society. Furthermore, he argued that the right to bequeath accumulated property to children was divinely ensured. "Nature appoints the descent of their [parent's] property to their children who then come to have a title and natural right of inheritance to their father's goods, which the rest of mankind cannot pretend to" (Locke, 1988, p. 207). Likewise, Locke felt that a father should inherit a child's property if the child died without issue. If, however, a person died without any kindred, the property should be returned to society. Government was established at the will of the people and was charged with protecting these rights, according to Locke. However, government had an even higher responsibility—to ensure the benefit of all society. When societal and individual rights clashed, suggested Locke, it was the civil government's duty to exercise its *prerogative* in order to ensure the common good.

The idea that inheritance was a "natural right" was refuted nearly a century later by English jurist William Blackstone. In his *Commentaries on the Law of England* (1769), Blackstone wrote that possession of property ended with the death of its owner; thus, there was no natural right to bequeath property to successive generations; therefore, any right to control the disposition of property after death was granted by civil law—not by natural law—primarily to prevent undue economic disturbances. Blackstone thus concluded that the government had the right to regulate transfers of property from the dead to the living. His interpretation of law "has served as the legal foundations upon which death taxes in Anglo–American tax systems rest" (Fiekowsky, 1959; p. 22).

The belief that government was responsible for the protection of the general good, espoused by John Locke and others, laid the foundation for the Utilitarian movement in English social philosophy. Jeremy Bentham, one of the greatest proponents of Utilitarian philosophy, rejected the idea of natural rights. Instead, he stressed the higher goal of ensuring the general welfare. He and his followers believed in a government that played an active role in moving society toward that goal. Bentham, therefore, advocated strong regulation of inheritances " 'in order to prevent too great an accumulation of wealth in the hands of an individual' " (Chester, 1982, p. 18).

Yet the idea of government actively engaged in promoting the general welfare was rejected by economist Adam Smith, a contemporary of both Blackstone and Bentham, and the father of classical economics. Smith believed that an unregulated economy, driven by the natural interplay of selfish, individual desires, would produce the greatest good for society. Although he seemed to accept the government's right to tax inheritances, he argued against it. He called all taxes on property at death "more or less unthrifty taxes, that increase the revenue of the sovereign, which seldom maintains any but unproductive labor, at the expense of the capital of the people, which maintains none but productive" (Smith, 1913, p. 684). Later, economist David Ricardo, writing in the early 19th century, reinforced the idea. He suggested that English probate taxes, legacy duties, and transfer taxes "prevent the national capital from being distributed in the way most beneficial to the community" (Ricardo, 1819, p. 192).

These then, are the somewhat divergent philosophies from which Thomas Jefferson, in drafting the Declaration of Independence, developed his idea of God-given, or natural, rights that emphasize personal and political freedoms. Jefferson argued that the use of property was a natural right, but that the right was limited by the needs of the rest of society. Furthermore, he also argued that property ownership ended at death. Although he did not call for abolishing the institution of inheritance, he did advocate a strong role for government in its regulation. As in other areas of American life, Jefferson heavily influenced later thinking about property rights, inheritance, and taxation by governmental bodies.

The Stamp Tax of 1797

In general, early American government adopted a laissez-faire approach to the economy, an approach advocated by Adam Smith. However, when Congress needed to raise additional funds in response to the undeclared naval war with France in 1794, it chose a death tax as the source of revenue. The Stamp Act of 1797 was enacted to finance the naval buildup necessary for the national defense. Federal stamps were required on wills offered for probate, as well as on inventories and letters of administration. Stamps also were required on receipts and discharges from legacies and intestate distributions of property (Zaritsky and Ripy, 1984). Duties were levied as follows: 10 cents on inventories and the effects of deceased persons, and 50 cents on the probate of wills and letters of administration. The stamp tax on the receipt of legacies was levied on bequests larger than $50, from which widows (but not widowers), children, and grandchildren were exempt. Bequests between $50 and $100 were taxed 25 cents; those between $100 and $500 were taxed 50 cents, and an additional $1 was added for each subsequent $500 bequest. In 1802, the crisis ended, and the tax was repealed (Repeal of Internal Tax Act, 1802). In 1815, Treasury Secretary Alexander Dallas proposed the resurrection of the tax to provide revenue for the war with England. The Treaty of Ghent, however, ended the war while the tax was still under consideration, and the tax subsequently was dropped (Zaritsky and Ripy, 1984).

In the years immediately preceding the war between the states, revenue from tariffs and the sale of public lands provided the bulk of the federal budget. Inheritance taxes, however, were a source of revenue for many states. Early in the 19th century, Supreme Court Justices John Marshall and Joseph Story defended an individual's natural right to own property; however, their belief that inheritance was a civil, not a natural, right affirmed the states' right to regulate inheritances (Chester, 1982). Later, U.S. Supreme Court Justice Roger Taney, a Jackson appointee, described the inheritance tax in the case of *Mager v. Grima* (1850). "[I]f a state may deny the privilege [of inheritance] altogether," he wrote, it may, when it grants that privilege, "annex to the grant any conditions which it supposes to be required by its interests or policy" (p. 494).

The Tax Act of 1862

The advent of the Civil War again forced the federal government to seek additional sources of revenue, and a federal inheritance tax was enacted in the Tax Act of 1862. However, the 1862 tax differed from its predecessor, the stamp tax of 1797. In addition to a document tax on the probate of wills and letters of administration, the 1862 tax package included a tax on the privilege of inheritance. Originally, the tax only applied to the devise of personal property, and tax rates were graduated based on the legatee's relationship to the decedent, not on the value of the bequest or size of the estate. Rates ranged from 0.75 percent of bequests to ancestors, lineal descendants, and siblings, to 5 percent on bequests to distant relatives and those not related to the decedent. Estates of less than $1,000 were exempted, as were bequests to the surviving spouse. Bequests to charities were taxed at the top rate, despite pleas from many in Congress that the tax should be used to encourage such gifts (Office of Tax Analysis, 1963). In addition, the stamp tax ranged from 50 cents to $20 on estates valued up to $150,000, with an additional $10 assessed on each $50,000 or fraction thereof over $150,000.

Far from a source of controversy, the inheritance tax was praised in the *Congressional Globe* as a "large source of revenue which could be most conveniently collected" (Office of Tax Analysis, 1963, p. 2). Senator James McDougall of California argued that the tax was the least burdensome alternative for raising needed revenue because "those who pay it, never having had it, never feel the loss of it" (Paul, 1954, p. 15). According to *The Internal Revenue Record and Customs Journal*, the 1862 tax was "one of the best, fairest, and most easily borne [taxes] that political economists have yet discovered as applicable to modern society" (1869, p. 113).

The mounting cost of the Civil War led to the reenactment of the 1862 Revenue Act, with some modifications. These changes, established in the Internal Revenue Law of 1864, included the addition of a succession tax—a tax on bequests of real property—and an increase in legacy tax rates (see Table 4.1). In addition, the tax was applied to any transfers of real property made during the decedent's life for less than adequate consideration, thus establishing the nation's first gift tax. Wedding gifts were exempted. Transfers of real property to charities, again, were taxed at the highest rates. Bequests to widows, but not widowers, were exempt from the succession tax, as were bequests of less than $1,000 to minor children.

TABLE 4.1. 1864 Death Tax Rates

Relationship	Rates on real property (%)	Rates on legacies (%)	Increase in legacies over 1862 (%)
Lineal issue, ancestors	1.00	1.00	0.25
Siblings	2.00	1.00	0.25
Descendants of siblings	2.00	2.00	0.50
Uncle, aunt, and their descendants	4.00	4.00	1.00
Great uncle, aunt, and their descendants	5.00	5.00	1.00
Other relatives, not related	6.00	6.00	1.00
Charities	6.00	6.00	1.00

The end of the Civil War and subsequent discharge of the debts associated with the war gradually eliminated the need for extra revenue provided by the 1864 Act. Therefore, in 1870, the inheritance tax was repealed (Internal Tax Customs Duties Act). The probate tax was modified in 1867 to exempt all estates less than $1,000 (Internal Revenue Act of 1867) and repealed in 1872 (Customs Duties and Internal Revenue Taxes Act). Between 1863 and 1871, the tax had contributed a total of about $14.8 million to the federal budget (see Table 4.2; Fiekowsky, 1959). In an important victory, the Supreme Court upheld the constitutionality of the federal inheritance tax in *Scholey v. Revenue Service* (1874). The court ruled that the inheritance tax was not a direct tax but an excise tax authorized by Article I, Section 8 of the Constitution.

The 1864 Act, although altered by subsequent legislation, introduced several features that later formed the foundation of the modern transfer tax system. Some of these features included the exemption of small estates, the taxation of certain lifetime transfers that were testamentary in nature, and the special treatment of bequests to the surviving spouse. The idea of using tax policy to encourage bequests to charitable organizations also was advanced in the debates surrounding the structure of the inheritance tax (Paul, 1954).

Inheritance Taxation and the Industrial Revolution

The repeal of the Civil War inheritance tax was achieved with little public notice. However, inheritance and the responsibility of government to ensure equal opportunities for its citizenry would invoke intense debates by the close of the century. The postwar period was one of unprecedented economic and population growth. It was also one that saw enormous changes in the American way of life. The industrial revolution was at hand and, as

TABLE 4.2. Death Tax Receipts, Total Tax Receipts
in the United States, for Fiscal Years 1863-1871

Year	Total tax receipts (millions)	Death tax receipts (millions)	Death taxes as percentage of total
1863	41.0	0.1	0.1
1864	117.1	0.3	0.3
1865	211.1	0.5	0.3
1866	310.9	1.2	0.4
1867	265.9	1.9	0.7
1868	191.2	2.8	1.5
1869	160.0	2.4	1.5
1870	185.2	3.1	1.7
1871	144.0	2.5	1.7

Americans sought the fruits of mass production, the growth of industry spurred the development of large urban centers and provided new jobs for both natural-born citizens and the ever-increasing number of immigrants (Bruchey, 1988).

The growth of industrial America and, with it, the prosperity of entrepreneurs who pioneered in the creation of new products and services came at a time when declining prices for agricultural products were hurting American farmers in the West and in the South. The wealth of the country increasingly became concentrated in the hands of industrialists as investments in stocks began to supplant those in real estate. Because tariffs and real estate taxes formed the basis of government finances at the federal and state levels, the burden of supporting government fell disproportionately on farmers, whereas the wealth of the industrial giants was relatively untouched. These events brought about a series of important political and social movements, including a renewed discussion of the institution of inheritance (Paul, 1954).

In Europe, the growing discontent with the concentration of national wealth in the hands of relatively few privileged families, and with the perpetuation of that wealth through bequests, coincided with the rise of communism (Chester, 1982). In England, economist John Stuart Mill (1994) urged limits on the rights of individuals to bequeath property to heirs. He argued that inheritance of property had its roots in feudal society where land was used, but not owned, by the family. The death of a family member had little effect on the use of the land. This was not the case in "modern" society, where grown children left their parents' homes and pursued independent lives and, therefore, no longer held a claim on their parents' property. Mill, therefore, proposed "fixing a limit to what anyone may acquire by mere favor of others without exercise of his facilities," adding that "if he desires any further accession of fortune, he shall work for it" (Mill, 1994, p. 35). Thus, Mill condoned a graduated tax on inheritances as a proper limiting mechanism. In agreement with Locke and Bentham, he proposed eliminating bequests to nonfamily members.

In America, the populist movement also was calling for limits on inheritance and changes in tax laws to make the very wealthy "pay their fair share." Writers such as Joseph Kirkland, Mark Twain, William Dean Howells, and others were addressing the evils of capitalism and the plight of the farmer. Reformers such as Joseph Pulitzer, publisher of the *New York World*, embraced the cause of the people rather than that of "purse-proud potentates" (Paul, 1954, p. 30). Pulitzer urged the elimination of tariffs, because tariffs protected businesses and their owners from competition and put the burden of taxation disproportionately on consumers. That sentiment was echoed by many in Congress, including Congressman Henry George, who advocated an income tax in "an attempt to tax men on what they have, not on what they need" (Paul, 1954, p. 31). Other reformers, such as Charles Bellamy, a utopian socialist writing in 1884, called for limits on inheritance, especially a limit on the amount of property that could be distributed by will (Chester, 1982). "Steep [inheritance] taxes ... would decrease the number of social drones," according to Professor Gustavus Meyer, author of *The Ending of Hereditary American Fortunes*. "Heirs would have less funds to indulge in lavish expenditures, and the tax burden would be shifted from the laboring and consuming public" (Office of Tax Analysis, 1963, p. 7). Richard T. Ely, author of *Taxation in American States and Cities*, hailed the inheritance tax as a tax that was "in accord with the principles of Jeffersonian Democracy and with the teachings of some of the best modern thinkers on economic and social topics" (Office of Tax Analysis, 1963, p. 7).

One of the outstanding proponents of a substantial federal inheritance tax was industrialist Andrew Carnegie. In his essay, "The Gospel of Wealth," he advised that "the thoughtful man" would rather leave his children a curse than the "almighty dollar" (1962, p. 21) The parent who leaves his son enormous wealth generally deadens the talents and energies of the son and tempts the son to lead a less useful and less worthy life than he otherwise would, according to Carnegie. He did not advocate leveling the wealth distribution, however. Rather, he strongly believed that individuals should be encouraged to amass great wealth and spend it, not on opulent living, but on important, carefully planned works for the public good. Carnegie also advocated a confiscatory inheritance tax, which, he suggested, would force the wealthy to be more attentive to the needs of the state—to use their money for noble causes during their lifetimes. Dismissing arguments that a large inheritance tax would diminish the incentive to accumulate wealth, Carnegie maintained that for the class whose ambition it is to leave great fortunes, "it will attract even more attention, and, indeed, be a somewhat nobler ambition, to have enormous sums paid over to the State from their fortunes" (p. 22).

Defenders of material accumulation and of the right to bequeath wealth to successive generations found refuge in the philosophy of social Darwinism. Related to the writings of the naturalist Charles Darwin, social Darwinism was first proposed in England by Herbert Spencer and later popularized by William Graham Sumner in the United States. Foremost, Sumner argued that government should not interfere with an individual's natural right to struggle for survival. Therefore, he saw no problem with inequalities in the concentration of wealth that arose through the course of that struggle. Those who wanted either to limit the ability to accumulate wealth or to limit the amount of wealth that might be passed on to future generations were, according to Sumner, merely envious of the wealthy and had no right to dictate social policy (Chester, 1982). Sumner viewed a competitive economy as an essential component of a democratic society. Indeed, the discipline imposed by competition was viewed widely as a necessary mechanism for the development of character (Bruchey, 1988).

Reformers achieved the passage of the Income Tax Act of 1894. The value of all personal property acquired by gift or inheritance was included in this graduated tax, which had a top rate of 2 percent. Critics of the tax heralded it as a blow to American democracy and predicted that it would lead ultimately to anarchy. Economist David A. Wells called it "a system of class legislation, full of the spirit of communism," whereas the *North American Review* called it the fulfillment of the "wildest socialist dream" (Paul, 1954, p. 34). The income tax was quickly appealed to the United States Supreme Court in the case of *Pollock v. Farmers Loan and Trust Company* (1895) and declared unconstitutional as an unapportioned direct tax.

Estate Tax of 1898

In 1898, progressive reformers—still stinging from the defeat of the federal income tax—proposed a federal death tax as a means to raise revenue for the Spanish–American War. Unlike the two previous federal inheritance and probate taxes levied in times of war, the 1898 tax proposal provoked heated debate. Supporters of the tax, including Congressman Oscar Underwood of Alabama, used the debate to further their populist agenda. "The inheritance tax is levied on a class of wealth, a class of property and a class of citizens that do not otherwise pay their fair share of the burden of government," Underwood said (Office of Tax Analysis, 1963, p. 11). However, conservatives, such as Congressmen Henry Cabot Lodge and Steven Elkins, opposed the tax. They suggested that the tax would force businesses to liquidate their assets and destroy incentives to accumulate wealth, incentives that were essential to the growth of capital markets (Paul, 1954).

Despite strong opposition, the inheritance tax was made law by the War Revenue Act of 1898. A duty on the estate itself, not on its beneficiaries, the 1898 tax served as a precursor to the present federal estate tax. Rates of tax ranged from 0.75 percent to 15 percent, depending both on the size of the estate and on the relationship of legatee to decedent (see Table 4.3). Only personal property was subject to taxation. A $10,000 exemption was provided to exclude small estates from the tax; bequests to the surviving spouse also were excluded.

In the case *Knowlton v. Moore* (1900), the U.S. Supreme Court declared the constitutionality of the 1898 inheritance tax. The 1898 Act was amended in 1901 to exempt certain gifts from inheritance taxation, including gifts to charitable, religious, literary, and educational organizations, and gifts to organizations dedicated to the encouragement of the arts and the prevention of cruelty to children (War Revenue Reduction Act, 1901). The end of the

TABLE 4.3. 1898 Death Tax Rates

	$10,000 under $25,000 (%)	$25,000 under $100,000 (%)	$100,000 under $500,000 (%)	$500,000 under $1,000,000 (%)	$1,000,000 or more (%)
Lineal issue, ancestors, siblings	0.75	1.125	1.50	1.875	2.25
Descendants of siblings	1.50	2.25	3.00	3.75	4.50
Uncle, aunt, and their descendants	3.00	4.50	6.00	7.50	9.00
Great uncle, aunt, and their descendants	4.00	6.00	8.00	10.00	12.00
All others	5.00	7.50	10.00	12.50	15.00

Note: Estates under $10,000 were exempt from the tax.

Spanish–American War came in 1902, and opponents of the tax wasted no time in enacting its repeal later that year (War Revenue Repeal Act, 1902). Although short-lived, the tax raised about $14.1 million (see Table 4.4, Fiekowsky, 1959).

Prelude to the Modern Estate Tax, 1900-1916

The years immediately preceding and following the turn of the 20th century saw an unprecedented number of mergers in the manufacturing sector of the economy. A new form of ownership, the holding company, caught on and by 1904 was responsible for 86 percent of large mergers (Bruchey, 1988). The result of these mergers was a concentration of wealth in a few powerful companies and in the hands of the businessmen who headed them. Along with such wealth came great political power, and the rise of plutocracy fueled the growth of the progressive movement into the early part of the twentieth century.

The debate that had surrounded the enactment and repeal of both the 1894 income tax and the 1898 inheritance tax gave new credence to the idea of federal taxes as a means of addressing societal inequalities. Under the influence of Carnegie and others, the general public accepted the notion that large inheritances led to idleness and profligacy, states that contradicted their Puritanical worldview. America was founded on the belief that each citizen should begin life with an equal opportunity to succeed and that the economic well-being of the community required that each member earn his or her own living (Bittker and Clark, 1990). The inheritance tax was proclaimed an appropriate tool for ensuring the fulfillment of this manifesto.

By 1906, the progressive movement had an ally in the White House. President Theodore Roosevelt, in his annual message to Congress, endorsed an inheritance tax and suggested that its "primary objective should be to put a constantly increasing burden on the inheritance of those swollen fortunes which it is certainly of no benefit to this country to perpetuate" (Bittker and

TABLE 4.4. Death Tax Receipts, Total Tax Receipts in the United States, for Fiscal Years, 1899-1902

Year	Total tax receipts (millions)	Death tax receipts (millions)	Death taxes as percentage of total
1899	273.5	1.2	0.5
1900	295.3	2.9	1.0
1901	306.9	5.2	1.7
1902	271.9	4.8	1.8

Clark, 1990, p. 3). In the spring of that year, he again called for a progressive tax on all fortunes beyond a certain amount, either given during life or devised, or bequeathed at death. The tax would be directed at "malefactors of great wealth, the wealthy criminal class," according to Roosevelt (Paul, 1954, p. 88). Later in 1906, he endorsed both an inheritance tax and a graduated income tax; however, he was unable to convince a majority of the Congress to enact the reforms (Bittker and Clark, 1990).

In 1909, newly elected President Taft, although unenthusiastic about an income tax, endorsed the inheritance tax. A special session of Congress was called in March 1909 to address the revenue needs that had arisen due, in part, to the bank panic of 1907. In that session, Representative Sereno Payne, the Republican chairman of the House Ways and Means Committee, proposed a graduated inheritance tax. The tax was both correct in principle and easy to collect, according to Payne (Paul, 1954). However, after the enactment of a corporate excise tax, the inheritance tax was dropped by the U.S. Senate. Efforts to enact an income tax that year also were derailed.

The debate over the institution of inheritance, as well as debate over the most suitable source of federal revenues, continued until the passage of the Sixteenth Amendment to the Constitution. With the Sixteenth Amendment came the enactment of the federal income tax. The establishment of a national income tax served, at least temporarily, to pacify the public's need to redress the inequalities in wealth which arose as a result of America's industrialization (Office of Tax Analysis, 1963). However, the election of Woodrow Wilson in 1912 would serve as a catalyst to the eventual passage of a permanent federal estate tax.

In his inaugural address, President Wilson pledged to ensure equality of opportunity for every American. According to Wilson, government was an instrument to be used by people to promote the general welfare (Paul, 1954). Espousing that view, he instituted a number of reforms, including the Clayton Act (1914), which prohibited unfair labor practices, and the Federal Reserve Act. Wilson also created the Federal Land Bank, which made low-interest loans to farmers. He opposed high tariffs and, at the advent of World War I, moved to eliminate such tariffs on U.S. allies. The elimination of tariffs caused a loss of federal revenue, a loss that was amplified by the buildup of armaments and supplies following the sinking of the U.S. passenger ship *Lusitania*. Facing a deficit of $177 million, Congress was forced to find additional sources of revenue, and, once again, a form of inheritance tax was considered a prime candidate (Office of Tax Analysis, 1963).

The Modern Estate Tax

In May 1916, Representative Cordell Hull of Tennessee introduced a proposal for a federal estate tax in response to what he called "an irrepressible conflict" between the rich and the poor. He suggested that, compared to the nonwealthy, the wealthy should pay a larger share of the cost of government. Hull proposed an excise tax on estates prior to the transfer of assets to the beneficiaries, rather than an inheritance tax. This, according to Hull, would form "a well balanced system of inheritance taxation between the federal government and the various states" and could be "readily administered with less conflict than a tax levied upon the shares" (Paul, 1954, p. 107). Although an inheritance tax, with graduated rates for each recipient, encourages greater dispersion of the estate, the proposed estate tax eliminated the burden imposed by an inheritance tax on estates with fewer beneficiaries (Bittker and Clark, 1990).

Understandably, reaction to Hull's estate tax was mixed. Having long advocated limits on inheritance, prominent economists such as John A. Ryan, Richard T. Ely, Wilford F. King, and E. R. A. Seligman supported the estate tax. In contrast, the *New York Times* declared the tax a "frank project of confiscation." Harvard economist C. J. Bullock called it a "fiscal crime" (Paul, 1954, p. 108). However, on September 8, 1916, Congress enacted an estate tax that would survive, in large part, to the present (Revenue Act of 1916).

The Revenue Act of 1916

The federal estate tax was applied to net estates, defined as the total property owned by a decedent, the gross estate, less deductions. Although a $50,000 exemption was allowed for all residents, the exemption was not available to nonresidents owning taxable property in the United States. This relatively high filing threshold was adopted in deference to the right of states to tax small estates. According to the Act of 1916, the gross estate included all property, both personal and real, owned by a decedent; life insurance payable to the estate; transfers made for inadequate consideration; transfers made in contemplation of death—within two years of death; and transfers that took effect on or after death. Also included in the gross estate was all joint property, unless proof could be supplied supporting the contribution of the co-owner. A deduction was allowed for administrative expenses and losses, debts, claims and funeral costs, as well as for expenses incurred for the support of the decedent's dependents during the estate's administration. The tax rates were graduated from 1 percent on the first $50,000 of net estate to 10 percent on the portion exceeding $5 million. According to the act, taxes were due one year after the decedent's death, and a discount of 5 percent of the amount due was allowed for payments made within one year of death. A late payment penalty of 6 percent was assessed unless the delay was deemed "unavoidable."

The 1916 estate tax was appealed to the United States Supreme Court in *New York Trust Company v. Eisner*. The plaintiff argued that, unlike the earlier inheritance taxes that applied only to the receipt of property, the new estate tax was an infringement on the states' right to regulate the process of transferring property at death. Justice Oliver Wendell Holmes, in upholding the tax, reasoned that "if a tax on property distributed by the laws of a state, determined by the fact that distribution has been accomplished, is valid, a tax determined by the fact that distribution is about to begin is no greater interference and is equally good" (256 U.S., p. 348) Thus, the federal estate tax became a lasting component of the federal tax system.

Significant Tax-Law Changes: 1916 to the Present

Since its inception in 1916, the basic structure of the modern federal estate tax, as well as the law from which it is derived, has remained largely unchanged. However, in the eight decades that followed the Revenue Act of 1916, the U.S. Congress has enacted several important additions to, and revisions of, the modern estate tax structure (see Figure 4.1). There have also been occasional adjustments to the filing thresholds, tax brackets, and marginal tax rates (see Table 4.5). The first such addition was a tax on *inter vivos* gifts, a gift tax, introduced by the Revenue Act of 1924. The new tax was imposed because Congress realized that wealthy individuals could avoid the estate tax, invoked at death, by transferring wealth during their lifetimes; that is, due to *inter vivos* giving, the estate tax's inherent capacity to redistribute wealth accumulated by large estates effectively was circumvented, and a source of revenue was removed from the federal government's reach. The Congressional response was a gift tax applied to lifetime transfers.

The first federal gift tax was short-lived, however. Due to strong opposition to estate and gift taxes during the 1920s, the gift tax was repealed by the Revenue Act of 1926 (Zaritsky and Ripy, 1984). Then, just six years later, when the need to finance federal spending during the Great Depression outweighed opposition to gift taxation, the federal gift tax was reintroduced by the Revenue Act of 1932 (Zaritsky and Ripy, 1984). A donor could transfer $50,000 free of tax over his or her lifetime, with a $5,000 per donee annual exclusion from gift tax.

The Revenue Act of 1935 introduced the optional valuation date election. Although the value of the gross estate at the date of death determined whether an estate tax return had to be filed, the act allowed an estate to be valued, for tax purposes, one year after the decedent's death. With this revision, for example, if the value of a decedent's gross estate dropped significantly after the date of death—a situation faced by estates during the Depression—the executor could choose to value the estate at its reduced value after the date of death. The optional valuation date, today referred to as the *alternate valuation date*, later was changed to six months after the decedent's date of death.

Most outstanding among the pre-1976 changes to estate tax law were the

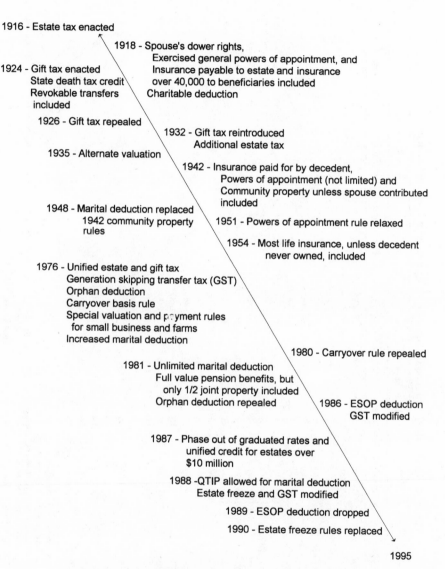

FIGURE 4.1.   Significant tax law changes, 1916–1995.

TABLE 4.5. Estate Tax Law Changes Affecting Filing Requirements and Tax Rates, 1916-1995

Year	Basic tax				Supplemental tax			
	Exemption	Initial rate	Top rate	Top bracket	Exemption	Initial rate	Top rate	Top bracket
1916	50,000	1	10	5,000,000				
1917	50,000	2	25	10,000,000				
1918–23	50,000	1	25	10,000,000				
1924–25	50,000	1	40	10,000,000				
1926–31	100,000	1	20	10,000,000				
1932–33	100,000	1	20	10,000,000	50,000	1	45	10,000,000
1934	100,000	1	20	10,000,000	50,000	1	60	10,000,000
1935–39	100,000	1	20	10,000,000	40,000	2	70	50,000,000
1940[a]	100,000	1	20	10,000,000	40,000	2	70	50,000,000
1941	100,000	1	20	10,000,000	40,000	3	77	10,000,000
1942–53	100,000	1	20	10,000,000	60,000	3	77	10,000,000
1954–76	60,000	3	77	10,000,000				
1977[b]	120,000	18	70	5,000,000				
1978	134,000	18	70	5,000,000				
1979	147,000	18	70	5,000,000				
1980	161,000	18	70	5,000,000				
1981	175,000	18	70	5,000,000				
1982	225,000	18	65	4,000,000				
1983	275,000	18	60	3,500,000				
1984	325,000	18	55	3,000,000				
1985	400,000	18	55	3,000,000				
1986	500,000	18	55	3,000,000				
1987–95[c,d]	600,000	18	55	3,000,000				

[a] Ten percent was surtax added.
[b] Unified credit replaces exemption.
[c] Tax rate was to be reduced to 50 percent on amounts beginning in 1988, but was postponed until 1992, then repealed retroactively in 1993 and set permanently to the 1987 levels.
[d] Graduated rates and unified credits phased out for estates over 10,000,000.

estate and gift tax marital deductions, as well as the rule on "split gifts," introduced by the Revenue Act of 1948. Indeed, the estate tax marital deduction, as enacted by the 1948 Act, permitted a decedent's estate to deduct the value of property passing to a surviving spouse, whether passing under the will or otherwise (Zaritsky and Ripy, 1984). However, the deduction was limited to one-half of the decedent's adjusted gross estate—the gross estate less debts and administrative expenses. In a similar manner, the gift tax marital deduction allowed a "donor [spouse] to deduct one-half of the inter-spousal gift, other than a gift of community property" (Zaritsky and Ripy, 1984, p. 16). Furthermore, the Act of 1948 introduced the rule on "split-gifts," which permitted a nondonor spouse to act as donor of half the value of the donor spouse's gift. The rule on split gifts effectively permitted a married couple to transfer twice as much wealth tax free in a given year.

With few other exceptions, the Congressional Record remained free of reference to the estate tax and the entire transfer tax system until the enactment of the Tax Reform Act (TRA) of 1976. By creating a unified estate and gift tax framework that consisted of a "single, graduated rate of tax imposed on both lifetime gift and testamentary dispositions" (Zaritsky and Ripy, 1984, p. 18), the act eliminated the cost differential that had existed between the two types of giving. Prior to the act, "it cost substantially more to leave property at death than to give it away during life" (Bittker and Clark, 1990, p. 20) due to the lower tax rate applied to *inter vivos* gifts. The TRA of 1976 also merged the estate tax exclusion and the lifetime gift tax exclusion into a "single, unified estate and gift tax credit, which may be used to offset gift tax liability during the donor's lifetime but which, if unused at death, is available to offset the deceased donor's estate tax liability" (Zaritsky and Ripy, 1984, p. 18). An annual gift exclusion of $3,000 per donee was retained.

The 1976 tax reform package also introduced a tax on generation-skipping transfers (GSTs). Prior to passage of the act, a transferor, for example, could create a testamentary trust and direct that the income from the trust be paid to his or her children during their lives and then, upon the children's deaths, that the principal be paid to the transferor's grandchildren. The trust assets included in the transferor's estate would be taxed upon the transferor's death. Then, any trust assets included in the grandchildren's estates would be taxed at their deaths. However, the intervening beneficiaries, the transferor's children in this example, would pay no estate tax on the trust assets, even though they had enjoyed the interest income derived from those assets. Congress responded to the GST tax leakage in the TRA of 1976. The act added a series of rules, applied to GSTs valued at more than $250,000, which were designed to treat the termination of the intervening beneficiaries' interests as a taxable event (Zaritsky and Ripy, 1984). In 1986, Congress simplified the GST tax rates and increased the amount a grantor could transfer into a GST tax free, from $250,000 to $1 million. As with the gift tax exclusion, "married persons may combine their [GST tax] exemptions, thus allowing the couple a $2,000,000 exemption" (Bittker and Clark, 1990, p. 31). Overall, the GST tax "ensures that the transmission of hereditary wealth is taxed at each generation level" (Bittker and Clark, 1990, p. 30).

The Economic Recovery Tax Act (ERTA) of 1981 brought several notable changes to estate tax law. Prior to 1982, the marital deduction was permitted only for transfers of property in which the decedent's surviving spouse had a terminable interest—an interest that grants the surviving spouse power to appoint beneficiaries of the property at his or her own death. Such property is, ultimately, included in the surviving spouse's estate. However, the ERTA of 1981 allowed the marital deduction for life interests that were not terminable, as long as the property was "qualified terminable interest property" (QTIP), defined as "property in which the [surviving] spouse has sole right to all income during his or her life, payable at least annually, but no power to transfer the property at death" (Johnson, 1994, p. 60). To utilize the deduction, however, the QTIP must be included in the surviving spouse's gross estate. The 1981 Act also introduced unlimited estate and gift tax marital deductions, thereby eliminating quantitative limits on the amount of estate and gift tax deductions available for interspousal transfers.

The ERTA of 1981 increased the unified transfer tax credit, the credit available against both the gift and estate taxes. The increase, from $47,000 to $192,800, was to be phased in over six years, and the increase effectively would raise the tax exemption from $175,000 to $600,000 over the same period (Johnson, 1990, p. 20). The ERTA of 1981 also raised the annual gift tax exclusion to $10,000 per donee; an unlimited annual exclusion from gift tax was allowed for the payment of a donee's tuition or medical expenses (Bittker and Clark, 1990). Finally, through ERTA, Congress enacted a reduction in the top estate, gift and GST tax rates from 70 percent to 50 percent, applicable to transfers greater than $2.5 million. The reduction was to be phased in over a four-year period. However, later legislation—both the Deficit Reduction Act of 1984 and the Revenue Act of 1987—delayed the decrease in the top tax rate from 55 percent to 50 percent until after December 31, 1992. Then, in 1993, Congress again revised the top tax rate schedule, imposing a marginal tax rate of 53 percent on taxable transfers between $2.5 million and $3 million, and a maximum marginal tax rate of 55 percent on taxable transfers exceeding $3 million. The higher rates were applied retroactively to January 1, 1993 (*IRS Legislative Affairs*, 1993).

The Revenue Act of 1987, also called the Omnibus Budget Reconciliation Act of 1987, introduced legislation to eliminate estate tax avoidance schemes known as "estate freezes." An estate freeze "involved division of ownership of a business into two parts: a frozen interest and a growth interest" (Miller,

1988, p. 1336). By selling or giving away the growth interest, the interest that held the potential for becoming valuable if the business prospered, "a taxpayer could maintain control of the business and continue to enjoy the income from the business while excluding any future appreciation in its value from his gross estate" (Miller, 1988, p. 1336). The 1987 legislation mandated treating the transferor's frozen interest as a retained life estate in the growth interest that was transferred. Therefore, the growth interest would be included in the owner's gross estate upon his or her death. In 1988, with the passage of the Technical and Miscellaneous Revenue Act, Congress revised its antifreeze legislation to include a different, and stricter, approach toward the valuation of business interests transferred prior to death (Miller, 1988). These rules, however, proved to be too restrictive. The Revenue Reconciliation Act of 1990 repealed all prior estate-freeze legislation and, in its place, substituted strengthened gift tax rules dealing with the valuation of the growth interest at the time of the transfer. The 1990 Act also established specific rules for valuing the retained interest for estate tax purposes (Johnson, 1994).

Current Estate Tax Law

According to current estate tax law, a federal estate tax return must be filed for every deceased U.S. citizen whose gross estate valued on the date of death, combined with adjusted taxable gifts made by the decedent after December 31, 1976, and total specific exemptions allowed for gifts made after September 8, 1976, equals or exceeds $600,000. The estates of nonresident aliens also must file if property held in the United States exceeds $60,000. All of a decedent's assets, as well as the decedent's share of jointly owned and community property assets, are included in the gross estate for tax purposes. Also considered are most life insurance proceeds, property over which the decedent possessed a general power of appointment, and certain transfers made during life that were (1) revocable, or (2) made for less than full consideration. An estate is allowed to value assets on a date up to six months after a decedent's death if the value of assets declined during that period. Special valuation rules and a tax deferment plan are available to an estate that is primarily comprised of a small business or farm.

Expenses and losses incurred in the administration of the estate, funeral costs, and the decedent's debts are allowed as deductions against the estate for the purpose of calculating the tax liability. A deduction also is allowed for the full value of bequests to the surviving spouse, including bequests in which the spouse is given only a life interest, subject to certain restrictions. Bequests to charities also are fully deductible. A unified tax credit of $192,800 is allowed for every decedent dying after December 31, 1986. Credits also are allowed for death taxes paid to states and other countries, as well as for any gift taxes the decedent may have paid during his or her lifetime. The estate tax return (Form 706) must be filed within nine months of the decedent's death unless a six-month extension is requested and granted. Taxes owed for GSTs in excess of the decedent's $1 million exemption and taxes on certain retirement fund accumulations are due concurrent with any estate tax liability. Interest accumulated on U.S. Treasury bonds redeemed to pay these taxes is exempt from taxation.

Transfer Taxes and Estate Planning

As the federal transfer tax system has become more complex, individuals have increasingly turned to estate planners for tax-minimization strategies. Estate planners, in turn, keep their clients apprised of tax-law changes that may have an adverse effect on testamentary arrangements already in place. This has made estate planning more of a process than a one-time event. Tax-law provisions can have a significant impact on both the ownership of assets during one's lifetime and the disposition of an estate at death. Occasionally, legislative intervention is specifically intended to influence bequest patterns. Such was the case with the enactment of the GST tax. In other instances, changes in the tax code seeking to provide relief to specific segments of the population or those made in response to revenue needs will have a bequest effect. Allowable deductions, tax credits, and tax rates all play a role in bequest decisions.

Tax-law changes associated with the ERTA, which applied to decedents dying on or after January 1, 1982, provided for an unlimited deduction from the value of the gross estate for bequests to a surviving spouse; prior to that, the deduction was limited to one-half the adjusted gross estate. Figure 4.2 shows the full value of property bequeathed to surviving spouses as a percentage of the decedents' distributable estates (total gross estate less expenses; debts; and federal, state, and foreign death taxes) for selected years between 1972 and 1992. The percentage rises from about 60 percent prior to 1982 to about 70 percent after 1982 and passage of ERTA. This suggests a significant change in bequest behavior among married persons, with more property passing to the surviving spouse and, perhaps, a reduction in the amount bequeathed to others, including children and charities. Careful estate planning, however, may allow a decedent to take advantage of tax-avoidance strategies and maintain his or her bequest goals. A popular strategy is to form a trust known as an "A-B trust." Here, the estate planner creates one trust in the amount of the decedent's tax exemption ($600,000), sometimes called a Unified Credit Trust, and puts the rest of the estate into a second, usually larger, QTIP trust. Income from both trusts is directed to the surviving spouse

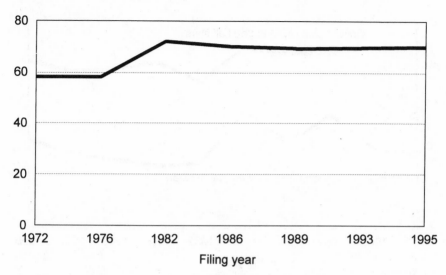

FIGURE 4.2.   Marital bequests as a percentage of distributable estate, 1972–1995, for married decedents with estates of $600,000 or more in constant 1987 dollars.

for life; however, the smaller trust is really set aside for the children. The surviving spouse typically is given more access to the principal of the second trust and may have limited powers to appoint beneficiaries. Upon the death of the second spouse, the remainder passes to the children. Thus, the first decedent takes advantage of the unlimited marital deduction but ensures that the children will eventually benefit from the estate.

The value of property bequeathed to charities, as well as the number of decedents making gifts to charities, declined after ERTA (see Figure 4.3). This may represent a shift in bequests from charities to the surviving spouse as a result of the unlimited marital deduction. A reduction in the top tax rate from 77 percent and increases in the unified credit since 1977 also may explain the decrease in charitable bequests. Studies of charitable giving at death have shown that tax rates seem to exert an influence on the size of charitable bequests, as well as on the number of charitable organizations named as beneficiaries (Joulfaian, 1991). This is so because the amount of tax savings attributable to the deduction decreases as rates decline. Charitable bequests from decedents with relatively small- and medium-sized estates seem particularly sensitive to changes in the rate structure (Boskin, 1976; Clotfelter, 1985).

Federal estate taxes also encourage individuals to begin transferring wealth well before death in order to minimize the size of their estates.

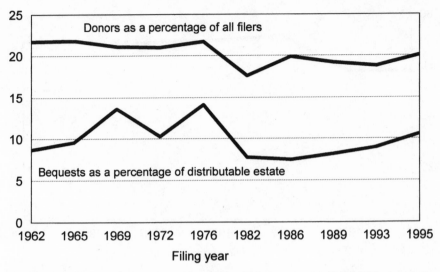

FIGURE 4.3.   Charitable bequest data, 1962–1995, for estates of $600,000 or more in constant 1987 dollars.

Lifetime giving may be an important component of an individual's overall bequest strategy. Federal gift tax law allows a donor to make annual gifts up to $10,000 per donee without incurring a transfer-tax liability; married couples are allowed up to $20,000 per donee. Children are usually the primary recipients of these transfers. There are a variety of trust instruments and financial arrangements that may be used in conjunction with gift giving to remove assets from the estate. These affect the timing and the amount of the tax liability, as well as the types of assets and degree of ownership eventual beneficiaries receive.

Current Transfer Taxation: Criticisms and Proposals

Eight decades since the introduction of the modern federal estate tax, and two centuries since discussions of inheritance and taxation first appeared in America, the current transfer tax system, including estate, gift, and GST taxes, remains a topic of Congressional, academic and popular discourse. Furthermore, the fundamental tenets of current discussions find their roots in the historic arguments of early thinkers, such as Adam Smith, David Ricardo, and Jeremy Bentham. Although the transfer tax system often is cited as a negative influence on the accumulation of capital stock in the U.S. economy, as well as a negative influence on the vitality of small business, the system is preserved in a form that differs little from its origins.

The scope of the transfer tax system, as measured by federal revenue flows, is quite narrow. Although it is reasonable to argue that a federal tax is levied, at least in part, for its contribution to federal budget inlays, the revenue derived from estate and gift taxes does not contribute significantly to total budget receipts. "Taxes on property transfers have never provided significant revenues in this country and have been reduced to an insignificant proportion in recent years," according to economist Joseph A. Pechman, former senior fellow at the Brookings Institution (1983, p. 226; see Figure 4.4). With few exceptions, revenue from federal estate and gift taxes has lingered between 1 and 2 percent of federal budget receipts since World War II, reaching a postwar high of 2.6 percent in 1972. Recent data also demonstrate the small role that transfer taxes play as sources of federal revenue. In 1994, as well as in the preceding four years, federal estate and gift taxes made up only 1 percent of budget receipts.

The scope of the transfer tax system, as measured by the size of the population directly affected by the system, is also quite narrow (see Table 4.6). The number of estate tax filers with taxable estates—filers who incurred a tax

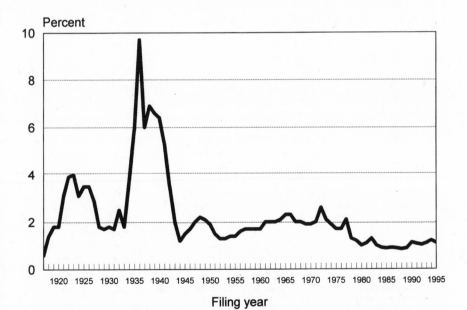

FIGURE 4.4.   Estate and gift taxes as a percentage of total federal receipts, 1917–1995.

TABLE 4.6. Estate Tax Returns as a Percentage of Adult Deaths,
Selected Years of Death, 1934–1993
(Starting with 1965, number of returns is based on sample estimates)

Selected year of death	Total adult deaths[b]	Taxable estate tax returns	
		Number	Percentage of adult deaths
	(1)	(2)	(3)
1934	983,970	8,655	0.88
1935	1,172,245	9,137	0.78
1936	1,257,290	12,010	0.96
1937	1,237,585	13,220	1.07
1938	1,181,275	12,720	1.08
1939	1,205,072	12,907	1.07
1940	1,237,186	13,336	1.08
1941	1,216,855	13,493	1.11
1942	1,211,391	12,726	1.05
1943	1,277,009	12,154	0.95
1944	1,238,917	13,869	1.12
1946	1,239,713	18,232	1.47
1947	1,278,856	19,742	1.54
1948	1,283,601	17,469	1.36
1949	1,285,684	17,411	1.35
1950	1,304,343	18,941	1.45
1953	1,237,741	24,997	2.02
1954	1,332,412	25,143	1.89
1956	1,289,193	32,131	2.49
1958	1,358,375	38,515	2.84
1960	1,426,148	45,439	3.19
1962	1,483,846	55,207	3.72
1965	1,578,813	67,404	4.27
1969	1,796,055	93,424	5.20
1972	1,854,146	120,761	6.51
1976	1,819,107	139,115	7.65
1982	1,897,820	34,446	1.82
1983	1,945,913	34,883	1.79
1984	1,968,128	30,447	1.55
1985	2,015,070	22,324	1.11
1986	2,033,978	21,939	1.08
1987	2,053,084	18,059	0.88
1988	2,096,704	20,751	0.99
1989	2,079,035	23,002	1.11
1990	2,079,034	24,456	1.18
1991	2,101,746	26,277	1.25
1992	2,111,617	27,243	1.29
1993[a]	2,168,120	32,002	1.48

[a]Preliminary.

[b]Total adult deaths represent those of individuals age 20 and over, plus deaths for which age was unavailable. For 1993, total deaths are for adults age 25 and older and for the 12-month period ending with November.

Sources: For years after 1953, Statistics of Income–Estate Tax Returns; Estate and Gift Tax Returns; Fiduciary, Estate and Gift Tax Returns; and unpublished tabulations, depending on the year. For years prior to 1954, Statistics of Income—Part I. Adult deaths are from the National Center for Health Statistics, Public Health Service, U.S. Department of Health and Human Services, Vital Statistics of the United States, unpublished tables.

liability—reached a high of 139,115 in 1976; the estate tax exemption in that year was $60,000. Since the introduction of the $600,000 estate and gift tax exemption in 1987, the annual number of taxable estate tax returns has not exceeded 32,000. In 1994, 31,918 taxable estate tax returns were filed for decedents, a number that represents only 1.4 percent of the adult deaths that occurred in that year, according to preliminary 1994 death statistics by the National Center for Health Statistics (see Table 4.6 footnote). The number of estate tax decedents with tax liabilities during 1995 was 31,692. Preliminary estimates for the number of adult deaths for 1995 are not available.

Clearly then, the transfer tax system neither provides a significant portion of federal budget inlays nor subjects a significant portion of the U.S. population to federal taxation. For these and other reasons, the system is the object of much criticism. The assertion that the estate tax is a *voluntary tax*, a term first employed by Columbia law professor George Cooper in his 1979 study of estate-planning techniques, is foremost among the criticisms of the tax. By labeling the estate tax "voluntary," Cooper suggests that, far from imposing an unavoidable tax, estate tax law really provides numerous methods for tax avoidance. Today, tax avoidance schemes fall into three basic categories. First, the "technique of estate freezing keeps free of tax the future growth in an individual's wealth by diverting that growth to the next generation" (Cooper, 1979, p. 4). Second, the "creation of tax-exempt wealth takes advantage of special provisions in the tax code that exempt certain assets from taxation" (p. 4). Finally, the "reduction or elimination of tax on existing wealth is made possible by a package of techniques for gift-giving, manipulating valuations and exploiting charitable deductions" (p. 5). Cooper concludes that "because estate tax avoidance is such a successful and yet wasteful process,... the present estate and gift tax serves no purpose other than to give reassurance to the millions of unwealthy that entrenched wealth is being attacked" (p. 82), reassurance that, he later suggests, is merely superficial. The annual costs of estate tax-avoidance schemes, including lawyer fees, accountant fees, costs of subscriptions to estate planning magazines, and opportunity costs of individuals involved in tax-avoidance activities, have been shown to represent a large percentage of the annual receipts from estate and gift taxes. A 1988 study showed that tax-avoidance costs approach billions of dollars annually, which, according to the study's researchers, represent "an inordinately high social cost for a tax that only yielded $7.7 billion in 1987" (Munnell, 1988, p. 19).

Our present system of taxing wealth transfers also is criticized for its effect on capital accumulation in the U.S. economy. In his examination of the federal transfer tax system, Richard Wagner (1993), professor of economics, suggests that "[b]y reducing the incentive that people have to save and invest, transfer taxation reduces capital formation which, in turn, reduces wages and job creation from what they would otherwise be" (p. 6). This argument echoes one asserted by Adam Smith in the late 18th century and David Ricardo

in the early 19th century. Indeed, according to both of these early economists, transfer taxes decrease investment in capital and thereby decrease
productivity and wages as heirs are forced to liquidate business assets to pay
the tax. In his study of the social costs of transfer taxation in the United States,
Wagner estimated that, in the absence of federal transfer taxation since 1971,
jobs would have increased by 262,000, capital investment would have increased by $399 billion, and gross domestic product would have increased by
$46 billion.

Federal transfer taxes often are cited as impediments to the livelihood of
small businesses and farms. Indeed, "small businessmen and farmers have
always felt that the estate tax is especially burdensome" (Pechman, 1983, p.
242), given that their estates may consist of little more than their businesses.
These businessmen, and their Congressional representatives, assert that
"[h]eavy taxation or a rule requiring payment of taxes immediately after the
death of the owner–manager would necessitate liquidation of the enterprise
and loss of the business by the family" (Pechman, 1983, p. 242). Congress has
responded to such concerns by introducing certain tax-relief provisions. In
1976, for example, Congress suggested that "additional relief should be provided to estates with [liquidity] problems arising because a substantial portion of the estate consists of an interest in a closely held business or other
illiquid assets" (U.S. Senate Report, 1976). Thus, in 1976, Code Section 6166
was passed. Under 6166, an executor is permitted to "elect to pay the Federal
estate tax attributable to an interest in a closely held business in installments
over, at most, a 14-year period" (Beerbower, 1995, p. 5).

During 1995 and 1996, the impact of estate taxation on small business,
and other estate tax issues, including the very existence of the tax, were once
again topics of discussion in Congress, as well as in the 1996 Presidential
election. Several bills addressing the federal estate tax were introduced during
the 104th Congress, 1995–1996. In April 1995, the U.S. House of Representatives passed one such bill, H.R. 1215, a proposal to increase the unified credit
against the estate and gift tax, as well as to provide a cost-of-living adjustment
for such credits (U.S. Library of Congress, 1996). In addition, the bill proposed
to provide an "inflation adjustment for the alternate valuation of certain farm
and business property, the gift tax exclusion, the generation-skipping tax
exemption, and the estate tax on closely held businesses" (U.S. Library of
Congress, 1996). The bill called for a gradual rise in the unified credit and,
therefore, a gradual rise in the effective exclusion for estate and gift tax
purposes, from the current $600,000 to $700,000 in 1996, $725,000 in 1997,
and $750,000 in 1998, after which the exclusion would be adjusted for
inflation. Although the Senate Finance Committee held hearings on the measure, the Senate did not pass a bill.

Congress submitted other, similar bills during its 104th session. H.R. 62, although never passed, sought "to increase the unified estate and gift tax credit to an amount equivalent to a $1,200,000 exemption" (U.S. Library of Congress, 1996). The Senate considered S.628, the Family Heritage Preservation Act. That bill proposed a complete repeal of federal estate, gift and GST taxes. While introducing the bill to the legislative body, the senate sponsor of S.628 called the federal estate tax "one of the most wasteful and unfair taxes currently on the books," further suggesting that the tax "penalizes people for a lifetime of hard work, savings, and investment." The tax "hurts small business and threatens jobs ... [and] causes people to spend time, energy, and money finding ways to avoid the tax," said the senate sponsor.

The 1996 presidential election also served as a forum for discussion of the federal estate tax. The need for estate tax relief was among the campaign themes of Republican presidential nominee Robert "Bob" Dole. At a campaign rally in Alamogordo, New Mexico, in early November 1996, Dole addressed the tax on death transfers. "[F]or those who work all their lives — kids work, the wife works, the husband works, you scrimp and save, and you finally have a little business or a little farm or a little ranch, and somebody passes on," Dole said, according to the Federal News Service (In the News, 1996, p. 2). "We don't think you should have to sell part of the ranch to pay the estate taxes. We're going to start providing estate tax relief." Dole and his running mate, Jack Kemp, outlined a 14-point pledge that contained a promise to "increase the estate tax exemption from $600,000 to $1.6 million and eventually eliminate the estate tax on family-owned businesses, farms and ranches," according to U.S. Newswire (p. 8).

During the first term of his administration, President Bill Clinton supported modification, not the complete elimination, of the federal estate tax. At hearings before the Senate Finance Committee in June 1995, then-Deputy Assistant Secretary of Tax Policy at the Treasury Department, Cynthia G. Beerbower, said that the Clinton administration "recognizes that the levels of the unified credit and various other estate and gift tax limitations have not been increased since 1987" (1995, p. 5). The administration is "willing to work with Congress to maintain an estate and gift tax system that exempts small- and moderate-sized estates, and that helps keep intact small and family businesses, so that they can be passed on to future generations" (p. 6), according to Beerbower.

In November 1996, the Clinton administration won a second term in office, and the Republicans retained the majority in Congress. These events, and recent negotiations about filing thresholds, tax brackets and marginal tax rates in the federal transfer tax system, suggest that the system will continue to find a place in national dialogue.

Conclusion

Today, some tax theorists work to convince Congress that transfer taxes should play a larger role in the federal revenue system because, they argue, "death taxes have less adverse effects on incentives than do income taxes of equal yield" (Pechman, 1983, p. 225). Indeed, "income taxes reduce the return from effort and risk taking as income is earned," according to Pechman, whereas "death taxes are paid only after a lifetime of work and accumulation and are likely to be given less weight by individuals in their work, saving, and investment decisions" (p. 226). There are economists who also reject the postulate that moderate transfer taxes have an adverse effect on capital accumulation. Embracing an idea first proposed by the mid-19th-century English economist J. R. McCulloch, they argue that transferors adjust their bequest plans when faced with transfer taxes (Fiekowsky, 1959). According to McCulloch, the death tax causes individuals who plan to make significant bequests to increase savings so that their heirs can pay the taxes without adversely affecting the transferred assets. When transfers involve business assets, McCulloch might have argued, a testator would ensure the continuance of a business by increasing the bequest amount in order to cover the cost of transfer taxes.

Still, Congress and the public seem hesitant to increase the scope of the transfer tax system. "The equalization of the distribution of wealth by taxation is not yet accepted in the United States," suggests Pechman (1983, p. 227). Chester (1982) attributes this to what he calls the "lottery phenomenon: the strong desire of the majority of Americans to have a chance to 'win big' by inheriting wealth, thus vaulting without exertion above the mass of men" (p. 51). Pechman also suggests that misconceptions regarding the scope of transfer taxes may also be a factor. "[E]state and gift taxes are erroneously regarded as especially burdensome to the family that is beginning to prosper through hard work and saving," according to Pechman, who further suggests that "the merits of wealth transfer taxes will have to be more widely understood and accepted before they can become effective revenue sources" (1983, p. 227).

More than 300 years after John Locke and his contemporaries sought to define the relationship between civil government and the governed, Americans struggle for consensus concerning government's ideal role in the regulation of wealth transfers. There is resentment over the use of transfer taxes as a source of revenue and as a tool for influencing the distribution of personal wealth. There is also the belief that the revenue and redistributive goals of transfer taxes are entirely appropriate to an altruistic nation that promotes the welfare of its citizens. Even economists are divided. Neoclassical economists assert that the disruption to businesses resulting from transfer taxes has cost the economy billions of dollars in lost productivity and hundreds of thousands of new jobs. Yet many tax economists argue that transfer taxes are less harmful than income taxes and have great appeal "on social, moral, and economic grounds" (Pechman, 1983, p. 226). Disputes over the economic effects and propriety of transfer taxes have spanned many centuries, and the fervor on which those disputes are founded is no less present today.

ACKNOWLEDGMENTS: The views expressed in this paper are those of the authors alone and in no way reflect the opinions of the Internal Revenue Service or the Treasury Department. The authors would like to thank Thomas Petska, Michael Alexander, Jeffrey Rosenfeld, and Jenny Wahl for their helpful comments during the editing phase of the project and Dorothy Wallace for preparing the data tables and graphs.

References

Beerbower, C. G. (1995). Statement of Cynthia G. Beerbower, Deputy Assistant Secretary (Tax Policy) Department of the Treasury, before the Senate Finance Committee. Washington, DC: Office of Public Affairs.

Bittker, I., & Clark, E. (1990). *Federal estate and gift taxation.* Boston: Little, Brown.

Boskin, M. J. (1976). Estate taxation and charitable bequests. *Journal of Public Economics, 5,* 27-56.

Bruchey, S. (1988). *The wealth of the nation.* New York: Harper & Row.

Carnegie, A. (1962). *The gospel of wealth and other timely essays.* Cambridge, MA: Belknap Press of Harvard University Press.

Chester, R. (1982). *Inheritance, wealth, and society.* Bloomington: Indiana University Press.

Clotfelter, C. T. (1985). *Federal tax policy and charitable giving.* Chicago: University of Chicago Press.

Cooper, G. (1979). *A voluntary tax?* Washington, DC: Brookings Institution.

Customs Duties and Internal Revenue Taxes Act of 1872 §36, 17 Stat. 256.

Economic Recovery Tax Act of 1981, Public Law 97-34.

Eyre v. Jacob, 14 Grat. 422 (1858).

Fiekowsky, S. (1959). *On the economic effects of death taxation in the United States.* Doctoral dissertation, Harvard University, Cambridge, MA.

In the news. Federal News Service, November 4, 1996.

Income Tax Act of 1894, 28 Stat. 509, 553.

Internal Revenue Act of 1867, 14 Stat. 169.

Internal Revenue Law of 1864 §124-150, 13 Stat. 285.

The Internal Revenue Record and Customs Journal (1869), 9(15), 113.

Internal Taxes. Customs Duties Act of 1870 §27, 16 Stat. 269.

IRS Legislative Affairs. September 17, 1993. Draft.

Johnson, B. W. (1994). Estate tax returns, 1989-1991. *Compendium of Federal Estate Tax and Personal Wealth Studies.* Washington, DC: U.S. Government Printing Office.

Joulfaian, D. (1991). Charitable bequests and estate taxes. *National Tax Journal,* 44(2), 169-180.

Knowlton v. Moore, 178 U.S. 41 (1900).

Locke, J. (1988). *Two treatises of government.* Cambridge, UK: Cambridge University Press.

Mager v. Grima, 49 U.S. 490 (1850).

Mill, J. S. (1994). *Principles of Political Economy and Chapters on Socialism*. Oxford, UK: Oxford University Press.

Miller, J. A. (1988). Gift wrapping the estate freeze. *Tax Notes*, December 19, 1135-1341.

Munnell, A. H. (1988). Wealth transfer taxation: The relative role for estate and income taxes. *New England Economic Review*, November/December, 3-26.

New York Trust Company v. Eisner, 256 U.S. 345, 348.

Office of Tax Analysis. (1963). *Legislative History of Death Taxes in the United States*. Unpublished manuscript.

Paul, R. E. (1954). *Taxation in the United States*. Boston: Little, Brown.

Pechman, J. A. (1983). *Federal tax policy*. Washington, DC: Brookings Institution.

Political writer. *National Desk*, October 31, 1996.

Pollock v. Farmers Loan and Trust Company, 158 U.S. 601 (1895).

Revenue Act of 1916, 39 Stat. 756.

Revenue Act of 1924, 43 Stat. 253.

Revenue Act of 1926, 44 Stat. 9.

Revenue Act of 1932, 47 Stat. 169.

Revenue Act of 1935, 49 Stat. 1014.

Revenue Act of 1948, 62 Stat. 110.

Revenue Act of 1987, Public Law 100-203.

Revenue Reconciliation Act of 1990, Public Law 101-508.

Ricardo, D. (1819). *On the principles of political economy and taxation*. Georgetown, DC: Joseph Milligan.

Scholey v. Revenue Service, 90 U.S. 331 (1874).

Smith, A. (1913). *An inquiry into the nature and causes of the wealth of nations*. New York: E. P. Dutton.

Stamp Act of 1797, 1 Stat. 527.

Tax Reform Act of 1976, Public Law 94-455 §§2001-2009.

Tax Reform Act of 1986, Public Law 99-514.

Technical and Miscellaneous Revenue Act of 1988, Public Law 100-647.

U.S. Library of Congress. (November 6, 1996). *Thomas, legislative information on the Internet*. (Available from the Internet at http://thomas.loc.gov).

U.S. Senate Report 94-938. (1976). 94th Congress, 2d Sess. 18.

Wagner, R. E. (1993). *Federal transfer taxation: A study in social cost*. Costa Mesa, CA: Center for the Study of Taxation.

War Revenue Act of 1898, 30 Stat. 448, 464.

War Revenue Reduction Act of 1901, 31 Stat. 956.

War Revenue Repeal Act of 1902, §7, 32 Stat. 92.

Zaritsky, H., & Ripy, T. (1984). *Federal estate, gift, and generation skipping taxes: A legislative history and description of current law*. (Report No. 84-156A). Washington, DC: Congressional Research Service.

5

Women and Inheritance in America

Virginia and New York as a Case Study, 1700–1860

Joan R. Gundersen

Probate records have proved to be an especially fruitful source for historians trying to reconstruct the socioeconomic world of early American women. The specific bequests and itemized inventories found in these records lend themselves to both quantitative and qualitative readings on questions as diverse as attitudes towards women (Gundersen and Gampel, 1982) and wealth stratification (Tompsett, 1974). Concerns about women's property rights, especially for married women, are of particular interest for scholars studying the status of women. Coverture, that doctrine of English common law that merged the interests of husband and wife (especially in areas of property), has often been seen by feminists and scholars as a symbol of women's status as nonbeings in the law (Flexner, 1959). Others, seeking to recover a role for women as actors in history, have pointed to equity law as a modifier of coverture (Beard, 1946). In all of these discussions, the right of

JOAN R. GUNDERSEN • Dean of Social Science Division, Elon College, Elon College, North Carolina 27244.

Inheritance and Wealth in America, edited by Robert K. Miller, Jr., and Stephen J. McNamee. Plenum Press, New York, 1998.

women to hold, control, inherit, and alienate property are seen as essential to determining women's status.

A close study of the patterns of women's inheritance in two states, New York and Virginia, can help to illuminate the ways community values, formal law, and socioeconomic conditions affected women's property rights. No two states can be seen as "typical" of the larger whole; however, a compelling case can be made for focusing on these two particular colonies (states) from 1700 to 1860. Virginia was the most populous colony in 1750, and the oldest. It had a well-developed county court system modeled on the English common law county courts. Furthermore, the county justices also acted as judges in equity when necessary, and Virginia's laws had been reviewed in the 1750s for compliance with English legal traditions. Despite its origins as a Dutch colony, New York, by 1750, also had fully accepted English legal traditions and implemented procedures for hearing cases in both equity and in common law. Like Virginia, it had a Anglican elite and a provincial culture consciously modeled on that of England. Among the middle and northern colonies, it was notable for its sizable slave population and a strong agricultural base. Thus, both colonies had much in common in the colonial period. With functioning traditions of equity and common law, New York and Virginia were among the best colonies for scholars to use to explore women's property status.

What makes such a comparison even more interesting is that their experiences diverge in the nineteenth century. New York abandoned equity and became a leader in women's rights with its passage in 1848 of a Married Woman's Property Act. Virginia took a more conservative course. Neither New York nor Virginia are "typical" of their region, but both were influential. The legislation passed by these states was frequently copied by others. New York and Virginia both produced outstanding jurists, whose legal writings and opinions were often cited in other states. Thus, decisions about inheritance in these two states had an influence felt well beyond their borders. Furthermore, that influence was spread by the large numbers of citizens from those states who moved West and became settlers in the upper South and Midwest.

It should not be surprising, therefore, that Virginia and New York have been well studied by legal and social historians of the colonial, revolutionary and early national periods. There are numerous careful studies making use of local probate records for both states. Because probate records are local in nature and voluminous, most studies focus on one or two counties, and cover only a single time period. Few are comparative. This chapter makes extensive use of these detailed studies, supplementing them with additional work in Virginia records, in order to weave together a comparative, long-term interpretation of women's experience with inheritance.

Although the legal divergence that Virginia and New York experienced after 1800 might lead one to assume that patterns of women's inheritance would also diverge, this chapter illuminates the way families manipulated inheritance provisions to reach desired social outcomes regardless of the law, and suggests ways in which law, inheritance, and social values form a complex formula shaping women's status. Only when families could not adequately manipulate old forms were new legal forms affecting inheritance introduced. For New York, those conditions occurred in the 1840s. In Virginia, such changes did not occur until Reconstruction. Furthermore, the changes adopted were essentially conservative, leaving the assumptions about male headship of families intact until challenged by a revived women's movement in the 1970s.

Background

Virginia and New York provide good case studies for shifting patterns of inheritance over a century and a half (1700–1860). Dutch law and settlers helped to provide an alternative tradition to the English common and statutory law in the earliest years in New York. As a royal colony after 1684, New York became among the most anglicized of the colonies legally, but remained ethnically diverse. In the 19th century, the state led the way by passing married women's property laws. New forms of wealth tied to a commercial economy were very evident in New York. Virginia began with English traditions and settlers but had recognizable pockets of settlement by Germans, French, Scots, and others. As these groups assimilated, the state's white population became more homogeneous. Although the kinds of agriculture and marketing systems changed, Virginia remained an agricultural state, with much of its wealth invested in slaves. The forces of the American revolution affected both states, but the commercial revolution helped to shape different outcomes. In the first half of the nineteenth century, Virginia resisted any changes to women's status, thus providing a contrast to the New York experience. This chapter explores both the substance of the patterns of women's inheritance and the shifting family and societal values that underlay them.

Families chose their inheritance strategies in response to the legal options available to them in Virginia and New York. New Yorkers and Virginians pursued their own goals in distributing property, which did not always coincide with the goals of the select group of legislators, judges, and lawyers who defined the legal rules of inheritance. The bedrock of inheritance practices were the rules governing distribution of the estates of those who died intestate. However, families could circumvent the intestate laws by use of a will or by gifts of property before death. The 1540 Statue of Wills and later English laws had given the testator great freedom to dispose of real and personal property through a will (Shammas, 1995, p. 108). About one-fourth of New York men chose to write wills, and between one-fourth and two-fifths of the men in the Chesapeake did so (Narrett, 1989, p. 217). Evidence in wills and deeds documents that many families distributed property to children before the parents' deaths (Gundersen, 1976). Thus, inheritance patterns in the two colonies become a fascinating way to unpack the relationship and meaning of property to families and to the state, especially as they affect women's property rights and legal status.

The English common law doctrines of heir-at-law, coverture, and dower[1] lie at the heart of the legally defined inheritance systems of both New York and Virginia by 1750. Describing English and colonial practice, however, is complicated, because English law varied from county to county. Thus, colonial law not only had unique American modifications, but also varieties of English practice from which to choose (Salmon, 1986, p. 3). In English law, males received preference as heirs-at-law, but at each level of kinship, women took preference over more distant male heirs. For example, the oldest male child was a man's heir-at-law. He would inherit all of the real property under intestate rules, and a double share of personal property. The daughters inherited equally if there were no sons. They thus received preference over their father's brothers. In practice, 35–40 percent of daughters were thus heiresses-at-law, given the odds that a couple would have no surviving male children (Spring, 1990, pp. 274–275).

Since almost all women married in colonial America, the English practices of coverture and dower shaped their experience of inheritance. The only sure way for a woman to benefit from an inheritance was to be single. Under coverture, a married woman's existence in civil matters merged with that of her husband's. She filed suits jointly with him; once the couple had issue, he had a life claim on land she owned at the time of their marriage and absolute control over all property acquired during their marriage (subject to dower). He controlled personal property outright (Salmon, 1986, p. 16). Although men had control of a couple's property, wives had dower rights (an undivided one-third life interest in all real property owned by the couple). Women had to relinquish dower rights before a land transaction was complete, and the dower modified property distribution of both estates for intestate men and for those who had written wills. In Virginia and New York, widows could elect to claim their "thirds" rather than accept a legacy in a will, although English widows lost that right in 1690. They could also sue for damages if property had been sold without their relinquishment of rights. The doctrine of "paraphernalia" created a small reserve of personal property (clothes, jewels and household tools) for women. A husband had to grant paraphernalia to his wife even if otherwise disinheriting her. Paraphernalia was likewise shielded from creditors' claims on the husband's estate. (Gundersen and Gampel, 1982, pp. 120–126; Shammas, Salmon, and Dahlin, 1987, pp 32–35; Shammas, 1995, p. 108; Narrett, 1989, p. 74).

Although the legal procedure of entail was officially gender-neutral, its impact on women's inheritance depended on the use families made of it. To entail real property meant to specify its descent through more than one generation of heirs, and thus to prevent its being sold or given to others. Under such provisions, the heir enjoyed the use of the property but not its ultimate disposal. Ultimately, the use of entail did limit women's inheritances by individuals specifying descent to male heirs, even if the initial devise was to a woman. For example, a father might give his daughter an estate and then entail it so that it passed to her oldest male child and his male descendants. Entail in practice thus could bar a daughter from inheriting land. Families often compensated female heirs with a marriage "portion" of personal property (Spring, 1990, p. 286). English law allowed heirs to "dock" (break) entail through a series of legal procedures that could be complicated and expensive, but in such cases the goal was sale of the property, not its passage to female heirs.

Law in Colonial New York and Virginia

The basic law of inheritance in both New York and Virginia was intestate law. This governed the distribution of property for all those who died without a will. The death of a married woman without a separate estate had little effect on property transfers. Her husband already owned all personal property. Any lands she brought to the marriage became his for life, and any property acquired during marriage became solely his. When a male died, both colonies gave all land to the oldest male child, and a widow received her dower—a one-third life interest in land. Both colonies split personal property between the wife and children. In New York, the widow received one-third, and the children got shares in two-thirds, with the oldest son receiving a double share. Virginia law gave the widow her "thirds," and all children equal shares in the rest. If there were no children, Virginia widows received one-half of the personal property. The rest went to blood relatives of the deceased man. Reserving the widow's thirds, the laws of both colonies passed land to blood kin of the male. Even if the husband wrote a will, a woman retained the right to a one-third life interest in lands. Virginia guaranteed her an equal share with children in personal property, no matter what the husband's will did, whereas New York made no such protection (Shammas et al., 1987, p. 32). New York's laws were the least egalitarian of any of the colonies.

Virginia was unique among the American colonies in treating slaves as real property for most of the eighteenth century. Because intestate laws gave widows only a one-third life interest in real property as opposed to an outright share of personal property, Virginia widows had a reduced control over a major source of wealth. It also meant that daughters did not share in the slave property with sons unless there was a will (Hening, III, 371-376, 334-335, IV 222-228, V, 432-448, 568, VII, 118-120; Shammas et al., 1987, p. 35). On the other hand, if slaves had been designated personal property, married women would have had no legal claim on such property while their husbands were alive. Many families chose to entail slaves, by specifying a grandchild who would receive the slave upon the death of the testator's daughter. (See, for example, William Ford will, November 19, 1751, Goochland County deeds.) This actually protected the woman's heirs from dissipation of the estate by her husband. The status of slaves as real property also allowed Virginians to give daughters slaves rather than land and yet feel that all their children had received a portion of real property.[2]

As changes in English law in the early modern period[3] limited women's inheritance rights and control of property under common law, the use of equity law increased. Equity (or chancery) law was practiced in courts in four American mainland colonies, including Virginia and New York.[4] Other colonies applied some equity procedures in their common law courts (Salmon, 1986, p. 11; 1982, pp. 655-722). Under equity provisions, a woman could create through pre- or postnuptial agreements with her husband, a separate estate that was not under his direct control. These estates could give women direct control of property or put it under the control of trustees. Depending on the provisions of the equity trust, married women could devise property in that trust. Others writing wills could create equity trusts as a part of their devises to ensure women would retain ownership of their inheritances. Not all uses of prenuptial agreements or other equity strategies, however, gave women control of their inheritances. Wealthy English families increasingly used "strict settlement" documents at the marriage of a daughter, which arranged for land to pass directly to her male offspring, or to convert the woman's family "portion" to cash. As personal property, cash became the immediate possession of her husband (Spring 1990, pp. 278-285).

Virginia and New York families and courts used variations on these English legal doctrines. Although such full, formal equity provisions were uncommon in Virginia and New York, families in the two colonies did "settle" or promise property to children at the time of marriage. Many wills include mention of property already in the hands of married children, or made to younger children bequests explicitly designed to match the property already settled on older, married children. Still other families made full legal gifts at marriage and gave their older children token sums (1 shilling to 20 shillings) while making younger children the heirs by will. The property transferred, however, followed the trends in England. Women's property became increasingly mobile—slaves, household items such as featherbeds, and cash. It also immediately passed to the control of the son-in-law. The legal battles surrounding Peter Harris's estate in Virginia were rare, but the practices they bring to light were not. When Peter Harris died in 1775, his son Henry challenged his father's last will as made while incompetent. Widow Elizabeth Harris and Charles Clarke were then ordered by the court to produce a previous will. What became clear through these legal battles is that Peter Harris did not wait until he died to distribute the shares in his estate, and that the portions given to children followed the general pattern of settlements in England. What differed was the informal nature of the agreements. Each child received promises at marriage. The fact that two married children thought that they each had five slaves still due them, but had only oral testimony to back their claims, confirms the informal nature of Peter Harris's distribution. In his will, the daughters received all of their shares in slaves, money, and personal property. The sons received land, slaves, and personal property. Furthermore, part of the daughters' "inheritance" in slaves was passed directly to their children. Henry had given the five disputed slaves to his wife Elizabeth, with instructions that she might dispose of them as she saw fit among their children (Cumberland County Wills, August 28, 1775).

Alternate Traditions

Despite the strong English base for their inheritance laws, Virginia and New York families were very aware that quite different assumptions about property, especially for married women, operated in other European countries and their colonies. They were also aware of the partible inheritance statutes in force in New England (Ditz, 1990, pp. 243-246). Many German and Huguenot (French Protestant) immigrants settled in New York and Virginia, bringing with them values reflective of community property traditions (Narrett, 1989, pp. 100-125; Gundersen, 1976). German immigrants to the colonies often complained about the unfairness of inheritance laws toward widows and daughters (Smith, 1995, p. 149). German law, for example, assumed that each spouse brought property to a marriage and that this property belonged to their "blood" kin, not a spouse. The spouse had rights of some kind to all property acquired during the marriage, and both daughters and sons had inheritance rights (Roeber, 1993, pp. 47-152). As the British empire expanded through conquest and purchase, the British acquired territories in which the inhabitants were familiar with a different system of inheritance. Parts of the British "New World" empire had previously been under Spanish, French, or Dutch law, not to mention the very different traditions of the original inhabitants of the Americas (Seed, 1995, pp. 159-161). New York was one of the colonies acquired through conquest, and in 1700, there were still a number of families trying to distribute property through inheritance applying values shaped by Dutch traditions.

Under the inheritance practices of Dutch New York, single women were independent actors, and a married woman was under a husband's guardianship but retained her rights to act alone, with his consent, and inherited under a version of community property rules. All property held by the couple was as joint tenants (excluding trusts and legacies clearly given to one person). At the death of one member of the couple, the survivor received half the property and the other half went to the deceased's heirs (children or blood kin). Those writing wills could not disinherit children, including daughters; children received equal shares in at least one-third of the estate (if four or fewer children) or one-half if there were more than four surviving children. Most families did not wait for the death of a spouse to distribute property but gave their children their shares as they married. Antenuptial agreements could reserve control of property so that it was not part of the community holdings of a couple. Married women could write wills to dispose of their half of an estate, or they could choose to sign a joint will with their husbands. In Dutch New York, women most often appear as signers of joint wills rather than writing a separate one (Narrett, 1992, pp. 41–56).

Dutch families were greatly concerned about the impact of British law on inheritance after the British conquest. The British originally assured the inhabitants of New Amsterdam that they would honor the Dutch traditions of inheritance, but the Duke's Laws promulgated in 1665 had modeled intestacy rules on those of New England. These granted the wife her "thirds"; the children received the rest, with the eldest son getting a double share. The British lost control of the colony briefly, but when they returned, several of the prominent men in the colony refused to swear an oath of allegiance to the British crown in 1675 without some guarantee that Dutch inheritance practices would be honored. Governor Andros jailed the men and eventually seized one-third of their estates. Local courts, however, did honor joint wills, women's wills, and marriage contracts, and followed Dutch customary law when settling estates. Dutch families, however, increasingly wrote wills to ensure that their wishes and not British intestacy rules would govern inheritance. The Charter of Liberties issued for New York in 1683 stipulated that English intestate rules would now apply to real estate. In 1691, British-style courts were set up in New York, and British rules of inheritance began to be enforced, although not strictly. By 1754, the courts were regularly applying the English rules of distribution of intestate estates, but not until 1774 was New York law clear on this point (Narrett, 1992, pp. 6–13, 127–128). New York courts continued to honor Dutch joint wills until the revolution. In practice, however, the number of such wills declined rapidly after 1700. Some people may have been afraid that the wills would be challenged; in other cases, the decline may have been a result of natural adoption of English custom by a younger generation (Gundersen and Gampel, 1982, p. 118).

Although Dutch legal forms declined rapidly after 1700 in New York, families continued to honor Dutch values. Dutch families, for example, often required the eldest son to buy out the shares of other children in order to ensure that daughters received a fair share. In the first quarter of the century, 70 percent of Dutch men gave their wives all of their estate, whereas only 43 percent of those of English descent in New York did so. Although the percentages declined over the course of the century, in the third quarter of the century, nearly half (43 percent) of the men of Dutch descent still continued to give their wives the whole estate, whereas only one-fourth (27 percent) of those of British descent did so (Narrett, 1992, pp. 95-98). The bequest of the whole estate to wives reflected Dutch assumptions of community property and the assumption that the wife would make her own will, properly taking care of any children.

German and Huguenot immigrants in Virginia and other colonies also turned to formal wills to express traditional values in patterns of inheritance at odds with the English/colonial legal provisions for intestates. A study of German immigrant wills shows that women tended to give land to daughters, that sons gave shared titles in land to siblings for token considerations, and that parents often turned over their land before death. Christopher Saur, a Pennsylvania German printer, whose German-language almanacs circulated widely in the colonies, used the almanacs in the 1750s to explain Pennsylvania inheritance law (and by extension the laws of other colonies) to new immigrants. Saur emphasized both that the widow's third was inadequate compensation for a woman's contribution to the family estate, and that men would have to make careful provision in wills to prevent unscrupulous sons from encroaching on that third. Migration to Virginia, however, disrupted the idea of maternal and paternal streams of property. Lands in Germany, including those owned by women, were left behind. In Virginia, men alone patented frontier lands settled by their families; thus, migrants began in Virginia with only a paternal stream of property. Virginia Germans avoided primogeniture, and although most tried to keep the home farm intact, testators tried to ensure that all children received shares, and the home plantation might be given to any of their children. There was no pattern by birth order or sex. Over half of the male testators with daughters in the Hebron area, for example, made sure that those daughters received land. In later generations, testators required that daughters receive compensation from the estate when giving the land to sons (Roeber, 1993, pp. 149-193).

Virginia Huguenots expressed similar values through their wills. First-generation immigrants were the most likely to give their wives sole control of an estate or land as an outright gift rather than as a life interest. Similarly, the first-generation Huguenots living at Manakin in Virginia were more likely to give daughters a share of land than their English neighbors or later generations. Over time, Virginia Huguenot families granted widows smaller shares and ones more in line with English intestate provisions. The percentage of wives receiving an unencumbered share dropped. Twenty-four percent of Virginia Huguenot wives received an unencumbered share in wills filed before 1749. By 1776, only 3 percent did. Sole heirs dropped from 14 to 2 percent, and widows with life interests rose from 26 to 41 percent in the same period. Families also translated earlier continental traditions of shares in land for all children to shares for sons, with daughters limited to personal property and slaves (Gundersen and Gampel, 1982, p. 122). Virginia's unique designation of slaves as real property in the first half of the 18th century may have allowed Huguenot fathers to feel that they had maintained older traditions even though sons and daughters received different kinds of "real" property. The behavior of Connecticut testators supports this assumption. The partible provisions of Connecticut inheritance laws meant sons and daughters all received shares (with the eldest son getting double). Families there assigned equal-value bequests but tended to give the sons that value in land and daughters their share in personalty. When the personal estate was too small to be equal, then daughters received small amounts of land (Ditz, 1990, pp. 249-251).

Colonial Wills

Individuals who were content with the distribution of property under the intestate laws did not need to write wills. Thus, the number of people who did write wills is a measure of those who wished to pursue other patterns of distribution. Many individuals, of course, died without making wills, because they legally had no status to transfer property. Married women, for example, had no legal status to transfer property unless they had a separate estate. The persistence of New York Dutch joint wills after English takeover is one exception to this rule and is a good illustration of families continuing to follow traditions at odds with colonial law. Slaves, themselves claimed as property by others, were not able to write wills or legally transfer any possessions they may have acquired. Given that Virginia's enslaved population grew from about 10 percent of the population to nearly 50 percent by the American Revolution, this was a serious disqualification of a substantial portion of the Virginia population. In New York, about 20 percent of the population was enslaved and thus disqualified from devising or inheriting property. Children were another group barred from writing wills, at least until they were in their teens. A portion of the adult, free population in both Virginia and New York (perhaps 5-20 percent) was simply too poor to have more than a small personal estate. Thus, the number at risk to write wills was probably less than 12 percent of the population of the colony at any given time. What is striking is the high proportion that chose to do so. In Goochland, Chesterfield, Powhatan, Cumberland, and Chesterfield Counties of Virginia during the 18th century, over four times as many estates were administered under provisions of a will than were administered under court-appointed intestate procedures. Among Huguenot families associated with Manakin settlement, the percentage was even higher. In New York City from 1664–1775 (with a population growing from about 500 to 12,000 during that period) there were 1,500 wills filed (Narrett, 1989, p. 94). The trends were similar; property increasingly came to daughters in liquid forms easily controlled by their husbands (Narrett, 1992, pp. 125–126, 145). Regardless of ethnicity, a majority of men in 18th-century Virginia and New York seem to have desired a more equitable pattern of property division among children than expressed in the intestate laws. But their values also put daughters on a lesser (although equal among themselves) level of inheritance.

Widows also received declining shares as the century progressed, a trend Virginia and New York shared with other colonies (Dayton, 1995, pp. 69–104); Tompsett, 1974; Ditz, 1990). Childless married men overwhelmingly passed their property to their wives throughout the period in both colonies regardless of ethnicity. In families where there were children, however, women's control over, and share in, the estate declined over the 18th century. One way that the control declined was that more property passed to widows as life interests or only for the duration of their widowhood, as opposed to fee simple ownership. In Albemarle County, Virginia, for example, after 1750, almost half of the widows with children received bequests limited to their widowhood. Before 1750, in the Cumberland-Chesterfield area, 38 percent of the testators made their wives sole heir or gave them an unencumbered share including land. Only 26 percent of the wills limited the widow to a life interest. From 1750–1776, 41 percent of the widows received life interests, and only 5 percent of the testators made the widow sole heir or gave her an unencumbered share. New York widows also increasingly were limited to maintenance or had a reduced share in property after children came of age (Gundersen and Gampel, 1982, pp. 122–123; Smith, 1980, p. 240; Deen, 1972).

Despite the decline, at no time before the revolution did the number of widows receiving at least the equivalent of their "thirds," through a husband's will, drop below half. In Amelia, Prince Edward, and Mecklenburg Counties of Virginia, for example, over 77 percent of widows whose husbands wrote wills received more than dower. Widows in New York, like their Virginian sisters, received at least their "thirds" in three-fourths of the cases. However, in the neighboring Chesapeake colony of Maryland, women receiving less than dower rose from 35 percent in midcentury to 57 percent by 1775 (Speth and Hirsch, 1982, pp. 16-21; Gundersen and Gampel, 1982, p. 123; Carr, 1989, p. 177). Virginia and New York testators followed the lead of Marylanders by reducing bequests to widows, but not as drastically. More men made room, board, and maintenance provisions for their wives in lieu of dower, but such cases remained a minority. The reason for limiting the widow's inheritance was not poverty, for wealthier families were less likely to give widows their "thirds" or more. Husbands gave women enough for a very comfortable subsistence, but then passed more assets on to their children. This was especially true when the widow came from a second marriage, or when there were adult children and the widow may have been elderly (Shammas, 1989, p. 143; Main, 1989, pp. 82-88).

One indication that women generally received the equivalent or more than what they would have received under intestate measures is the small number who chose to renounce such legacies and claim their dower right. In both New York and Virginia, such actions were unusual, but they happened just enough to confirm that courts would grant such requests when made, and that women knew they had the right. In Maryland, 17 percent of widows from 1740-1784 renounced bequests in order to claim dower (Lee, 1984, pp. 87-91). Another measure of awareness of dower rights is the procedures developed in each colony to waive dower rights when a couple sold land. In Virginia, for example, women had to go to court and relinquish their rights in front of the justices of the peace. The hearing was private to ensure that the woman had not been coerced into the sale (Speth and Hirsch, 1982, pp. 9-10; Salmon, 1986, pp. 18-19). After midcentury, however, the percentage of women appearing in person declined as courts sent justices to women's homes for private interviews (Gundersen, 1986, p. 17). New York did not move to protect such rights until the end of the century (Shammas et al., 1987, p. 74).

The changing pattern of bequests to widows in the 18th century reveals a growing assumption that women's proper role was as a dependent within a family rather than as a contributor to the family estate, either through their labor or through property they brought to a marriage. Land and slaves were essential to earning a living in the largely agricultural economies of the day. Even urban families depended on land for rents or as the site of business and home. Slaves provided skilled labor for many businesses. Although a dower life interest theoretically recognized a woman's contribution to the family enterprise, not all husbands did. The language some men used in wills written after 1750 illustrated their assumption that wives had no real interest in family property.

One Virginia woman, for example, had been given several slaves in her father's will. When her husband died, he assigned these slaves to her for her life, a practice he referred to as *lending* her his slaves for her lifetime (Gundersen, 1976). When a husband made a limited bequest, restricting a widow's inheritance to the duration of her children's minority or her widowhood, it both recognized her ability to run a farm or business and the husband's assumption that her appropriate role was as dependent—to a new husband or adult child. Some wills clearly assumed that women could not, or did not want to, run family businesses and farms. They directed that property be sold and the money or slaves be hired out to provide an income for a widow and/or children. Some widows controlled their own investments. In many wills, however, this became the duty of male executors. Provisions for maintenance alone carried this even further by simply making women dependent upon adult children. To some extent, an increase in the use of bequests stipulating maintenance rather than control of property (even if only a life interest) reflected a rising life expectancy. This meant that more widows were old enough to have adult children or to be ready to retire and thus not want control of a farm. The small number of widows who renounced more limited bequests to claim their dower in land may be evidence that most men understood their wives' abilities and desires; thus, few women felt compelled to challenge the bequests. But as the number of limited bequests went up, so did the number of women unwilling to accept them.

Even if widows did not receive direct ownership of land, they could have effective control for many years as the executors of administrators of estates. In Virginia, courts gave the widow priority as the administrator of an intestate husband's estate. A majority of those men who wrote wills in both New York and Virginia made their widows one of the executors of the estate. Over the course of the 18th century, the percentage of estates leaving administration to the sole control of widows declined throughout the colonies. In Virginia, for example, the percentage of men naming women as one of the executors ranged from 71 to 57 percent (depending on the county) at midcentury. It dropped to about 43 percent by the revolution. In New York, the decline in widows as sole executors occurred earlier. In the seventeenth century, with heavy Dutch influence, 75 percent of the men named their wives sole executor, but from 1751 to 1775, only 24 percent did so (Gundersen, 1986, p. 19; Speth and Hirsch, 1982, p. 23; Smith, 1980, p. 239; Narrett, 1989, pp. 118–119; Ditz, 1986, pp. 144–148). The decline in women's control of property through administration of the estate may also be a part of the lengthening life spans of colonists. Older colonists were more likely to have adult sons, whom they could include as executors, but at least one analysis of estate patterns in Maryland could find no strong correlation by family size, age of the couple, or wealth (Main, 1989, p. 77).

Despite the limitations on married women's property in both Virginia and New York, some women themselves had property for others to inherit and wrote wills. Generally, in the eighteenth century, colonial women owned about 10 percent of the wealth and men 90 percent. This was actually a more skewed wealth distribution than in England, where women's estates were about 20 percent of all probated (Shammas, 1989, pp. 138–139). Even if few in number, those women who did own property in the colonies usually wrote wills. One hundred twenty-five widows in New York City, for example, wrote wills between 1664 and 1775. The average age of women testators was much higher than that of men. Seventy percent of the eighteenth-century New York widows who wrote wills were sixty years of age or older. Forty-five percent were seventy or older. Only 32 percent of the men were sixty or older, and just 13 percent were seventy years or older. Widows distributed their property differently than had their husbands. Because the husband's will often had provided the family "portion" to each child, the widow could view her bequests as discretionary. Widows tended to favor daughters and granddaughters, a not surprising action, given that their property included clothes, jewels, and work tools such as looms or spinning wheels often used by women. For example, Ann David of King William Parish, Virginia, left her recently widowed daughter, Maryanne Burton, all of her clothes, flax and cotton (spun and unspun), linen loom, and sidesaddle. Her other married daughter, Ann Easley, received a mirror. Grandson Lewis Burton was to have £5 for schooling. Son Peter and the two daughters were to split the sale of her remaining estate. With basic family inheritances already distributed to children, New York widows were more likely to emancipate their slaves by will and to give bequests to grandchildren, women friends, and philanthropic causes than were men (Cumberland County, Virginia, Wills, November 26, 1750; Narrett, 1992, pp. 155–187, 239).

Inheritance during the American Revolution

The final quarter of the eighteenth century, filled with economic changes and the dislocations of the War for Independence, resulted in a reordering of inheritance in ways that made property more fluid and put sons and daughters on a more equal footing. Balancing this were even greater limitations on married women's inheritances. The most visible change in both Virginia and New York was the elimination of primogeniture. New York and Virginia had been laggards in eliminating primogeniture compared to other colonies. English legal practices had been more deeply embedded in their court systems than in New England. Connecticut intestate law, for example, had long given all children shares in an estate, with the oldest son receiving a double share (Ditz, 1990, p. 243). New York's inheritance law of 1787 gave all children equal shares, both in realty and personal property, in an intestate estate. Virginia's law of 1785 did the same. Those who benefited from the change were younger sons and all daughters of parents who died without a will. Because most families with land had used wills to escape the restriction of primogeniture before the war, the change was more symbolic than actual. In many families, one heir bought out the shares of the others. Unless women chose to remain single, the shift in law gave women little real control over their inheritances. When a daughter's inheritance was converted to liquid capital, it became the absolute property of a spouse. Even when she inherited land and retained a claim upon it, her husband controlled the property during the marriage (Shammas et al., 1987, pp. 64–67; Shammas, 1995, p. 129; Salmon, 1986, pp. 440–450; Orth, 1992, pp. 33–36).

Although the War for Independence resulted in a short-term rise in the number of young men dying, the pattern of bequests in New York and Virginia wills seemingly was unaffected by the demographic shift. However, more men may have died without wills, thus putting pressure on the legislatures to remove primogeniture. Men writing wills who died when their children were all young tended to leave the estate in the control of the widow until all children were of age, or allow the widow to grant shares as they came of age. Because young men had had less time to acquire land for children's portions, daughters generally shared only in the movable property and slaves. Widows had a short-term gain in control of property in Virginia, but their own share remained the increasingly standard third for life.[5] Thus, while gaining in informal control, their actual inheritances did not increase. The Virginia pattern of bequests contrasts with wartime Maryland, where there was an increase in the number of daughters granted life (or until marriage) interests in land that ultimately went to a son. The land of Maryland testators thus had to first provide for a daughter's support before the son could claim his inheritance. At times, the son also died before being able to claim that land (Lee, 1989, pp. 319–321).

The widow received the traditional dower protection of a one-third life interest in land. New York improved the widow's standing by granting her either a one-third interest (if there were children) or a one-half interest (if childless) in personal property, thus joining Virginia in granting the widow a claim to personal property, an increasingly important concern given the growth of commercial forms of wealth in the new nation. The widow could renounce a bequest in the will and choose a one-third interest in land if she chose. Land that had come to the couple by gift, descent, or devise had to pass to a blood relative of the original grantor. This provision resembled Dutch inheritance rules. While barring a widow from any claim on land inherited by her husband, it also ensured that land that she had inherited passed to her children. In 1785, Virginia explicitly debarred all married women from writing wills but retained the traditional "thirds" for realty, personal property, and slaves. The ability to entail slaves to protect women's inheritances had ended in 1775, and in 1792 slaves were declared personal property, thus becoming the husband's at marriage. In 1792, Virginia disadvantaged widows more by restricting personalty to a life interest. In the past, this had been outright ownership. The intestate provisions became more important because, by the 1790s, widows' shares in wills went down, and they were also less likely to have control of the property as an executrix.[6]

The dower was eroded in a number of ways in the years immediately after the revolution. Some states abolished the right entirely, something that neither New York or Virginia did. In most states, the dower, however, became liable for a husband's debts, or the income from the property could be claimed for the debts. Furthermore, the widow lost protection of "paraphernalia" as states made all of a couple's property subject to debt actions. This made a woman's inheritance much less secure and allowed property granted to her by her family to be eroded before widowhood. Because of coverture, she had little she could do to prevent a wastrel husband from encumbering her estate (Kerber, 1980, pp. 124–147).

Illegitimacy, Adoption, and Inheritance

Changes in the statutes covering those born outside a legal marriage also affected inheritance in the Revolutionary Era. Although Spanish law granted fathers the right to legitimatize bastards without marrying the mother (and thus make them heirs of an estate), English and colonial law had considered children born outside legal marriage to be the child literally of no one. Such children did not inherit from either the mother or the father. During the revolution, illegitimacy rates rose. Virginia was a pioneer in giving illegitimate children inheritance rights to their mothers' estates, passing such a law in 1785. New York was one of 12 states to follow suit by 1830. Most of the states to do so were slave states, where free African-American mothers were barred from marrying the fathers of their children (because the men were either slaves or were white). The Virginia statute went further than many of the other laws, recognizing the mother's right to a child's estate if the child died without heirs, and the right of the child to claim inheritances through the mother's line of kin. If a father later married the mother and acknowledged paternity, the child gained full inheritance rights. In 1837, Virginia courts extended the rights of illegitimate children even further by allowing a half-sister born out of marriage to claim the estate of her half-brother who had died intestate and without heirs. Judges in *Garland v. Harrison* (1837), ignored an earlier Virginia court decision to follow the precedent set by a Connecticut court giving those born outside legal marriages the right to claim a position as blood kin and thus be considered heirs-at-law. In both Virginia and New York, the absolute power of wills meant that fathers could grant bequests to children born out of marriage (or their mothers), and a few did so. It also took a positive bequest in a will to transfer property to an adopted child. Thus, fathers could not adopt illegitimate children to smooth inheritance rights. In 1857, a New York Court upheld for the first time a signed agreement making an adopted child an heir (Grossberg, 1985, pp. 199–269; Shammas et al., 1987, p. 70; Narrett, 1989, pp. 171–172).

The changes in inheritance rights for illegitimate children affected women more than men. The children themselves, of course, were nearly evenly divided among boys and girls, but these laws affected their mothers more than their fathers. Maternity was never at issue. What these laws did was to recognize maternal kinship for purposes of inheritance in all cases. Paternal inheritance rights remained dependent upon a bequest by will and entirely in the control of the father. The laws allowed women who were supporting children without paternal help to ensure that any property they owned could pass to their children, and gave them a similar claim on property acquired by their children. It did, however, give an incentive to fathers to transfer some property to the mothers of their children, because that property could now pass more easily to their child.

Emancipation and Inheritance

One other change during the Revolutionary Era had a major effect on the inheritances of women in New York. In 1796, New York passed a gradual emancipation law. The law did not free those currently enslaved, but it made children born after a set date free when they reached adulthood. Thus, by the 1840s, there would be a larger number of free black women able to inherit or to pass property to others. Few of the children of slaves, however, could expect to receive a substantial inheritance. For women from slaveholding families, however, emancipation brought a major change. Inasmuch as daughters tended to inherit personalty, including slaves, gradual emancipation disproportionately reduced their inheritances. Although they retained claims to slaves already born, they lost the claim to future progeny. Furthermore, families had to turn to other forms of property to provide a daughter's share.

In Virginia, the changes affected women's claims to wealth. Virginia did not pass a gradual emancipation law but for a short time following the American Revolution, a number of slaveholders did emancipate slaves by deed or will. No systematic study exists to suggest whether those who chose to emancipate their slaves had heirs. However, as an absolute reduction in the kind of property women often received as a marriage portion or bequest, emancipation affected women's inheritances most. The portion of an estate inherited by a widow in Virginia declined well into the 1790s.

Antebellum Virginia

Although Virginia retained dower rights, and even granted dower claims of the wives of Tories whose lands were confiscated, dower's value was greatly reduced by the limitation of personal estate to a life interest rather than outright ownership in the 1792 law (Kerber, 1980, p. 124; Shammas et al., 1987, pp. 64–65, 120–121). From 1784 to 1800, women wrote only 7 percent of recorded wills, a measure of the small number who owned property not in a life interest. The Virginia intestate law reflected the priority that men placed on distribution of property to children (including younger sons and daughters) rather than wives. One measure of male contentment with Virginia's revised intestate laws was a drop in will writing. More men were content to let intestate rules govern their estates now that younger children were guaranteed a share in lands. This trend grew over the years, until about two-thirds of all men died intestate in the years 1841–1860 (Lebsock, 1984, pp. 130–133).

The growing identification of women with the domestic sphere left an increasing number of women unsure of their ability or the propriety of administering an estate. The decline in widows as executors or administrators of estates that began in the mid-18th century continued. A little more than half the men named their wives as an executor of their wills from 1784 to 1860. Before 1830, wealthier men were more reluctant to do so, fearing that remarriage would bring their estates under the control of the new husband. Legal changes from 1824 to 1835 resulted in new executors being named upon a widow's remarriage; thus, the number of widows managing sizable estates went up. The percentage of widows administering smaller estates, however, went down, possibly because wives asked not to be burdened. In Petersburg, Virginia, for example, only about 60 percent of those women who had an option of administering the estate chose to do so. Wealthier women and/or younger women were more inclined to take up the challenge (Lebsock, 1984, pp. 37–40, 121–122). The higher literacy of these groups may have been a factor in their decisions. Although Virginia's economy remained based in agriculture, estate administration increasingly required literacy.

As inheritance laws in Virginia increasingly favored daughters and limited wives, there was a rise in the use of antenuptial and postnuptial agreements in equity that reserved rights to property for a married woman. In Petersburg, Virginia, from 1784 to 1810, only 13 trusts for married women were created. From 1821 to 1860, nearly 600 were. This process was simplified during the late eighteenth century by the growing legal acceptance of equity arrangements that had no formal trustees. In effect, the woman's husband served as informal trustee. Virginia courts began recognizing equity arrangements without explicit trustees after 1800 (Salmon, 1986, pp. 112–115; Lebsock, 1984, p. 66). Courts in Virginia interpreted the documents setting up these separate estates very strictly. Only powers explicitly stated were conferred. Thus, only 18 percent of postnuptial agreements and 62 percent of prenuptial agreements in Petersburg, Virginia, gave women the right to will or sell their property (Shammas, 1994, pp. 13–14). Women in business for themselves at the time of marriage were more likely than other women to sign such agreements, but the use increased generally. From 1784 to 1825, only one out of every sixty-two women signed such agreements at marriage, and of those, one-third were in business. From 1821 to 1860, about one out every twenty-six made such agreements. Ironically, if women had actually controlled more property, the number of separate estates might well have risen. Women created five out of eighteen separate estates done by will (i.e., for a daughter or other female heir) in Petersburg, Virginia, before 1840, and fifteen of twenty-six executed and filed from 1840 to 1860. Overall, women established by will, deed, or gift, one-third of all separate estates in Petersburg, a proportion far above their actual occurrence among property owners (Lebsock, 1984, pp. 75–77).

Given the changes in Virginia's inheritance law, families modified the strategies they had used to convey wealth without altering the underlying goals. Men's wills continued to provide the basic property division among children and to provide for the widow. Because more men were satisfied with the intestate provisions, fewer wrote wills, and, more often, they did so in order to increase what their wives inherited. Ninety percent of the men who wrote wills, but had no children, did so to give their widows land in fee simple. Over 70 percent of the men who wrote wills directed that their children share equally in the estate, thus duplicating the intestate provisions. The interest in enlarging a widow's inheritance spread to those with children after 1830. Among poor or middle-class testators, the widow received some fee simple property about half the time. Overall, about 35 percent did so, an increase of 13 percent over the bequests made by testators from 1784 to 1830 (Lebsock, 1984, p. 44). The result was that widows at the end of the period were about as likely to inherit land in fee simple as they had been before 1750. The decline witnessed during the Revolutionary Era had been erased (Gundersen and Gampel, 1982, p. 122).

New York in the New Republic

In the New Republic, the experience of New York women and Virginia women diverged more radically than it had during the colonial period. New

York laws increasingly reflected that a growing commercial economy required liquid capital. As New York limited dower protections, and as estates came to have larger and larger shares in various forms of personal property, women had less opportunity to inherit or control the inheritance they received. If a woman was married, these forms of wealth passed directly to her husband. If he died intestate, she had no claim to these movable, liquid assets, even if they had been property given to her originally. Decisions by the New York Chancery Courts made prenuptial agreements nearly unenforceable, thus eliminating an important way to circumvent coverture. Even if New York courts had not undermined prenuptial agreements, the use of trusts to protect women's inheritance was declining, if the experience of nearby New Jersey is an indication (Friedman, 1964, pp. 41–44). In Virginia, the economy remained rooted in agriculture, with slaves as the most prominent form of capital investment, and the state retained dower and equity provisions.

If males carried the burden of distributing the majority of assets to the next generation, women in New York and Virginia who wrote wills had the luxury of granting favors to specific children. Over three-fourths of Virginia's female testators used their wills to favor daughters. This may have been an attempt to balance unequal distributions favoring sons, made at the time of the children's marriages, or it may reflect that the property women had to will was mostly property of interest to other women. Even if all of a woman's children were of the same sex, she tended to play favorites two-thirds of the time, thus reinforcing the image that women saw their property as more discretionary than did men. Not surprisingly, women also were more likely to leave special bequests to slaves, free specific servants by will, or protect them from being sold (Lebsock, 1984, pp. 130–135).

The lack of dower protection and equity estates, and the growing commercial economy took New York families down a different path. Like Virginia judges, those in New York recognized by 1818 the use of passive trusts or simple agreements between husband and wife as setting up a woman's separate estate. However, just ten years later, the sate assembly eliminated the separate estate as an option for couples marrying after that date. Husbands and wives could no longer make these agreements for themselves. Formal trusts reverted to simple ownership by the couple (i.e., under control of the husband). Trusts already in effect would be honored, but married women were forbidden to write wills unless the trust explicitly stated she had the power. Third parties, such as fathers, could still create trusts for their children, but unless the trust specified that it was to continue after a woman's marriage, the trust ended and the husband gained control of the property. The remnants of dower provided women with the only leverage to create a separate estate. A wife could still sign an agreement with her husband after marriage, but only to determine her right of "settlement" (i.e., dower rights of inheritance).

Such agreements did not always work to the benefit of women. Wealthy men sometimes used these agreements to limit a wife's claim on their estate. Courts could ask if a couple that successfully sued for an inheritance due the wife wanted a *portion* (i.e., her "third") to be placed in a trust. Some women who had been abandoned, separated, or could not count on their husbands for support, chose to shield an inheritance by petitioning the courts to recognize the inheritance as part of their dower. The court acted as trustee in these cases (Basch, 1982, pp. 74-93).

The growing commercial economy clearly affected New York inheritance patterns. By the time that the New York Assembly limited the use of trusts during a marriage, most trusts created by will were used to provide for widows and minor children. Often, the trusts included much more than a widow's third, but only until remarriage. Thus, rather than give her full control, the trust restricted a widow's control of property. Like Virginians, New York males seemed quite content with the intestate provisions, for only 5 percent of Westchester residents who died in 1825 chose to write wills. Women wrote a disproportionately high 27 percent of the Westchester wills, given how few women were in a position to sign a will at all. The action of the state assembly in 1828 barring married women from writing wills affected very few women, except by encouraging other states to follow suit. New Jersey passed such a law in 1847, for example. All of those who wrote wills in Westchester, for example, were single or widowed. New York's Dutch legal traditions had clearly vanished. By 1850, estates included larger amounts of stocks, bonds, and property rented to others. Rents, stocks, and bonds, of course, passed to the control of a woman's husband. Women's control over their inheritance was decreased even further by the use of trusts created by wills, especially for large and complex estates (Basch, 1982, pp. 100-105; Friedman, 1964, p. 36).

Because of the changes in equity law and the fact that more property passed to women in liquid forms immediately controlled by their husbands upon marriage, pressure grew more rapidly in New York for legal innovation than it did in Virginia. The economy in the New Republic was very volatile, with cycles of boom and bust. Economic downturns, called "Panics" in 1819, 1837, and 1857, for example, brought waves of foreclosure. Under such circumstances, families rightfully worried that a woman's inheritance might quickly be swallowed by claims of her husband's creditors. Given that women also were making more independent marriage choices, and fathers had less say in the selection of sons-in-law, it is not surprising that concern rose about the ability of sons-in-law to manage wisely. Coverture thus seemed a dangerous tradition to families concerned about the financial stability of their daughters (Basch, 1982, p. 27; Shammas, 1994, pp. 11, 24-26). In 1848, New York was a pioneer in developing women's separate estates through statute. The Married Women's Property Act of 1848 gave married women the right to receive by "gift, grant, devise, or bequest, from any person other than her husband and to hold to her sole and separate use, as if she were a single female, real and personal property, and the rents, issues and profits thereof, and the subject shall not be subject to the disposal of her husband, nor be liable for his debts." Judges minimized the impact of this law by ruling that it applied only to marriages contracted or property acquired *after* passage of the law. Furthermore, courts interpreted this law so conservatively that the assembly had to amend the act the next year to allow women to convey and devise the property the previous law had allowed them to "hold." The revision also allowed women to petition the court for personal control of funds held by the courts in trust for them (Basch, 1982, pp. 159, 204, 233).

Although the 1848 law protected some women's inheritances from improvident husbands, women who had married *before* 1848 remained unprotected. The potential inheritance represented by a married woman's dower claims in property acquired by the couple during marriage was unaffected by these laws. A husband had the power to reduce a woman's dower to nothing by squandering their joint assets or turning it over to creditors. If a woman did not draw up a will for her separate estate, the husband acquired all of it upon her death. Furthermore, in New York (as well as a number of other states), income generated from the inherited property could be seized by his creditors, even if the property itself inherited by the woman could not. Thus, feminists continued to press for further revision—revisions that would alter the basic rules used for centuries in English law—to determine inheritance and property rights. In 1860, the assembly passed a law that restructured inheritance by giving each spouse in a childless union a one-third interest in the estate of the other. If there were children, the survivor got all property during the minority of the child and then a one-third interest for life. The rest of the estate went to the child. This equality in inheritance, although based on traditional "thirds" in intestate cases, too radically reduced patriarchal power. Only two years later, the assembly revised the law, reinstating male rights to guardianship and men's larger rights to inheritance (Avery and Konefsky, 1992, pp. 326-327; Basch, 1982, pp. 176-236). The effect of the New York Married Women's Property Acts was gradual. Probate records would not show an increase in women's property holdings until the generation of women who married after 1848 began to die (Shammas, 1994, pp. 17-19). Women, of course, gained control of inherited property long before it was recorded as a part of their probate estate, but the impact of the laws was cumulative and slow.

Thus, in the nineteenth century, Virginia and New York families chose very different strategies to achieve the same end—protection of women's inheritances from bad management by a husband. Their concern was with protecting a family inheritance passed to a daughter rather than assuring equity for widows as contributors to a marriage. For Virginians, changes in inheritance law to give daughters and younger sons a greater share came at the expense of widows. Families concerned about protection of daughters turned to equity law in growing numbers. In an agricultural society, with much wealth held in the form of human capital, these provisions worked reasonably well to allay concerns of fathers for their daughters. In New York, a growing commercial economy led the legislature first to give males more control over assets held in a marriage and then eliminate most equity protections for women. But, as concerned fathers cast a skeptical eye on the skill of their sons-in-law as managers of their daughters' inheritances and marriage portions, they had to turn to legal innovation—the Married Women's Property Act. Not until after the Civil War would Virginia pass a similar measure. With slavery gone and a cash-based, commercial economy growing, equity and entail no longer were equal to the task.

By the end of the century, most states had passed Married Women's Property Acts. Further pressure to change the legal structures of inheritance dissipated despite the rarity of equity arrangements. Not until the feminist movement reorganized in the 1960s would serious agitation for more equal laws, and the focus on an equal rights amendment result in legal change.

Conclusions

From 1700 to 1750, both Virginia and New York adopted much of English traditional law on inheritance. In the process, they turned away from potential sources of innovation—New York's original Dutch legal system, the traditions brought by other immigrants, and the variations found in other colonies. Colonists instead turned to the law of wills to modify inheritance practices that favored sons over daughters, and older sons over younger ones. In turn, they also adopted practices of equity law that provided some opportunity to mitigate the disabilities of coverture for married women. Although these decisions set the parameters for women's inheritance in the late colonial period in the two colonies, even more important were the values that helped families determine desirable outcomes. Late colonial families were more interested in seeing their children well settled with property than they were in recognizing a wife's contribution to the family estate. Thus, families increasingly chose to limit widows' inheritances and control of estates in favor of their children.

Changes during the revolution further reduced women's inheritances. These included erosion of the protection dower could give to inherited property, the reduction of a widow's claim to personal property from outright ownership to a life interest, and the increasing practice of bequeathing women forms of property, which passed immediately to the full control of her husband and carried no dower protections. Although the gradual emancipation law in New York and an increase in private emancipations in Virginia created a number of new individuals who had the legal right to inherit for the first time, the very conversion of human property into free individuals reduced other women's inheritances. Of all the Revolutionary Era changes, only the extension of some inheritance rights to children born outside of a legal marriage countered these trends limiting women's inheritances.

In the antebellum years, New York's increasingly commercial economy with liquid assets increased the threat coverture posed to securing a woman's inheritance from her father. Creditors' demands to have access to the whole of a couple's assets resulted in the 1828 New York law eliminating a major form of separate estates for married women. Equity thus no longer offered shelter, and by 1848, New York legislators were willing to experiment with a Married Women's Property Act that granted married women a passive, separate estate for property she inherited, while leaving her under coverture in other ways. In contrast, Virginia expanded the use of separate estates under equity law, refusing to pass a Married Women's Property Act until after the Civil War. By then, emancipation, industrialization, and reconstruction had made equity a cumbersome alternative. What is striking, however, is that despite the difference in legal stratagies chosen in the antebellum period, the reality of women's inheritances was quite similar in Virginia and New York. In both states, conservative male courts and legislatures ensured that law reinforced the assumptions of women's dependence by reducing women's control of estates. In both states, widows continued to receive reduced inheritances in order to give children more, and the number of women administering estates dropped. Both Virginia and New York widows had the freedom to give special bequests to favorite children and grandchildren, because their husbands had already provided the basic portions for the children. Thus, even though the tools were different in each state, the outcomes were the same, because New York and Virginia men shared common ideas about who within their families should own and control different kinds of property. Having eliminated legal preferences for sons over daughters in inheritance and secured the rights of married women to control inheritances they received as daughters, the states had no incentive to recognize the wife as her husband's equal in inheritance. Only New York came close in 1860, but that law was quickly repealed.

Afterword

After the Civil War, most states adopted Married Women's Property Acts. The few that did not were states with inheritance traditions traceable to

Roman law—through Spain or France. These legal traditions already recognized a wife's separate right to property brought to a marriage. Eventually, even community property states passed Married Women's Property Acts in order to protect married women's wages and property acquired after marriage (Hall, 1989, pp. 158-159). By 1900, the effect of these laws across the United States was to give women more disposable property. The number of women writing wills increased, and the use of separate estates declined rapidly. Women also regained lost ground as administrators of estates (Friedman, 1964, pp. 41-52; Avery and Konefsky, 1992). However, these laws did not remove coverture, and they left men in a privileged place as heads of families. They did make it possible for men to distribute property to their daughters with some degree of security, and for married women to retain their wages, thus siphoning off pressure for further reform.

When women's advocates began documenting the many inequities in civil law as part of a revived feminist movement in the 1960s, other aspects of coverture and property rights seemed more pressing than reform in inheritance law. Changes, however, did occur. When the U.S. Congress sent the Equal Rights Amendment (ERA) to the states for possible ratification, state laws came under close scrutiny. Many states made lists of the laws that would need to be changed, including the unilateral nature of women's separate estates under the Married Women's Property Acts and the unparallel claims that husbands and wives had on each other's estates (women's right of dower and men's right of curtsey).[7] Some states revised their law codes to comply with the ERA, assuming its eventual passage. Those revisions remained after the amendment was defeated.

Even more to the point, the Supreme Court turned a 1971 case involving inheritance into a landmark decision for women's rights. In *Reed v. Reed*, an Idaho state statute giving fathers precedence as administrators of their children's estates was challenged by a mother who claimed that her Fourteenth Amendment rights of due process and equal protections were violated by the statute. The court was urged in some of the briefs presented to use *Reed v. Reed* as an opportunity to declare sex a "suspect" category requiring "strict scrutiny" in cases raising Fourteenth amendment claims. The court ruled unanimously for the mother, finding no reasonable basis for the state to assume that a father was automatically better qualified than a mother to administer a child's estate. However, the justices were unwilling to consider sex a suspect category (Hall, 1989, p. 329). Thus, the U.S. Supreme Court, while signaling to all the states that inheritance statutes needed to be written in gender-neutral language, had followed in the footsteps of Virginia and New York justices by construing the law narrowly and minimizing the impact of the decision for women. Even so, the decision was the first in a series of sex discrimination suits that expanded constitutional rights of women in the 1970s.

Notes

1. An "heir-at-law" is literally the person designated to inherit real estate according to prevailing statutes. After 1540, a will took precedence over statute in determining actual inheritance. "Coverture" is the application of the common law doctrine that merged a married woman's interests with those of her husband for the duration of the marriage and gave the husband actual control of her interests. It did not obliterate her rights, but it suspended independent action during the marriage. "Dower" was the legal protection to provide support for women and recognize their property interests in a family's economic holdings. It was defined by English law as a one-third, undivided life interest in all properties held by the couple during marriage.

2. See, for example, the John Martin will, May 15, 1739, Goochland County Deeds.

3. Historians use a variety of dates for this period. I am using *early modern period* to mean the years from the Reformation through the Enlightenment, about 1500–1800.

4. Equity law developed in the medieval period from feudal claims of the crown to control over certain categories of estates, especially those of minors. In time, it became a network of courts handling technical matters of inheritance and property. The courts relied on judge-made law but theoretically were to weight "justice" more heavily than legal forms. This is what earned the courts their label as "equity" courts. By the nineteenth century, equity courts had ironically gained a reputation as the most bureacratic of all English courts. Its judges were called "Chancellors," hence "Chancery Court." The terms *chancery* and *equity* are used interchangeably in the American colonies.

5. The will sample is part of a large study still under way by the author. It consists of over 300 wills filed between 1700 and 1800 in Virginia. The sample includes all extant wills of Virginia testators descended from the Huguenot refugees who settled at Manakin. It also includes a sample of every fifth will in the will books of the counties in which the Manakin community was located. This ensured a comparative base of English-origin planters.

6. Shammas et al., 1989, pp. 64–65, 120–121; Salmon, 1986, pp. 151–156; An act concerning wills, *Acts of the Virginia Assembly*, 1785, pp. 46–51; An act concerning dower and jointures of widows, ibid., p. 54. Section 1. reads in part: "That every person aged twenty-one years of upwards, being of sound mind, and not a married woman, shall have power of his will and pleasure, by last will and testament in writing to devise all the estate, right, title, and interest, to possession, reversion, or remainder, which he had or at the time of his death shall have, or, in, or to lands, tenements, or hereditaments, or annuities, or rents charged upon issuing out of them; ..." No provision was made for married women to write wills to transfer property in equity trusts; thus, only by explicit mention in a trust arrangement would a woman be able to exercise this right.

7. A husband's right of curtsey gave him a life interest (if they had offspring) in all land held by the wife.

References

Avery, D., & Konefsky, A. J. (1992). The daughters of Job: Property rights and women's lives in mid-nineteenth-century Massachusetts, *Law and History Review, 10*, 325-356.

Basch, Norma. (1982). *In the eyes of the law: Women, marriage and property in nineteenth-century New York.* Ithaca, NY, and London: Cornell University Press.

Beard, M. R. (1946). *Woman as force in history: A study in traditions and realities.* New York: Macmillan.

Carr, L. G. (1989). Inheritance in the colonial Chesapeake. In R. Hoffman & P. J. Albert (Eds.), *Women in the age of the American Revolution* (pp. 155-208). For the United States Capitol Historical Society by the University of Virginia Press.

Dayton, C. H. (1995). *Women before the bar: Gender, law and society in Connecticut, 1639-1789.* Chapel Hill: Institute of Early American History and Culture, University of North Carolina Press.

Deen, J. W. (1972). Patterns of testation: Four tidewater counties in colonial Virginia. *American Journal of Legal History, 16*, 154-176.

Ditz, T. (1986). *Property and kinship: Inheritance in early Connecticut, 1750-1820.* Princeton, NJ: Princeton University Press.

Ditz, T. (1990). Ownership and obligation: Inheritance and patriarchal households in Connecticut, 1750-1820. *William and Mary Quarterly*, 3rd ser., *43*, 235-265.

Flexner, E. (1959). *Century of struggle: The women's rights movement in the United States.* Cambridge, MA: Belknap Press of Harvard University.

Friedman, L. M. (1964). Patterns of testation in the 19th century: A study of Essex County (New Jersey) Wills. *American Journal of Legal History, 8*, 34-53.

Grossberg, M. (1985). *Governing the hearth: Law and the family in nineteenth-century America.* Chapel Hill and London: University of North Carolina Press.

Gundersen, J. R. (1976). *"In the name of God, amen": Wills, women and property in Virginia.* Paper presented at Women Historians of the Midwest Conference on Women's History, St. Paul, MN.

Gundersen, J. R. (1986). Kith and kin: Women's networks in colonial Virginia. Paper presented Citadel Conference on the History of the South, Charleston, SC.

Gundersen, J. R., & Gampel, G. V. (1982). Married women's legal status in eighteenth-century New York and Virginia. *William and Mary Quarterly*, 3rd ser., *39*, 114-134.

Hall, K. H. (1989). *The magic mirror: Law in American history.* Oxford, UK: University of Oxford Press.

Hening, W. W. (Ed.). (1809-1823). The statutes at large; being a collection of all the laws of Virginia.... Richmond, VA.

Kerber, L. K. (1980). *Women of the republic: Intellect and ideology in revolutionary America.* Chapel Hill: Institute of Early American History and Culture, University of North Carolina Press.

Lebsock, S. (1984). *The free women of Petersburg: Status and culture in a Southern town, 1784-1860.* New York and London: W. W. Norton.

Lee, J. B. (1984). *The social order of a revolutionary people: Charles County, Maryland, 1733-86.* Doctoral dissertation, University of Virginia.

Lee, J. B. (1989). Land and labor: Parental bequest practices in Charles County, Maryland, 1732-1783. In L. G. Carr, P. D. Morgan, & J. B. Russo (Eds.), *Colonial Chesapeake society* (pp. 306-341). Chapel Hill: Institute of Early American History and Culture, University of North Carolina Press.

Main, Gloria L. (1989). Widows in rural Massachusetts on the eve of the Revolution. In R. Hoffman & P. J. Albert (Eds.), *Women in the age of the American Revolution* (pp. 67-90). Charlottesville: United States Capitol Historical Society by the University of Virginia Press.

Narrett, D. (1989). Men's wills and women's property rights in colonial New York. In R. Hoffman & P. J. Albert (Eds.), *Women in the age of the American Revolution* (pp. 91-133). Charlottesville: United States Capitol Historical Society, University of Virginia Press.

Narrett, D. (1992). *Inheritance and family life in colonial New York City*, Ithaca, NY, and Cooperstown, NY: Cornell University and the New York State Historical Association. 1988, pp. 306-341.

Orth, J. (1992). After the Revolution: "Reform" of the Law of Inheritance, *Law and History Review, 10*, 33-44.

Roeber, A. G. (1993). *Palatines, liberty, and property: German Lutherans in colonial British America*. Baltimore: Johns Hopkins University Press.

Salmon, M. (1982). Women and property in South Carolina: The evidence from marriage settlements, 1730-1830. *William and Mary Quarterly*, 3rd ser., *39*, 655-722.

Salmon, M. (1986). *Women and the law of property in early America*. Chapel Hill: Institute of Early American History and Culture, University of North Carolina Press.

Seed, P. (1995). American law, Hispanic traces: Some contemporary entanglements of community property. *William and Mary Quarterly*, 3rd ser. *52*, 157-162.

Shammas, C. (1989). Early American women and control over capital. In R. Hoffman & P. J. Albert (Eds.), *Women in the age of the American Revolution*, Charlottesville: United States Capitol Historical Society, University of Virginia Press.

Shammas, C. (1994). Re-assessing the Married Women's Property Acts. *Journal of Women's History, 6*, 9-30.

Shammas, C. (1995). Anglo-American household government in comparative perspective. *William and Mary Quarterly, 52*, 104-144.

Shammas, C., Salmon, M., & Dahlin, M. (1987). *Inheritance in America from colonial times to the present*. New Brunswick, NJ and London: Rutgers University Press.

Smith, D. B. (1980). *Inside the great house: Planter family life in eighteenth-century Chesapeake society*. Ithaca, NY, and London: Cornell University Press.

Smith, D. S. (1995). Behind and beyond the law of the household. *William and Mary Quarterly*, 3rd ser. *52*, 145-150.

Speth, L., & Hirsch, A. D. (1982). *Women, family, and community in colonial America: Two perspectives*, Women and History, Number 4, Institute for Research in History and the Haworth Press.

Spring, E. (1990). The heiress-at-law: English real property from a new point of view. *Law and History, 8*, 273-296.

Tompsett, C. H. (1974). A note on the economic status of widows in colonial New York. *New York History, 55*, 319-332.

6

Ethnicity and Inheritance

REMI P. CLIGNET

Sociologists hold diverging views of the logic governing the acquisition and the transfer of wealth. Some researchers focus on material and objective factors, others on symbolic and subjective forces. When Marx, who represents the materialist position, argues that the *value* and the *nature* of assets shape both the conception that their owners have of the world, and more specifically, their definition of their domestic rights and obligations (cited in Newby, Bell, Rose, and Sanders, 1979, p. 24), he reminds us that market forces have an impact on wealth transfers. Differences in rates of returns on investments, risks incurred as a result of their acquisition or of their management, and rates of liquidity and transfer of specific kinds of assets condition choices made by individuals in building their estates as well as in disposing of them during or at the end of their lives.

A subjectivist perspective (Thompson, 1979) suggests that neither material nor symbolic objects have intrinsic value. Rather, their value is a mere social construct that individuals elaborate in order to justify and perpetuate their socioeconomic and/or cultural status. In this second perspective, the primary task of analysts consists of assessing how the ordering of assets mirrors and affects the ordering of eligible heirs. According to this perspective, sociologists should identify the role of inheritance as one of the mechanisms that social categories (gender, religious affiliation, social class, nationality, birth cohort) utilize in order to make and legitimate status claims.[1]

REMI P. CLIGNET • ORSTOM, Institut Français de Recherche Scientifique pour le Developpment en Cooperation, 213 rue La Fayette, 75480 Paris Cedex 10e, France.

Inheritance and Wealth in America, edited by Robert K. Miller, Jr., and Stephen J. McNamee. Plenum Press, New York, 1998.

Between these two perspectives, other social scientists posit the independence of the objective processes governing the acquisition of wealth and of the subjective processes regulating its intergenerational transfer. In a capitalist society, the acquisition of wealth is driven by rationality and the attempt to maximize profit. Yet wealth acquisition does not preclude the need for its legitimation through the use of significant, but "nonrational" symbols, to use here the very terms of Weber (1968). To reiterate Weber's own example, even though neighboring Polish and German farmers shared the same soil and, hence, the same opportunities or constraints, they have maintained distinct patterns of inheritance. Norms for deciding *which* share *which* eligible heir should receive, and *when*, vary with the culturally relative interpretations of opportunities and constraints, rights and duties.

Against this theoretical background, the purpose of this chapter is to assess the influence of ethnicity on the acquisition and the transfer of wealth in contemporary America. The amounts and kinds of economic capital available for transfers are affected by national origin.[2] Yet the notions of national origin and of social class tend to overlap. Both the overall duration of the American experience acquired by various national groups and their prestige, relative to dominant groups of Anglo–American origin, condition the size of the share of the American "pie" claimed by each of these groups. Immigrant communities do not have equal access to the most rewarding educational opportunities or to the juiciest occupational or residential "plums." Furthermore, their economic progress varies (Lieberson, 1980). As an illustration, differences in the nature and the value of the assets owned by, say, the WASPs and the Vietnamese result from differences in the duration of their respective American experience. Moreover, the rank-ordering of national groups in terms of prestige operates independently of duration of experience, as illustrated by WASP and African-American differences in wealth, despite similarity of time of arrival in the New World.

Besides externally imposed conditions, such as economic opportunities and status rankings, wealth transfers are also conditioned by internal cultural differences among ethnic groups themselves.[3] Such cultural differences include the nature of the assets preferred by individuals at various moments of their lives, their choice of a particular instrument of transfer, and the shares they assign to their heirs.

In view of the dearth of pertinent data, the first section of the chapter is devoted to pointing out the conditions under which ethnicity or national origin remains likely to influence the formation of individual wealth and its transfer to heirs in contemporary America. In the following sections of this chapter, I will assess the evidence pertaining to the impact of ethnicity and national origin on the composition of estates, the functions of wills, and on the mode of division of the estate.

Prerequisites to the Impact of National Origin
or Ethnicity on the Formation
and the Transfer of Wealth in Contemporary America

The impact of national or ethnic origin on wealth transfers depends on several factors. First, ethnic inequalities, in terms of access to collective assets such as educational or health amenities, should be considered separately from the patterns that govern the way the familial groups of each ethnic group divide their wealth among eligible heirs. In other words, interethnic variations in the nature or the value of the capital accumulated or transferred should not mask differences within ethnic or national groups themselves. Splitting bequests *evenly* among heirs or making distinct bequests as a function of each heir's skills, needs, aspirations, or other factors generates differing opportunities for upward mobility. In turn, the relevant norms of each national group not only affect individual life chances, but also the long-term ethnic distribution of collective assets.

Independent of these objective contrasts, there are also ethnic disparities in the invidious comparisons that heirs establish between their shares and those of both their siblings and their counterparts in other ethnic groups. Inconsistencies between the dominant American ideology and the world-views of the immigrants' countries of origin influence the extent to which immigrants themselves emphasize the unique nature of their cultural outlook. But the effect of these inconsistencies also depends on their evaluation. Having been exposed to the myths of the melting pot and of the American dream, some immigrants internalize the American ideals of mobility and individualism. Others, however, see the system of values typical of their own country as preferable. They view as irreplacable the preeminence of the group over the individual and of tradition over progress taught in their Old World values system.

Yet, far from being invariant, the impact of ethnicity or national origin on the acquisition and the transfer of familial wealth is not the same for all the rungs of the socioeconomic ladder. This effect is maximal at the lower end of the continuum. First, the importance individuals attach to rationality and to economic results increases with the amount of resources already available to them. Conversely, modest wealth holders are more inclined to emphasize legitimacy as a criterion for evaluating the acquisition or the sale of assets and their transfers to heirs. In other words, individuals with limited means are more likely to do things defined as right by their various reference groups (Goody, 1973, 1976). In addition, the holders of large estates often hold ecumenical views as to (1) the most attractive forms of wealth, (2) the most attractive procedures to transfer them, and (3) the solutions most likely to minimize conflicts with the Internal Revenue Service or among eligible heirs.

Even though these testators enjoy larger and more loose-knit networks, they use the services of lawyers who all share the same vision of the world. Therefore, the inheritance practices of wealthy testators should be more rational and less diverse than those of their less fortunate fellow citizens.

It remains necessary to identify the lines along which the resulting variations of heirship practices take place and, hence, to ascertain the salience of national or ethnic origin in relation to other possible reference groups such as gender, age or cohort, and social class. This salience is a function of three factors. First, it depends on the residential concentration in the same residential community of immigrants with the same ethnic background. The more accentuated the boundaries between ingroups and outgroups, the more likely it is that individuals sharing both the same national origin and the same territory will retain the same language and the same lifestyle. The phenomenon will be particularly visible in the case of ethnic "ghettos." Thus, it will prevail among the inhabitants of rural as well as urban villages, whose majority do not speak English and rely on go-betweens with a high status in the local community (such as clergymen) for dealing with the outside world.

Roeber (1987) shows in this regard the importance of the role played by Catholic priests in the early German settlements of Pennsylvania. Indeed, these priests wrote wills in English with the purpose of enabling their parishioners to respect local laws while satisfying their own sense of familial obligations.[4] The impact of these priests on the perpetuation of the status achieved by early settlers was enhanced by the fact that the settlers themselves sought to have the best of two worlds. They used their earnings for maintaining or for acquiring properties both in their new communities and in their countries of origin. As a result, they continued to have good reasons to remain familiar with the laws governing property rights back home. The situation is unlikely to have changed. The greater the ties maintained with the "old country," and particularly the greater the aspirations toward returning home after retirement, the more likely it is that individuals will organize their lives in their American ghetto around the perpetuation of the rules that prevailed in their place of origin at the time of their emigration.[5]

In addition, the salience of national origin as a determinant of heirship practices depends on the frequency and the form of exogamic marriages in the ethnic group under consideration. The perpetuation of national or ethnic identity is maximal whenever spouses share the same origin and hold congruent socialization values. Alternatively, even though the perpetuation of ethnic patterns of inheritance becomes clearly more problematic as ethnically mixed marriages are more frequent, the ensuing decline should still be selective. The effects of interethnic marriages should not be the same when the alien spouse is the groom and when it is the bride. As socialization is primarily a female function, the children of a woman marrying outside her national group should be more likely to retain this group's lifestyle than the offspring of any of her also brothers marrying a stranger. The difference, furthermore, should be particularly marked whenever the first type of heterogamous couple lives around the bride's relatives. On the other hand, given the interaction among the effects of gender stratification, social class, and ethnic ranking, one can suspect that, in many instances, it is the culture of the groom that is most likely to prevail. For instance, to the extent that the American dominant culture places a German origin higher than a Russian background, a German man marrying a Russian woman has more chances to impose German values on his wife than a Russian man marrying a German woman has a chance to retain a Russian lifestyle. In other words, "mixed bloods" and, more specifically, ethnically mixed marriages are unlikely to form a homogeneous social category.[6]

Last, the persistence of national or ethnic identity reflects the concentration of each category of immigrants in particular occupational niches. Whenever members of a national group are particularly numerous in specific occupational groups, the access to which they control, the ensuing shared material conditions make it more likely that their familial groups will retain the norms originally governing their heirship practices. In America, for instance, as shown by the work of Tarver (1952) or of Salamon and her associates (1980) and of Carroll and Salamon (1988), farmers are likely to retain such norms and models, *inter alia* because they groom early the heir they have selected. By the same token, one can infer that the self-employed persons (e.g., artisans, shopkeepers) who live in urban ethnic enclaves should be in a position to do the same.

To conclude, the persistence of ethnic or national models regulating the acquisition and the transfer of specific assets probably varies across the rungs of the wealth ladder. Furthermore, although this persistence is most salient in the case of ethnic communities highly concentrated in specific residential *and* occupational niches, it also fluctuates over time. Undoubtedly maximal for newly arrived immigrants whose limited resources enhance the need to do things "right," these models lose their initial salience among subsequent generations, before being partially or totally restored whenever material or ideological factors facilitate the renascence of ethnic identity and competition.

Ethnicity and Ownership

Different communities, as well as different groups within these communities, prefer certain types of assets and offer their own receipes for acquiring those assets. Not only do some social groups decry the possession of specific

objects as being immoral, but there are also significant differences in the
knowledge that their members acquire concerning the best deals to be made
with regard to their acquisition or their transfer.

Stephan Thernstrom's work (1964, 1973) illustrates cultural variations in
the relative preference given to home ownership as opposed to the acquisition of human capital. During the 19th century, early waves of Irish peasants
migrating to American cities were eager to acquire their homestead as quickly
as possible. In view of the uncertainties of an urban employment and of the
ensuing vagaries of family resources, Boston's Irish were prone to send their
firstborn children to work in factories as early as possible. They wanted to
accumulate enough cash and ensure the downpayment on the house they
intended to acquire while paying the subsequent annuities of the mortgage. In
contrast, their Jewish counterparts arrived in Boston during the same period—
accustomed as they were to be chased away from their communities of
origin—preferred to rent their residence, to remain mobile, and to use the
savings accumulated for enabling their children to acquire the formal schooling they saw as facilitating occupational upward mobility.[7]

The acquisition of life insurance offers another illustration of the conditions under which ethnicity affects the acquisition of distinct types of goods.
In some quarters, ownership of life insurance was treated as a form of vice
akin to gambling (Zelizer, 1979). In other social circles, however, this form of
capital was heralded as a particularly eloquent symbol of familial solidarity,
because the procedures that beneficiaries must follow for enjoying the capital
guaranteed by the policy are much simpler than those governing the transfer
of most valuables. For example, in two samples of German and Irish decedents drawn from 1920 and 1944 Internal Revenue Service (IRS) estates tax
lists, the incidence of life insurance policyholders climbs from 18 to 46
percent (Clignet, 1992). Other variables held constant, Irish decedents of
1920 were more likely than their German counterparts to hold insurance
certificates. Yet insofar as Germany has been one of the first industrialized
countries to launch a variety of insurance policies with the blessing of the
State, the sums invested in this asset were initially proportionately larger
among German- than Irish-Americans. In other words, the *value* of life
insurance certificates in relation to the overall size of individual estates was
greater for the 1920 German decedents than for their Irish counterparts.

To conclude, immigrants to the United States do not immediately adopt
American behaviors toward distinct forms of capital. Instead, they are likely to
continue to suscribe to the values imputed to distinct forms of capital in their
nation of origin. Their limited social networks prevent them from gaining
access to information concerning alternative sources of investments. As long
as the circulation of financial tips remains restricted, then ethnic differences
both in the relative number of individuals holding various kinds of assets and

in the relative, as well as the absolute, value of the relevant investments should persist. To be sure, these ethnic disparities should not take the same form or the same magnitude among nationalities long established in the United States such as German or Irish immigrants, compared to newcomers who have settled in North America since the end of World War II. Disparities should be more subtle among early established groups, because their enduring urban experience generates a more differentiated view of the investments deemed to be most desirable. In contrast, to the extent that more recently arrived national groups remain concentrated in specific occupational niches (e.g., fishing for the Vietnamese, a variety of cottage industries for the Koreans), they continue to run a more common set of economic risks (Cheung Moon Cho, 1990). Not only are they likely to individually accumulate less money than Americans whose ancestors arrived early in the New World, but they are also more likely to pool capital and reinvest in these restrictive niches.

Ethnicity, National Origin, and Testamentary Behavior

The persistence of national identity among American immigrants requires them to evenly stress social and economic reproduction. As a result, these groups should be more prone to draw wills. Indeed, individuals who retain a strong commitment to communal and familial values are more likely to take a stand with regard to the transfer of their assets and of their liabilities than their uprooted counterparts who view themselves as entrepreneurs and emphasize self-reliance accordingly. The contrast between these two populations should be particularly visible in the United States, where the official ideology minimizes the significance of intergenerational obligations and views inheritance as a vestigial behavior at odds with the development of the large-scale economic ventures that form the backbone of contemporary corporate capitalism (Gouldner, 1970; Clignet, 1992).

In a study that compared German and Yankee farmers in Illinois, Carroll and Salamon (1988) found that among farmers who passed away prior to 1901, no less than 90 percent of German estates were filed as testate (i.e., with a will) against only 21 percent of their Yankee counterparts. Originally, German and American orientations toward the perpetuation of familial groups were not the same, in part as a result of the distinct material circumstances of their respective arrival in the Midwest. The Germans settled in the area as a cohesive group of families, but not the Yankees. However, with the increased marginality of farming as an economic activity, and with the growing commitment of Yankee individuals toward a rural lifestyle, the two populations have become increasingly alike. Between 1901 and the date of the study (1981), the proportion of German estates filed testate varied within a narrow range, between 75 and 80 percent. In contrast, among the Yankees, the corresponding percentage increased from 44 percent for the estates filed between 1901 and 1930, to 66 percent for those filed between 1960 and 1981.

The transfer of land is more closely linked to familial values and feelings in the case of German than of Yankee farmers. The comments of these German and Irish farmers confirm in qualitative terms what the figures imply. A German respondent emphasizes that "keeping the land you inherit and the land your family has worked is very important" in contrast to a Yankee neighbor, who concedes more simply that "money should not be accumulated and just passed on to the heirs." Convergences in the attitudes and the behaviors of the two populations should not mask their distinctive orientations toward their communities and toward heirship. The corresponding differences have persisted until a recent past. Says a German farmer, "We knew our kids would stick together when we gave them the land," and another adds, "Even for the children and grandchildren who have moved away, this is their home," a stance that contrasts with the comment of an old Yankee farmer who regrets that "there is really nothing much [around here] to hold people together."[8] Furthermore, the two groups endow testacy with distinct functions. Regardless of the date of their wills, German testators use this particular legal instrument for ensuring the equality of heirs, even though it is already guaranteed by the relevant Illinois laws. In other words, German farmers use wills as a way of marking their appropriation of existing legal dispositions. In contrast, their Yankee counterparts have been increasingly prone to rely on testacy for asserting their desire to depart from existing local norms by favoring one or several eligible heirs at the expense of others. Thus, their behavior confirms the validity of the views of Maine (1954) concerning the functions of wills.

The differential use of testacy by the two groups of farmers is made even more evident when one examines the distribution of testacy by family size. Regardless of the dates considered, planned inequality characterizes Yankee testators with the largest number of eligible heirs, which confirms the pragmatic nature of their approach to transfers *mortis causa*. The purpose of their will is essentially to ensure the survival of the familial enterprise. In contrast, the relationship between family size and the disposition of wills is more unstable among German decedents. Even though the Germans are not insensitive to the opportunities and constraints of the economic cycle, they still attach more importance to legitimacy and to their commitment to the values typical of their culture of origin.

Finally, testators often use other instruments than wills when they decide to make intergenerational transfers early in their lives. Various cultures hold distinct views of death and its impact on intergenerational forms of interaction. For instance, although German and Irish decedents whose estates were processed in 1920 do not differ from one another in this regard. German decedents of 1944 seem to adopt a more modern view of family relations than their Irish counterparts (Clignet, 1992). Germans rely more frequently on gifts *inter vivos* to help some of their children when the need arises, whereas the Irish more often maintained their tradition of keeping heirs "on their toes" until the very last minute of their lives.[9]

To conclude, the evidence summarized here presents at least two problems. First, can we generalize the differential salience of testamentary behaviors between German and Yankee farmers to other forms of family-owned productive capital? Is what is true of German and Yankee farmers equally true of German and Yankee artisans or shopkeepers, even though they do not share comparable environments and do not face the same legal challenges? Second, are their similar contrasts among other national groups that have settled in the United States earlier or later and whose socioeconomic trajectories differ from those of the Germans and Irish studied by Carroll and Salamon?[10]

Ethnicity, National Origin, and the Treatment of Heirs

The concept of heritage embodies the set of norms that governs the manner in which decedents split the assets that form their estate in function of (1) their value and their functions, (2) the birth order and gender of all the eligible heirs, and (3) the needs, capabilities, or responsibilities of these heirs. As already suggested however, the notion of heritage does not exclusively refer to ethnicity or national origin. As gender, social class, religion, and age cohort represent other reference groups invoked by testators to justify the decisions they take concerning the transfer of their symbolic and material estate, the issue is to evaluate the relative weight of ethnicity or national origin in relation to these other sources of legitimation.

There is little reason to expect that various ethnic or national groups should endow distinct forms of wealth with the same value. For instance, Goody (1976) has shown that relations between the ranking of assets and the hierarchy of eligible heirs vary among ethnic groups. To be sure, the dissolution of national identity among some immigrants in the United States is probably already so far advanced that the corresponding populations of testators fully adhere to the dominant American practice of dividing shares equally among heirs. These testators want the executors of their wills to sell each and every component of the estate in order to ensure the formal equality of all shares. In contrast, other ethnic groups continue to differentiate income-producing assets from the remaining parts of the estate. The "favorite son" is often expected to run the family business, with his siblings receiving whatever is left in the estate. In other contexts, some ethnic groups will distinguish items of personal property and particularly jewelry, paintings, or smaller mementos that will be adjudicated (for particularistic reasons) independently of the major components of the estate that should be divided according to the rules corresponding to the will or to the laws of residence of the decedent.

Similarly, although some ethnic or national groups claim to abide by the principle of "share and share alike" (equality of bequests) at least among male heirs, others differentially distribute assets or liabilities as a function of their heirs' gender and/or birth order. In addition, different immigrant populations have not come to adopt the dominant practice of equality of shares at the same pace and under the same circumstances. This is at least in part because of contrasts in the geographic and social origin of their respective settlers (Alston and Shapiro, 1984).[11] Among early British immigrants, for example, one can distinguish the heirship strategies of aristocrats settled in the Carolinas or in Virginia from those of New Englanders. The former have retained the principle of impartibility for a longer period of time. They have continued to transfer their properties to only one child at the same time that the latter decided to divide their estates into equal shares.[12]

Today, parental behaviors regarding eldest sons and eldest daughters continue to vary across cultures. The Taiwanese, for instance, would like the firstborn male child to climb the highest rungs of the academic ladder by relying on the resources accumulated by the family as a result of the work of his younger female siblings. At the same time, the Taiwanese would like their oldest daughters to finance the studies of their younger brothers (Greenhalg, 1985). If such contrasts characterize the choices of the Taiwanese at home, it is reasonable to expect that, at least in the short run, those Taiwanese who have immigrated recently to the States would retain the same practice.

In addition, ethnic groups are also likely to hold distinct views regarding not only the kind and the value of the bequests that children born to successive marriages should receive from their parents but also the differential duties that paternal and maternal relatives owe to various kinds of heirs. Even though divorce rates climb across all national groups, all parents do not necessarily adopt the same behaviors toward the offspring born of the subsequent marriages of their sons and daughters.

Finally, the various ethnic or national groups differ from one another in terms of the rationales they invoke for rewarding or for punishing a particular heir. To the extent that McClelland's (1961) ideas on the cultural determinants of need for achievement are at least partially valid, we may expect reliance on *efficiency* as a factor affecting their selection of a specific heir to vary along cultural lines (Clignet, 1995). Indeed, national groups do not equally value entrepreneurship. There are comparable ethnic variations in the parental definitions of the needs experienced by individual heirs and, hence, in the relevant heirship strategies. As an example, ethnic groups differ both in the stigma they attach to the fact of an adult son or daughter remaining unmarried and in the measures they adopt to alleviate the ensuing plight. Furthermore, although there are also ethnic variations in the expectations concerning what sons and daughters should do in order to alleviate the financial and emotional pains of their aging parents, the reciprocal services that parents and children render to one another during their lifecycles should be more numerous and significant in the case of the newly arrived immigrants than among their more assimilated counterparts.

Unfortunately, the evidence available to document these speculations remains scanty. From a clinical perspective, Philip Roth's *Patrimony* (1991) raises a number of questions concerning the universality or the ethnic character of the major dilemmas experienced by testators and by their heirs. Is the author's apparent and reversible desire to forego his own share of the paternal estate a by-product of his junior position as the latest born son? And is such a desire universal or more salient among all patriarchal societies? Similarly, are Roth's reactions toward his father's discard of religious artifacts universal or ethnically specific? In the same vein, Mary Gordon in her novel *Final Payments* (1978) evokes the strength of the bonds that link a dying Irish widower to his only daughter. Are such bonds universal, or are they an exclusive property of the Irish family?

The available sociological evidence is restricted to farming communities. It concerns differences among Irish, German, and Yankee farmers settled in analogous communities of Illinois that offer the same opportunities and are devoted to the same types of crops (Salamon, 1980, 1988; Carroll and Salamon, 1988). The Irish retain the rule of unigeniture that prevails in their country of origin. Depending on the age at marriage of the decedent and his subsequent age differences with his successive male children, the farm goes to the oldest or the youngest son, who has then the obligation of compensating the remaining siblings who are excluded from existing sources of income. In contrast, the Germans who originate from a part of Germany that follows the rule of equal shares have retained the practice depending on favorable material opportunities. Among German decedents who had drawn a will prior to 1901, 78 percent had planned equal shares for their children. However, the practice of distributing equal shares among all heirs declined over time to 52 percent among their counterparts who drew a will between 1931 and 1960. Although the decline has nothing to do with the changing of family size (the average number of heirs has increased during the period of reference), it may be attributed to the declining availability of land.

During the same period, the percentage of Yankee farmers who drew a will in order to differentiate the sharers of their children climbed from one-third for those testators who passed away prior to 1901 to over 40 percent for the period prior to 1960. This, combined with the simultaneous decline in the average number of heirs among Yankee farmers, suggests convergences in the heirship strategies and demographic behaviors of the German and Yankee farming population. German farmers are more and more like their Yankee counterparts in that they seek to obtain maximal returns of their enterprise. Although those farmers deceased after 1960 have been inclined to grant undivided interest in the totality of their land, persisting forms of inequality tend to be gender related. Farmers expect their daughters to sell their shares in favor of the one brother who has taken over the farm.

One can compare these results that pertain exclusively to the practices of a *contemporary* but geographically and occupationally limited sample with those concerning the choices made by an *older* sample of more diversified decedents (Clignet, 1992). Although the limited size of the sample prevents a sophisticated statistical analysis, it looks as if among the cohort of testators deceased in 1920, the Irish were slightly more prone than the Germans to differentiate the shares they transferred to their children, even though the underlying distinctions were probably not exclusively based on gender or on matrimonial status. In other words, at least initially, the Irish probably held a more individualized view of the talents, needs, and merits of their sons and daughters. However, among the 1944 cohort of decedents, German testators have tended more often than their Irish counterparts to discriminate *against* their daughters, which would suggest that the familial groups of distinct ethnicity did not experience similarly the weight of the Depression. Some families responded to economic difficulties by underscoring their obligations toward their economically *weakest* relatives, whereas others emphasized the profits that could be derived from helping the most *efficient* eligible heir.

Yet a comparison between Korean immigrants in the United States and a control group of individuals who remained in Korea offers an even more significant test of the relative impact of ethnicity on patterns of inheritance (Cheung Moon Cho, 1990). Traditional Korean rules underlying intergenerational transfers deviate more markedly from the dominant American practice than the models used by European immigrants. The Korean inheritance system is more encompassing; the heir becoming the religious and political head of the familial group. It is also more markedly patrilineal, because the oldest son is the most likely beneficiary of the familial estate from which married daughters are excluded, being fully absorbed in their own husband's familial community. Nevertheless, as Korean immigrants to the United States are significantly more educated than their nonmigrant counterparts, they should adopt a more relativistic stance toward traditional norms, including those that govern familial life.

The migratory experience of Korean immigrants has exposed them to the more egalitarian American ideology. Thus, only a little over one-third of Koreans settled in the United States used birth order as a determinant of the shares to be assigned to *sons* as opposed to no less than two-thirds of their nonemigrating counterparts. Similarly, only 43 percent of the immigrants relied on gender as a determinant of the way estates should be shared, as opposed to almost three-fourths of the Koreans who stayed home. Furthermore, the two populations also differed in terms of defining both the duration of their obligations and the relative size of the shares to be assigned to the widow and her children. In Korea, marriage and the corresponding creation of a new residence traditionally mark the end of a child's dependence. In contrast, the economic success of emigrating Koreans and their awareness of the hurdles encountered by minorities induce them to lengthen the duration of their parental assistance (41 percent of them view these responsibilities as persisting beyond the marriage of their children, against only 8 percent of nonmigrating Koreans). In this sense, the constraints of a new environment reinforce familial bonds. Last, even though all Korean males report they would give a larger share of their estate to their spouses (two-thirds of nonmigrants and 60 percent of emigrants), their respective motivations are not necessarily alike. In Korea itself, patterns of marriage as well as gender differences in mortality are likely to maximize the obligations that widows must discharge toward their children, who are often quite young when their fathers pass away. Yet the economic advantages granted to surviving spouses are often fictitious, because additional assets often imply additional liabilities. In contrast, assertions of conjugal solidarity among Korean emigrants are probably eroded by the dominant American ideology that emphasizes intergenerational independence.

The evaluation of this whole array of contrasts requires, however, at least three caveats. First, formal schooling should be a more significant contributor of attitudes toward heirship than migratory experience per se. Although all forms of mobility soften the imprint of tradition, this is particularly true of the psychic "liberation" fostered by formal schooling.[13] Second, self-reported deviations from the traditional Korean model vary with the status occupied by respondents in the Korean social structure. For example, migrating Korean females tend to adopt a more egalitarian stance than their male counterparts, notably with regard to the ideal impact of birth order and gender on the size of the shares assigned to children. Furthermore, gender differences are also evident among native Koreans with respect to the duration of the support that parents should display toward their progeny. Men are likely to see a cutting point in their obligations (the entry of their offpsring in the labor market), whereas female respondents see their obligations as continuing *after* the marriage of their children. By contrast, there are no such cleavages among migrants. Last, among migrants themselves, there are also significant differences between the responses elaborated *in vacuo* toward the dominant ideological orientations of the host country and those verbal reports that refer explicitly to the dilemmas raised by the presence of sons and daughters who are supposed to ensure the material and symbolic continuity of the familial group. Whenever one probes the actual number and gender of their children, those respondents with many children and with a firstborn son are more likely to reaffirm their commitment to traditional rules.[14]

Conclusions

To conclude, ethnic or national identities continue to affect not only the nature and the value of the assets bought and sold by individuals at different moments of their lives, but also the instruments of transfer they use in order to bequeath their estate, their selection of heirs, and, finally, the nature as well as the amount of the shares they distribute.

The origin of this persisting influence is twofold. First, the continuing salience of national origin results from the competition among immigrant groups and, hence, from disparities in the material and symbolic resources available to each of these groups as a function of the duration of their American experience and of the status assigned to them by the remaining parts of the American society.

Moreover, the very distinction that the American culture establishes between the public and private realms of social life allows familial groups to retain the system of values prevailing in their country of origin. To be more specific, American forms of political decentralization encourage cultural diversity, at least as far as patterns of marriage, divorce settlements, and modes of inheritance are concerned.

Of course, both the concepts of ethnicity and national origin remain equally elusive, not only because they overlap to a degree, but also because both evoke simultaneously distributive phenomena and specific ethical or normative orientations. Indeed, the values concerning the reproduction of familial groups and familial ideals are also likely to be inspired by religious or ideological motivations (Michelat and Simon, 1977).[15]

The persisting impact of national origin or ethnicity on the creation and the transfer of domestic wealth in America raises two additional theoretical questions. First, the reproduction at work in the processes of intergenerational transfers is increasingly more often interpretative than mechanical (Bourdieu and Passeron, 1970). In other words, the growth of corporate capitalism and the subsequent growing number of wage earners prevents an ever-increasing number of heirs from wearing the full legal clothing corresponding to *all* the roles that the testator used to perform. Not only do the majority of such roles shrink and become obsolete, but also the environment obliges or induces a number of individuals to invent symbolic equivalences to the heirship practices of their forebears.

As an illustration, in contrast to the Japanese mourners who bring rice to the immediate relatives of the deceased (in order to maximize the time and the energy that the latter spend praying), their Nisei counterparts transform the obligation and offer some money rather than cooked rice (Yaganisako, 1978). The example is telling on two counts. The very label *Nisei* reminds all Americans that to be born out of the "old country" disqualifies some of the claims that individuals can make with regard to the binding power of their roots. In other words, it reminds us that the concepts of national origin or of ethnicity are relative. In addition, the substitution of money for cooked rice highlights the diffusion of formal rationality as the material basis of social life and reduces proportionately the tightness of the links between symbols of familial solidarity and what they stand for. In more general terms, the increasing power of interpretive rather than mechanical patterns of reproduction throws some additional light on the issue of whether both inheritance rules and practices are the exclusive by-products of prevailing material arrangements. Whenever sociologists assert that significant changes in the material basis of social life are sufficient to alter ethnic or national contrasts in modes of inheritance, they expect the full-fledged emergence of a postindustrial society to be accompanied by the irreversible erosion of ethnic differences. Alternatively, as other sociologists anticipate that cultural particularisms are likely to survive converging material arrangements, they expect contrasts in the patterns of transfers of material forms of capital to survive technological as well as symbolic revolutions. From their perspective, the rules accounting initially for the transfers of land should account as well for the subsequent rules and the practices governing the transfer of symbolic capital, notably formal schooling. Whether we look at past or current societies, these sociologists believe that the logic underlying the transfer of a scarce valuable is independent of its specific nature.

Second, to expect the impact of ethnicity on inheritance to decline with the passage of time makes it necessary to explain the pace of the underlying process and, notably, of ascertaining whether the evolution follows a linear or curvilinear pattern. In a number of cultures scattered around the world, it has been observed that *odd* generations are closer to one another than to their *even* counterparts. Correspondingly, grandchildren should be more often interested in following the behavioral examples of their grandparents than in conforming to the models set up by their own parents. The concept of sociological ambivalence is relevant here (Merton and Barber, 1963), because it highlights the constant tug-of-war between the desire to affirm one's national identity (notably, through the way one acquires and transfers certain types of assets), and the rewards associated with conformity to the American dream and to the relevant behaviors.[16] In short, the persistence of specific heirship strategies is the by-product of the interaction between the extent or the form of familial solidarities and the variety of pressures that the new environment exerts on migrants. In this sense, the perpetuation of national identity lies at the very juncture of a sociological time, which is made of the repetition of cycles, and of an historical time, which is made of unpredictable discontinuities. But the point is also that this juncture is not necessarily the same for the three aspects of inheritance considered here. Technological, legal, or economic innovations do not strike simultaneously and/or with the same intensity the models that govern the acquisition of wealth, the use of pertinent instruments of transfer, and the nature of the transfers themselves.

Notes

1. The concept of birth cohort is relevant here, insofar as the sharing of opportunities and constraints due to the sharing of the same age generate similar worldviews as well (Easterlin, 1980).
2. One should note that the distinction between ethnicity and national origin is often equivocal for at least two reasons. First, the definitions of these two terms differ often between the host society and the nation of origin of the individuals under consideration. In addition, the distinction itself varies over time. As an illustration, the distinction that Habakkuk (1955) underlines between the Bohemian and the Slovak inheritance traditions may still characterize the relevant behaviors of immigrants with one or the other of these backgrounds, even though they have ceased to use such labels to define their cultural identity.
3. One cannot sufficiently underline the dangers of reducing economic or cultural hierarchies to a mere distributive phenomenon. Whether one refers to gender, to social class, to religion, or to national origin, one evokes the need to explain the two distinct dynamics that govern the accentuation or the decline of contrasts in the resources and the outlook of the relevant categories. These dynamics are in part imposed by the behavior of outsiders, but they also result from the socialization of the ingroup's members to a wide range of significant economic and social practices.
4. As suggested by Maine (1954), the transcription of a practice in a written form also offers an opportunity for the corresponding go-between to get his or her own share of the estate. What is most remarkable is the universality of the phenomenon. In the United States, the existence of parishes organized along ethnic lines raises the question of ascertaining whether Catholics follow universal ideals or, rather, respond to the heirship models of their countries of origin.
5. One forgets too easily that all emigrants assess the community they leave behind in the context of a frozen time. They have been so busy adjusting to the new environment that they have not kept up with the changing practices or attitudes

of their "homes." For this reason, emigrants are often more conservative in their outlook than their nonmigrating counterparts.

6. The point is clearly demonstrated by Guyot (1993) as far as the children of French and Togolese partners are concerned. Because it has often been suggested that ethnic and gender stratification interact with one another in different ways, one can only deplore the lack of attention of the sociological community to the problem. For an example, see Alba (1990), who treats mixed marriages as a homogeneous category.

7. It is tempting to speculate about the limits within which national groups retain their preference for some assets in a new environment as well as about the limits within which they generalize the procedures they used initially for transfering older forms of capital for disposing of newer types of wealth such as human capital, that is, formal schooling. It makes sense to note that researchers such as Steelman and Powell (1989) have shifted the focus of their research from the analysis of intrafamilial inequalities in the transfer of human capital to the evaluation of interethnic disparities in this regard. Indeed, intrafamilial inequities are not universal.

8. This illustrates the significance of the distinction between specific heirship practices that depend on current economic situations and traditional heirship ideologies that are more specific and slower to change. For a more general argument and its empirical verification outside the United States, see Cole and Wolfe (1974).

9. Of course, the date of wills is a slippery variable, because one cannot know the number of successive versions of the document or ascertain the reasons that have induced changes in its content.

10. One could in this respect rank-order the various national groups present in the United States as a function of the date of their arrival, their numerical importance, and the size of their "share" of the American pie.

11. The early dominance of primogeniture in the Carolinas is particularly striking, because the first cohort of settlers was primarily composed of the late-born male children of aristocratic families who migrated to the New World because they had been excluded from the familial estate.

12. The diversity of intestate laws throughout the states of the union may be explained in terms of their respective ethnic composition, that is, the number of national groups present, their demographic importance, and the date of their arrival.

13. The psychic mobility generated by formal schooling explains why the relative stress placed upon self-reliance and upon sense of community varies as intensely among Americans as between them and strangers or newcomers. For a development, see Bellah, Madsen, Swidler, and Tipton (1985).

14. Once more, one encounters the difficulty of collecting data about the normative aspects of heirship. Unfortunately, Cheung Moon Cho has been mesmerized by the insensitivity of many American researchers to the distinction between rhetoric and practice, and this weakens somewhat the scope of his findings.

15. At least in France, Catholics are more sensitive to the notions of estate and cultural heritage than other religious groups. More generally, we can expect that religion or ethnicity generates specific time orientations and specific mediations between the importance attached to the past and to the future.

16. As an illustration, Wang, the owner of one of the largest computers companies, wanted to remain faithful to the Chinese ideal of primogeniture and transfer the ownership of the company to his eldest son, whom he had groomed to that effect. The major associates of Wang refused to go along and obliged Wang to disinherit his son. For details, see Cohen (1990).

References

Alba, R. (1990). *Ethnic identity: The transformation of white America*. New Haven, CT: Yale University Press.

Alston, L. J., & Shapiro, M. P. (1984). Inheritance laws across colonies: Causes and consequences. *Journal of Economic History, 44,* 277-287.

Bellah, R., Madsen, R., Swidler, A., & Tipton, S. (1985). *Habits of the heart: Individualism and commitment in the United States*. Berkeley: University of California Press.

Bourdieu, P., & Passeron, J. C. (1970). *La reproduction*. Paris: Editions de Minuit.

Carroll, E., & Salamon, S. (1988). Share and share alike: Inheritance patterns in two Illinois farm communities. *Journal of Family History, 13,* 219-232.

Cheung Moon Cho. (1990). The comparative study of inheritance among Korean Americans and Koreans. *Korean Journal of Population and Development, 19*(2), 201-219.

Clignet, R. (1992). *Death, deeds, and descendants: A study of inheritance in modern America* New York: Aldine de Gruyter.

Clignet, R. (1995). Efficiency, reciprocity, and ascriptive equality: The three major strategies governing the selection of heirs in America. *Social Science Quarterly, 76,* 274-293.

Cohen, D. (1990). The fall of the house of Wang. *Business Month*, February, 23-37.

Cole, J., & Wolfe, E. (1974). *The hidden frontier: Ecology and ethnicity in an Alpine valley*. New York: Academic Press.

Easterlin, R. (1980). *Birth and fortune*. New York: Basic Books.

Goody, J. (1973). Strategies of heirship. *Comparative Studies in History and Society, 15,* 1-19.

Goody, J. (1976). Introduction. In J. Goody, J. Thiersk, & E. P. Thompson (Eds.), *Family and inheritance* (pp. 1-17). Cambridge, UK: Cambridge University Press.

Gordon, M. (1978). *Final payments*. New York: Random House.

Gouldner, A. (1970). *The coming crisis in Western sociology*. New York: Basic Books.

Greenhalg, S. (1985). Sexual stratification: The other side of growth with equity. *Population and Development Review, 11,* 265-314.

Guyot, D. (1993). Contribution à l'analyse des relations entre stratifications sociale, raciale, et sexuelle: le cas des métis togolais. *Cahiers d'etudes Africaines, 131*(3), 403-418.

Habakkuk, D. (1955). Family structure and family change in nineteenth century Europe. *Journal of Economic History, 15,* 1-15.

Lieberson, S. (1980). *A piece of the American pie*. Berkeley: University of California Press.

Maine, H. (1954). *Ancient law*. London: Dent.

McClelland, D. (1961). *The achieving society*. Princeton, NJ: Van Nostrand.

Merton, R., & Barber, E. (1963). Sociological ambivalence. In E. Tiryakian (Ed.), *Sociological theories, values, and sociocultural change* (pp. 97-120). Glencoe, IL: Free Press.

Michelat, G., & Simon, M. (1977). *Classe, religion et comportement politique*. Paris: Presses de la Fondation Nationale des Sciences Politiques.

Newby, H., Bell, C., Rose, D., & Saunders, P. (1979). *Property, paternalism and power*. Madison: University of Wisconsin Press.

Roeber, A. (1987). The origin and transfer of German-American concepts of property and inheritance. *Perspectives in American History*, *3*, 115-171.

Roth, P. (1991). *Patrimony*. New York: Simon & Schuster.

Salamon, S. (1980). Ethnic differences in farm family land transfers. *Rural Sociology*, *45*, 290-308.

Salamon, S. (1988). *Prairie Patrimony Family, Farming, and Community in the Midwest*. Chapel Hill and London: University of North Carolina Press.

Steelman, L., & Powell, B. (1989). Acquiring capital for college: The constraints of family configuration. *American Sociological Review*, *54*, 844-855.

Tarver, J. (1952). Intra-family farm succession. *Rural Sociology*, *17*, 250-262.

Thernstrom, S. (1964). *Poverty and progress*. Cambridge, MA: Harvard University Press.

Thernstrom, S. (1973). *The other Bostonians*. Cambridge, MA: Harvard University Press.

Thompson, M. (1979). *Rubbish theory*. New York: Oxford University Press.

Weber, M. (1968). *Economy and society*. Glencoe, IL: Free Press.

Yaganisako, S. (1978). Variations in American kinship: Implications for cultural analysis. *American Ethnologist*, *5*, 15-29.

Zelizer, V. (1979). *Morals and markets*. New York: Columbia University Press.

7

Why Should Men Leave Great Fortunes to Their Children?

Class, Dynasty, and Inheritance in America

PETER DOBKIN HALL AND GEORGE E. MARCUS

In an important 1988 article, legal historian John Langbein identified what he regarded as fundamental shifts in the contemporary ethos and practice of wealth transmission in America. Langbein wrote,

> Whereas of old wealth transmission from parents to children tended to center upon major items of patrimony such as the family farm or the family firm, today for the broad middle classes, wealth transmission centers on a radically different kind of asset: the investment in skills. In consequence, intergenerational wealth transmission no longer occurs primarily upon the death of the parents, but rather, when the children are growing up, hence, during the parents' lifetimes (Langbein, 1988, p. 723).

This shift from testamentary to *inter vivos* transfers was due not only to changes in the nature of wealth itself, from land assets or shares in family firms to financial assets (stocks, bonds, bank deposits, mutual fund shares, insur-

PETER DOBKIN HALL • Program on Non-Profit Organizations, Yale University, 88 Trumbull Street, P.O. Box 208253, New Haven, Connecticut 06520   GEORGE E. MARCUS • Department of Anthropology, Rice University, Houston, Texas 77251.

Inheritance and Wealth in America, edited by Robert K. Miller, Jr., and Stephen J. McNamee. Plenum Press, New York, 1998.

ance contracts, and the like), but also, and more significantly, to human capital—the skills and knowledge that are the foundation of advanced technological societies.

One indicator of the shift, according to Langbein, has been an immense increase in investment in education: In 1870, only 2 percent of the population was graduating from high school; by 1970, the figure was 75.6 percent; during the same period, the total number of degrees conferred by college and universities increased more than a hundredfold (p. 731). Necessarily, these trends involved vastly increased expenditures for formal education, which grew from $9.2 million in 1840 to $282.1 billion in 1987. On this scale, such expenses "represent capital transfers in a quite literal sense: Amounting to nearly one-third of family income, "the money comes from savings, that is, from the family's capital; or debt is assumed, meaning that the money is borrowed from the family's future capital" (p. 733). To an increasing extent, such investment had become the essential "provision in life" that could rescue children from the harsh fate of becoming unskilled laborers. "In today's economic order," Langbein argues, "it is education more than property, the new human capital rather than the old physical capital, that similarly advantages a child" (p. 733).[1]

This shift from transferring wealth by will to *inter vivos* transfers in the form of investments in human capital has been paralleled by a striking change in what Langbein calls the "ethos of inheritance," in ways that have affected even the holders of great wealth. "The new pattern," he argues, "has become a social norm, a norm so powerful that it has begun to chip away at the ethos of older notions of inheritance" (p. 736). Citing a *Fortune* magazine story on inheritance, Langbein points to the views of a number of "extremely wealthy people who planned to leave their children only token inheritances," citing the example of Warren Buffet, the billionaire chairman of the Berkshire Hathaway holding company, who said he expected his children "to carve out their own place in this world." Declaring that it would be "harmful" and "antisocial," to set up his children with "a lifetime supply of food stamps just because they came out of the right womb" (p. 737), Buffett's intends to leave his fortune to charity. His sentiments were echoed by New York entrepreneur Eugene Lang, who intended to leave his three children no more than "a nominal sum" after college and to bequeath the rest of his $50 million to charity. "To me inheritance dilutes the motivation that most young people have to fulfill the best that is in them," he told the *Fortune* reporter. "I want to give my kids the tremendous satisfaction of making it on their own" (pp. 736–737).

Langbein regards Buffet and Lang as exceptional not only in their hostility toward conventional modes of inheritance, but also in their views about inheritance, which, he argues, "would have been inconceivable a century or more ago." "Can we imagine the twelfth Earl of Carlisle arranging for the dissipation of the family seat, in order to stimulate the thirteenth Earl to the challenge of reacquiring it?" Langbein asks. He suggests that these attitudes toward conventional wealth transmission are "not only quite exceptional," but also "historically very recent and also very American" (p. 737). Behind them, he believes, are two novel ideas: first, the assumption that wealth is largely fungible, that there is no great sentimental attachment nor any particular social significance to the family's existing patrimony; second, the notion that wealth should be regarded as a return on human capital rather than mere possession of property. These notions, Langbein argues, fit the new forms of wealth better than the old and American circumstances better than English or European. The disdain for customary modes of wealth transfer voiced by Buffett and Lang, he continues.

> presupposes that these gentlemen have already achieved for their children the characteristics wealth transfer of modern times, the investment in human capital through education. More and more, Americans expect personal wealth to take the form of earned income, that is, we expect it to be a return on human capital. Messrs. Buffett and Lang have taken that expectation to its limit; in their eyes, conventional wealth transfer has lost its legitimacy. The esteem associated with holding property really now applies only to earned income, to property that embodies the fruits of human capital. In this sense, the revolution in family wealth transmission, which is overwhelmingly an event of the broad middle classes, touches even the holders of great wealth. (pp. 737–738).

Langbein's overall assessment of changing patterns in American wealth transmission is insightful and substantially correct, but he errs in arguing that the shift from transfer of assets to investment in human capital and the "new ethos of inheritance" are particularly new. This chapter will suggest that the fundamental elements of Langbein's "revolution" actually emerged over the course of the past century and a half ago as strategies in the formation of certain urban elites, were elaborated on by the managers of dynastic family fortunes in the late 19th and early 20th centuries, and, in our own time, became models for the population as whole.

The Revolution in American Law, 1780–1880

The law of inheritance ought, Tocqueville believed, "to be placed at the head of all political institutions" because it exercised such an

> incredible influence upon the social state of a people: When the legislator has once regulated the law of inheritance, he may rest from his labor. The machine once put in motion will go on for ages, and advance, as if self-guided, towards a point indicated beforehand. When framed in a particu-

> lar manner, this law unites, draws together, and vests property and power
> in a few hands; it causes an aristocracy, so to speak, to spring out of the
> ground. If formed on opposite principles, its action is still more rapid; it
> divides, distributes, and disperses both property and power. Alarmed by
> the rapidity of its progress, those who despair of arresting its motion
> endeavor at least to obstruct it by difficulties and impediments. They
> vainly seek to counteract its effect by contrary efforts; but it shatters and
> reduces to powder every obstacle, until we can no longer see anything
> but a moving and impalpable cloud of dust, which signals the coming of
> the Democracy. (de Tocqueville, 1945/1840, I: pp. 50–51)

Moderating the force of partible inheritance posed special difficulties for
Americans of the late 18th century. For nearly 200 years, the legitimacy of
children's claims to paternal estates was the bedrock of the popular conception of testamentary justice. These attitudes had been reinforced by the
Revolution, which both promoted concepts of legal equality and explicitly
identified entail and primogeniture with the "tattered Gothic garment" that
Americans had repudiated in declaring their independence.

Although mechanisms capable of ensuring the intact transmission of
estates within families over long periods of time—primogeniture, entail, and
trusts—had long existed as a part of English law, Americans varied in their
willingness to permit their use or even to allow the creation of the legal
jurisdictions necessary for their enforcement. Thus, in 1804, we find the
Massachusetts Supreme Judicial Court declining to enforce a testamentary
trust on the grounds that "if the conveyance was in *trust*, this court could not
have compelled the execution of it; and, until the legislature shall think it
proper to give us further powers, we can do nothing upon subjects of that
nature" (*Prescott v. Tarbell*, 1804, p. 204).

Trusts require a special form of legal authority called *equity jurisdiction*. Unlike the Common Law, which is concerned with *past* acts, equity is
concerned with enforcing *future* acts. In addition, trusts involve coextensive
property rights that are divided between the trustee, who is the *legal* owner
(and has the right to buy, sell, or rent the property, as if it were his own),
and the beneficiary, who is the *equitable* owner (and has enforceable claims
on the use of the trust property) (Scott, 1939, I: pp. 3–8). Historically, neither
future acts nor the coextensive legal rights and equitable rights associated
with trusts were enforceable by the courts of most states after the Revolution.[2]

Despite this, family founders in the early republic appear to have viewed
trusts as a promising solution to the challenges of passing wealth intact
between generations while also ensuring that the capital it represented remained undivided and available for investment. A trust estate could be left in
the care of a trustee, who would manage and invest it for the benefit of a

testators' descendants. The property itself would remain undivided, but the descendants would receive, in more or less equal proportion, the shares in parental estates that they had reason to expect.

The nature of the law itself, as well as questions of judicial authority and architecture, preoccupied the legislatures of the Revolutionary and post-Revolutionary era. The Common Law, the collective body of judicial precedents stretching back into English history, was viewed by many Americans as a "tatter'd Gothic garment," tainted with feudal solicitude for aristocracy and church. Under Jefferson's leadership, Virginia in the 1770s undertook a "revisal of the laws" intended to entirely reject the English legal heritage, repealing the Common Law, and building from the ground up a legal system suitable to republican government.[3] Other states followed suit to a greater or lesser extent.

Although Massachusetts followed a generally less radical course than Virginia, the attitude of legislators toward equity was unyieldingly hostile (Curran, 1951, pp. 269–273). This hostility stemmed from a number of sources. Equity powers were regarded as unsuitable for a democratic state because of the independence it granted the judiciary and wide discretionary powers it permitted individual judges. Looking to English experience with chancery courts, which exercised equity powers, Americans were keenly aware of the protracted, inaccessible, expensive, and often incomprehensible nature of equity proceedings. Even lawyers distrusted it because of its seeming irrationality—citing the remark of the seventeenth century jurist Lord Selden that "equity is a roguish thing. 'Tis all one as if they should make the standard for measuring the chancellor's foot" (Quoted in *Encyclopaedia Britannica*, 1911, p. 727).

The result of this hostility was that the Massachusetts Constitution of 1780, though generally a very conservative document, explicitly denied the Commonwealth's courts equity powers. These were reserved, as in the old Province Charter, to the legislature—to which petitioners could appeal for equitable remedies.

Despite these discouraging prospects, efforts to grant equity powers to the courts were promoted by a handful of determined lawyers. Chief among them was Joseph Story, a young Jeffersonian representative from Salem (Curran, 1951; Newmyer, 1985; Langbein, 1993). In 1808, Story was named chairman of a committee to investigate and report on the matter. The committee drafted a bill proposing the establishment of a separate court of equity and offering a view of equity that was strikingly different from the traditional understanding.

In the report, Story argued that equity was more than a collection of irrationalities and that an Americanized equity, freed from the feudal institutions of Europe, would "operate with a constant and salutary influence"

(Story, 1851, pp. 163–164). Properly interpreted, it not only had broad application to a wide variety of issues, including commercial disputes, land titles, and wills, but also had a capacity to assume a "steady and well-defined shape" and to be "limited by fixed rules" of interpretation and application (p. 151). Without equity, Story warned, the country was in danger "of having our most valuable estates locked up in mortmain, and our surplus wealth pass away in specious or mistaken charities, founded upon visionary or useless schemes, to the impoverishment of friends, and the injury of the poor and deserving of our own countrymen" (p. 156). Without it, neither the interests of "idiots and lunatics, as to the guardianship of their persons, and the management of their estates, and the protection of their rights" — nor those of orphans — could be adequately safeguarded (p. 157).

Story's arguments resonated with wealthy Bostonians' desire to strike a balance between securing property and ensuring that their wealth remained a source of continuing vitality for their families and their class. On the one hand, equity, by protecting contracts from meddling legislatures and vexatious suits over estates and land titles, promised a legal transformation that could have far-reaching impacts on commerce, real estate, charities, and testation. On the other, it promised to ensure the free circulation of property essential to a growing entrepreneurial economy.

Despite Story's learned and eloquent report and the backing of influential politicians from both parties, the legislature defeated the "Act Providing for Relief in Equity." The bill was again introduced in 1810, but again defeated — a defeat "due in no small measure to Representative Story's own party, which won its first statewide victory in that year" (Curran, 1951, p. 274). The growing strength of the Republicans benefited Story's career; even his beliefs moved in a more conservative direction. In 1811, President Madison appointed Story to the U.S. Supreme Court. He had pursued his political ambitions as a leader of the party of Jefferson. Once on the bench, Story began handing down decisions that had far more in common with the ideas of the Federalists — ideas that promoted the growth of federal over state power, the strength and stability of institutional over popular power, and a legal infrastructure favorable to economic development.

As his reputation grew, Story began gathering influential allies in the legal profession and, perhaps more important, building his ties to powerful Boston mercantile interests (Story, 1981). As one biographer put it in describing Story's political transformation, he "not only joined Massachusetts conservatives but wished to lead them" (Newmyer, 1985, p. 163). Though neither wealthy nor well connected, his Harvard degree, his evident brilliance, and his outstanding service as a director of two Salem banks, drew him into the most powerful circle of Boston leaders. He became an intimate friend of John Lowell, the leader of Boston conservatism, and this brought him into contact with the "Merrimac Men," Cabots, Jacksons, Lees, and other relatives of Lowell, who were moving their mercantile fortunes into pioneering—and ultimately fabulously successful—industrial experiments. His aesthetic interests brought him friendship with the city's well-connected intellectual leaders, including publisher George Ticknor (who had married a textile fortune), Edward Everett (who married a daughter of insurance magnate Peter Chardon Brooks), and Josiah Quincy, Jr. (possessor of a private fortune based in Boston real estate).

Story's reward for his "apostasy" was closer involvement with Harvard, which was becoming the core institution of the emerging Brahmin class and the "intellectual nerve center of conservative ideas" (Newmyer, 1985, p. 165). In 1818, he was elected to the Board of Overseers; in 1827, he became a Fellow of the Corporation; and in 1829, he became Dane Professor of Law and, in effect, head of the Law School. His Harvard position strategically positioned him as a scholar, teacher, and jurist to exert an extraordinary influence on the thinking of the legal profession in and beyond Massachusetts. His ideas about equity, originally set forth in reports to the state legislature, were expanded into influential articles for popular audiences [including an important article in the *North American Review* (1820)] and into legal treatises [*Commentaries on Equity Jurisprudence as Administered in England and America* (1836)]. He was also elected to the boards of the constellation of merchant-funded eleemosynary organizations which, as the nineteenth century wore on, came to define the institutional boundaries of the emerging Brahmin class.

Though he had become a national figure, Story remained intensely engaged in Massachusetts politics. He continued to push the legislature to grant equity powers to the Supreme Judicial Court, with strong support from the most powerful elements in Boston's merchant class. In February 1817, with surprisingly little public comment or debate, the legislature was persuaded to grant the Supreme Judicial Court full equity powers in matters affecting trusts.

Law and Institutions

The creation of a legal environment favorable to trusts was in every sense an achievement of the emerging Brahminate. Against deeply rooted traditions and well-organized popular opposition, this influential minority succeeded in creating a juridical basis for passing on their wealth to future generations, for pooling their collective economic resources, and for building their identity and influence as a class. At the same time, both the process and the product by which these goals were achieved suggested the complexity of the merchant group's intentions: They did not want to create an aristocracy along the European model; despite their growing wealth, they continued to see themselves as a capitalist class. And largely self-made men themselves, they recognized, in their willingness to recruit talented outsiders such as Joseph Story, that their continuing vitality depended on their ability, in Holmes's words, "to drain off" the "promising young author and rising lawyer and large capitalist" from wherever they could be found (Holmes, 1957/1854, pp. 119-120).

Striking this balance between desire for exclusivity (the need to define themselves as a group and to pool their resources) and the need for inclusivity (the need to constantly recruit talented outsiders and to ensure that only the most competent of their own progeny assumed positions of responsibility) was no easy task. Boston, in fact, was unique among America's emergent urban elites in meeting the challenge. Although Philadelphia and New York were both larger and richer, enjoying incalculably greater access to the natural resources and interior markets essential to economic growth, their sharp religious divisions and imperfect legal architecture hampered the capacity of their elites to pool their resources for either economic or institutional purposes. Although Boston would never give rise to great fortunes on the scale of Stephen Girard or John Jacob Astor, neither Philadelphians nor New Yorkers (until the twentieth century) would create cultural and educational institutions as influential as Harvard, the Massachusetts General Hospital, or the Boston Museum of Fine Arts. Nor would either succeed in creating a class of leaders who, despite its relative lack of political power, would, over the course of more than a century, so firmly and successfully dominate the civic life of its respective regions.[5]

The legal environment and the institutions to which it gave rise were the crucial difference. Although New York's Chancellor James Kent was unquestionably the chief figure in Americanizing equity and in successfully elaborating equity jurisprudence in the Empire State, his efforts were hampered by Jacksonian opponents in the legislature, who passed statues limiting the proportion of estates decedents could leave to charity, who limited the size of institutional endowments, and who placed all the state's eleemosynary institutions—including churches—under state regulation. Although Kent's efforts assured wealthy New Yorkers an extraordinary freedom in their private testamentary arrangements, legal and political barriers—as well as ethnic and religious conflicts within the elite—prevented the establishment and funding of institutions with broad public influence.[6]

Philadelphians labored under similar disabilities. Dominated by back-country Democrats, the legislature after the Revolution annulled the State of Charitable Uses, removing the legal basis for the enforcement of charitable trusts, and steadfastly refused to grant state courts equity powers. Although Pennsylvania's "common law courts proved exceedingly imaginative in compensating by incorporating parts of equity law and procedure into their own proceedings," neither these expedients nor the informal arrangements wealthy Philadelphians used to create and enforce testamentary trusts were any substitute for the "steady and well-defined shape" of a body of jurisprudence "limited by fixed rules" of interpretation and application (Katz, 1971, 271).[7] Despite the city's impressive financial and intellectual resources, the development of great institutions of education and culture under elite patronage would not occur until the end of the nineteenth century. And, although Philadelphia's elite would produce outstanding individuals, it would never produce a steady stream of national leaders comparable to Boston's.[8]

Trusts, Endowments, and the Rise of Urban Elites, 1820–1880

The Massachusetts legislature established the judicial framework for equitable remedies, but the substance of equity was built up by precedents established on a case-by-case basis. Suits brought by Boston merchants not surprisingly loomed large in this process, since they, more than any other group, possessed estates large and complex enough to require the "special means" needed to counteract the erosive force of partible inheritance.

Cases defining the fundamentals of trust law came in three major waves, each roughly correlated with generational removes from the founders of the early family trusts. The first wave, which came before the courts in the 1820s, concerned the most basic features of trusts: their immunity from the claims of creditors and other third parties; the fiduciary responsibilities of trustees; and the length of time a private trust could be permitted to last before its *corpus* was distributed. The second wave in the 1850s, focusing on the rights of beneficiaries under trust estates, resulted largely from challenges to restrictive trust provisions by beneficiaries. The third wave, decided in the 1870s, was concerned with the immunity of estates from the claims of third parties—in particular, the validity of spendthrift trusts.

Few cases have had greater impact on the character of American trusts—testamentary and charitable—than *Harvard College and Massachusetts General Hospital v. Amory*, which set the "prudent man" standard for fiduciaries (Harvard College, 1829). Brought before the court in 1829, the case involved the will of Boston merchant John McLean, husband of Ann (Amory) McLean, who died in 1823, leaving the sum of $50,000 in trust and appointing his brothers-in-law, Jonathan and Francis Amory, as trustees. Income from the trust was to be paid to McLean's widow during her lifetime. On her death, the principal was to be divided between the college and the hospital.

The trustees invested the principal in the stock of manufacturing corporations, particularly the Boston and Merrimack companies, in which the Amorys and their kinsmen owned substantial interests. The college and the hospital took exception to this, claiming that, while the large dividends yielded by such investments benefited the widow McLean, they "disregarded the interests of the respondents" and exposed the estate to "total loss" because of their fluctuating value and because manufacturing companies did not enjoy limited liability, their exposure to risk. In effect, the plaintiffs asked the court to rule on two questions: (1) how much discretion trustees could be permitted in making investment decisions; (2) whether beneficiaries had the right to question the discretionary powers of trustees in these matters.

In this case, the court ruled against the college and the hospital. Justice Putnam's opinion considered the allegation that the Amorys had invested imprudently and to the detriment of the remaindermen by exploring the safety of all possible kinds of investment. He found that each had significant potential to fail:

> Do what you will, the capital is at hazard. If the public funds are resorted to, what becomes of the capital when the credit of the government shall be so much impaired as it was at the close of the last war (p. 459)?
>
> Investments on mortgages of real estate are not always safe. Its value fluctuates more, perhaps, than the capital of insurance stock (p. 460).
>
> Again, the title to real estate, after the most careful investigation, may be involved, and ultimately fail, and so the capital, which was originally supposed to be as firm as the earth itself, will be dissolved (p. 461).

Justice Putnam gave this litany of insecurity a ringing conclusion:

> All that can be required of a trustee to invest is, that he shall conduct himself faithfully and exercise a sound discretion. He is to observe how men of prudence, discretion and intelligence manage their own affairs, not in regard to speculation, but in regard to the permanent disposition of their funds, considering the probably income, as well as the probable safety of the capital to be invested (pp. 459–461).

Almost anticlimactically, Putnam went on to point out that the testator himself, "a man of extraordinary forecast and discretion, in regard to the management of property," whose "vast accumulation could not be ascribed to accidental causes, but to calculation and reflection," had obviously considered the securities questioned by the remaindermen prudent investments, since he had "invested nearly half his property in manufacturing stocks." His inclinations, Putnam suggested, were "entitled to great consideration" in assessing the decisions of his trustees—and seemed to justify their actions (p. 462).

Having vigorously defended the power of trustees to invest at their discretion, Putnam concluded by further protecting them from accountability to beneficiaries by declaring that they were not liable for losses resulting from their investment decisions:

> Trustees are justly and uniformly considered favorably, and it is of great importance to bereaved families and orphans, that they should not be

> held to make good, losses in the depreciation of stocks or the failure of the
> capital itself, which they held in trust, provided they conduct themselves
> honestly and discreetly and carefully, according to the existing circum-
> stances, in the discharge of their trusts. If this were held otherwise, no
> prudent man would run the hazard of losses which might happen without
> any neglect or breach of good faith (p. 465).

This decision expanded tremendously the power and independence of
trustees by giving them almost complete discretion to invest funds as they saw
fit, free from restraints from interested parties. At the same time, the standard
of prudence set for trustees by the court was, it appeared, the standard set by
their peers in Boston's financial community. The effect of this decision was to
introduce a degree of rationality into the investment process: A common
standard of prudence had the effect of making the investment process less
idiosyncratic and less subject to the interests of particular families—in effect
establishing the basis for pooling economic resources to serve the collective
interests of the merchant families as a group.

Most important, by sanctioning trustees' ability to invest in manufacturing, railroads, insurance, and other stocks, and by protecting them from the
threat of endlessly vexatious suits by disgruntled beneficiaries, the Court both
released family money into a common pool available for rational investment
in the broader economy and transformed trustees into key intermediaries in
this process. From this point on, particular individuals who specialized in
managing trust estates, the trustees of charitable endowments, and firms such
as the Massachusetts Hospital Life Insurance Company (MHLI) began to assume greater and greater centrality in Boston's financial community. By 1850,
the MHLI had become the largest financial institution in New England and a
key player in underwriting the region's textile and railroad industries (White,
1957). Specialized trust managers—Boston Trustees, as they came to be
known—could, by midcentury, be found on the boards of directors of virtually every major enterprise in and (as Boston's role as a center of investment
banking began to grow) beyond Massachusetts.[9]

Furthermore, Putnam's decision, in freeing capital from family control,
signaled the separation of management and ownership that was, as Berle and
Means would point out nearly a century later, the distinguishing characteristic
of the modern economic order (Berle and Means, 1933).[10] It was also, as it
turned out, the distinguishing characteristic of the modern class structure: By
placing capital under the best possible management, but also by consolidating
and rationalizing its use, this arrangement constituted one of the "special
means" that could assure that the millionocracy would not be merely a "per-
petual fact of money with a variable human element" (Holmes, 1961, p. 16).

Finally, the separation of ownership and management, with its stress on
competence, ensured that the financial core of the emerging Brahminate

would embody a capacity to continually recruit talented outsiders and thus help to maintain the group's vitality. Although Brahmin lore is replete with stories about wealthy Bostonians' genealogical obsessions, the ranks of the city's economic and cultural leadership were, in fact, constantly replenished by talented individuals who were not descendants of post-Revolutionary family founders. At the same time, scions of Boston merchant families did not hesitate to move out into the economic mainstream—banking in New York, managing railroads in Illinois, setting up mining ventures in Michigan—and, in so doing, assured Boston's elite a central role in the development of a national economy, not only as supplier of capital, but as the *avant garde* of managerial and later technological expertise (Kolko, 1967).

In the 1830s, the courts also made key decisions on the *duration* of trusts. One of the most emphatic criticisms of English law involved the extent to which—through entails, restrictive trust provisions, and the uncontrolled growth of endowed charities—the "dead hand" of the past had hampered the growth of a free economy and empowered oppressive aristocratic and ecclesiastical institutions. It also had important bearing on the merchant's capacity to strike the balance between inclusivity and exclusivity: Inability to limit the duration of trusts would, while preventing the partition of estates, set loose all the corrupting potential associated with great wealth passed on, generation after generation, to unworthy descendants.

In *Nightingale v. Burrell*, Chief Justice Lemuel Shaw, borrowing on recent English decisions, brought the Rule Against Perpetuities into American law. This rule prevented testators from creating estates "inalienable, though all mankind join in the conveyance ... a thing odious in the law, and destructive to the commonwealth" (Nightingale v. Burrell, 1833, p. 111). Although the Rule Against Perpetuities required that property vest at some point, there was endless litigation as to *when* the property should vest. The guideline adopted by Shaw required that property vest at some point within the following span of time: the lifetime of a person or persons living at the time of the declaration of trust, plus twenty-one years, plus nine months. In simple terms, the Rule set three generations from the testator as the maximum duration of a trust (Newhall, 1942). This posed no real impediment, however, to families determined to keep their fortunes locked up in trust. According to *Fortune* magazine's 1933 article on Boston, it became "the accepted practice for the young Forbes or Lowell whom the Rule Against Perpetuities would make outright owner of several millions of gilt-edged bonds to reestablish voluntarily his family trust. And failing the voluntary act, there [were] always enough uncles and aunts to see that the deed in any case was done" (Boston, 1933, p. 36).

The adoption of the Rule Against Perpetuities by Massachusetts courts presided over by men who increasingly favored or were related by blood or marriage to the Brahminate underscores the complexity of the merchant group's social goals. Anglophiles though they were, they were not seeking to become an aristocracy through the creation of "special means" that would entirely insulate them from the democratizing forces of partible inheritance or the rigors of the marketplace. They knew that their strength as a group depended on their continuing commitment to commerce and manufacturing.

There was a more immediately practical reason for the Brahminate to favor adoption of the Rule. If perpetuities were permitted, as each succeeding generation increased the number of beneficiaries to be supported by such trusts, the amount of income available to each would grow less over time. Perpetuities would, in other words, subject estates to the same problems of partition and diminished resources that the merchants were trying avoid in the first place. In addition, perpetuities would tend to reinforce the interests of individual families over those of the group as a whole. For if property could not vest, the primary reason for intermarriage within the group would disappear, because it would not be possible to consolidate estates in any meaningful sense. Without widespread endogamy, the children of merchant families would marry non-Bostonians and would scatter their talents—and their shares in family fortunes.

Even as the first generation of merchant family founders was dying off and its fortunes passing to a generation of heirs who enjoyed unprecedented privileges and wealth, the group remained keenly aware of the need to strike a balance between "an audacious will to power and the cautious reckoning of gain" (Story, 1972, p. 42). Not surprisingly, given the growing amount and economic significance of property held in trust, the direction of court decisions over time further increased the power of trustees and diminished the rights of beneficiaries.

Although Massachusetts went further than any other state in upholding the wishes of testators with regard to the disposition of their property, analogous developments had taken place in other states where commerce and industry had produced wealthy urban elites. As noted earlier, both in New York and Pennsylvania, urban upper classes had nurtured methods—albeit somewhat different ones—of keeping their estates intact and favoring the desires of testators over the claims of beneficiaries and creditors.

Opportunities to test the validity of Massachusetts' solicitude for the integrity of trust estates in a national arena did not arise until the 1870s. In 1875, a creditor brought suit against a "spendthrift" trust, claiming that devices that enabled beneficiaries to enjoy wealth without liability for debts were "void on grounds of public policy as being in fraud of the rights of creditors" (Nichols v. Eaton, 1875, pp. 721–722). The U.S. Supreme Court upheld the trust. Pointing out the public nature of testamentary and property records, the justices decided that it was incumbent upon creditors and assignees to determine the *bona fides* of persons to whom they extended credit. If they failed to do so, it was at their own risk (p. 726).

This decision outraged portions of the legal community. In *Restraints on the Alienation of Property* (1882), John Chipman Gray, an eminent Boston lawyer, a Brahmin, and Royall Professor of Law at Harvard, assailed spendthrift trusts as contrary to the public interest, legal precedents, and, ultimately, to national survival. "One of the worst results of the decision upholding the spendthrift trust," Gray declared, "is the encouragement it gives to a plutocracy, and to the accumulation of a great fortune in a single hand, through the power it affords to rich men to assure undisturbed possession of wealth to their children, however weak or wicked they may be" (p. v).[11] Fearing that such trusts would "perpetuate a privileged class whose power and wealth should not be endangered by the weakness or folly of particular members," Gray linked them to the rising tide of working class and agrarian radicalism:

> To a frame of mind and a state of public sentiment like this, spendthrift trusts are most congenial. If we are all to be cared for, and have our wants supplied, without regard to our mental and moral failings, in the socialistic Utopia, there is little reason why in the meantime, a father should not do for his son what the State is then asked to do for us all.... My modest task has been to show that spendthrift trusts have no place in the system of the Common Law. But I am no prophet, and certainly do not mean to deny that they may be in entire harmony with Social Code of the next century. Dirt is only matter out of place; and what is a blot on the escutcheon of the Common Law may be a jewel in the crown of the Social Republic. (pp. ix-x)

Gray's influential protest not only reiterated the tension between "an audacious drive for power" and the "cautious reckoning of gain" that had characterized Brahmin testation from its beginnings, but it also reflected the extent to which social Darwinism had heightened and sharpened these concerns in the post-Civil War period. Even before the war, pundits such as Oliver Wendell Holmes had fretted over the weakening tendencies of wealth. Criticizing Boston's "chryso-aristocracy," for its tendencies to "cheap dandyism," he fretted,

> Our young men must gild their spurs, but they need not win them. The equal division of property keeps the younger sons above the necessity of military service. Thus the army loses an element of refinement, and the moneyed upper class forgets what it is to count heroism among its virtues. Still I don't believe in any aristocracy without pluck as its backbone. Ours may show it when the time comes, if ever it does come. (Holmes, 1957/1854, pp. 244-245)

Holmes wrote these words in the spring of 1858. The young Brahmins—his own son included—would very soon have a chance to "earn their spurs."

But even the wartime heroism of the best and brightest of the young Brahmins, celebrated by Thomas Wentworth Higginson in *The Harvard Memorial Biographies* (1866, p. v) as a vindication of "those classes, favored in worldly fortune, which would elsewhere form an aristocracy," was insufficient to allay the anxieties of men like John Chipman Gray by the 1880s. The immense growth of new commercial and industrial fortunes, combined with rising economic turbulence and social disorder, intensified his concern that the Brahmin class would unfit itself for the ever harsher "struggle for existence." And he feared that spendthrift trusts would tip the balance between "audacious will" and "cautious reckoning" dangerously far in the direction of the latter—and that spiraling accumulation of wealth would give rise to the economic and social senility characteristic of decadent European aristocracies. Gray had no objection to the existence of classes. But, as a social Darwinist, he insisted that such groups must be founded in strength, competence, and force of will. As he wrote in comparing *laissez-faire* with newer social ideas, "The old doctrine was a wholesome one, fit to produce a manly race, based on sound morality and wise philosophy; and that new doctrine is contrary thereto" (Gray, 1882, p. x).

Wealth and Charity: The Public Dimensions of Private Wealth

The accumulation, consolidation, and transmission of wealth are private acts. But they inevitably have public dimensions. When one portion of a community proves to be more economically adept, it not only alters relationships between all groups but also each group's perception of itself. This is especially true in societies such as New England's, where strong egalitarian traditions, rooted in Puritanism and nurtured by the Revolution, remained strong.

Still very much engaged in making their money, the Boston families, who would by the 1850s, be labeled "Brahmins," had not yet acquired a distinct identity. They did not live in residential enclaves, generally avoided conspicuous displays of their wealth, and sent their children to play on the Common and to public schools such as the Boston Latin School. They were civically active: As citizens of means, they naturally maintained an intense interest in public affairs, running for elective office and serving on local boards and committees. To the extent that they conceived of themselves as a group at all, they appear to have framed their common purposes in public rather than private terms.

The 1830s marked the financial takeoff point for the families that would eventually constitute the core of Boston's "Brahmin" elite. The textile industry, still experimental in the 1820s, grew rapidly in the 1830s, thanks to tariff protection, inexpensive Southern cotton, growing domestic markets, and abundant capital. The leading firms, still closely held by a handful of interrelated extended families, produced an embarrassment of riches, a flood of wealth that grew faster than it could be spent. Funds were poured into new ventures: railroads, banks, real estate, iron, shipping, and lumber. But these only yielded more profits.

Boston's wealthiest families, despite their growing resources, lived austerely. They did not build great estates or entertain lavishly. Nor did they abandon active involvement in civic or economic affairs for more "aristocratic pursuits." But the scope and scale of their fortunes, which grew unremittingly, made it increasingly difficult to sustain the fiction that they were merely the better-off portion of a still-integral urban community. Not only were they rich, but also their wealth—thanks to trusts, to its increasingly corporate character, and to the growing extent to which its competent management was becoming distinguished from its enjoyment—seemed to become more permanent with each succeeding generation. As this occurred, spokesmen for the group became increasingly preoccupied with the problem of selecting and training competent leaders and managers from within the group and justifying the fact of possession in terms of the dominant egalitarian and democratic values of American society.

The merchants responded to these challenges by further increasing their commitment to the city's charitable and educational institutions. In part, this commitment represented an elaboration of the need to maintain and extend their public influence. At the same time, as more sons chose professional careers in preference to business, giving to educational and other institutions that helped to enhance the status of the professions, became itself a form of wealth transmission. To be sure, Harvard, Massachusetts General Hospital, the Athenaeum, and the host of other privately supported eleemosynary institutions founded and funded by the merchants provided public benefit. But the private advantages that accrued to the extended families of those who sat on their boards and contributed generously by gift and bequest to their fundraising efforts cannot be underestimated (Story, 1981, pp. 57–88).

By the 1830s, Harvard had become a central mechanism for socializing the sons of elite families—as well as for recruiting talented and ambitious young men into commercial and eleemosynary enterprises in which they were interested.[13] As young businessmen and professionals built their careers after graduation, service on corporate and charitable boards began to be regarded as an important indicator of leadership ability, as well as a testing ground for advancement to greater responsibilities in both the worlds of commerce and charity. By the 1850s, leadership in the emerging Brahminate had come increasingly to be largely defined not merely by possession of wealth, but by service on an elaborate hierarchy of boards of the city's increasingly well-endowed charitable, educational, and eleemosynary institutions. The most strategically important positions were held by individuals who linked the worlds of finance and benevolence, and who, through control of their own enterprises and through their power to invest the assets of testamentary trusts and institutional endowments, were able to collectively shape the city's economic direction, while at the same time assuring the continuing influence of its elite families. This move from mere wealth transmission toward systematic, often *inter vivos*, investment in the human capital necessary for sustaining the Brahmins and their influence was of immense significance and, more than anything else, denoted their transformation into a coherent and cohesive *class*.

In 1845, Harvard Treasurer Samuel Atkins Eliot attempted to summarize the remarkable commitment of Boston's wealth to benevolent purposes—a commitment that he regarded, and correctly so, as being unrivaled by any other American city. Eliot's purposes were twofold: first, he was attempting to show the role of private giving in the development of the city's charitable, cultural, educational, and religious life; second, he was trying to articulate and to justify the public role of private wealth. He began by stating that with Boston's impressive increase in population and wealth since 1830, it had "become a question of deep interest" to "enumerate the principal objects of Boston liberality" to see "how far, and in what particular ways, the character of Boston has been or is to be so affected by such a sudden development of its resources, and such an immense accession to its physical and commercial strength" (Eliot, 1845, pp. 135–159).

Eliot's findings gave him reason to praise the extraordinary liberality of his fellow citizens and the "great variety of purposes" for which money was voluntarily bestowed. These included "thirty-one societies or institutions having religious objects, twenty-six for purposes of literary education, and twenty-five for the relief of physical and moral wants," as well as thirty-one "other objects of more or less general interest" and "no less than thirteen subscriptions for monuments to the memory of as many honored individuals" (p. 149). He worried, however, about the "obvious effects arising from this multiplicity and subdivision of institutions of benevolence" (p. 149). Although conceding that interorganizational rivalries stimulated "the activity and industry of all," leading not only to higher levels of giving, but also to "an unseen under-current of kindness and active benevolence which may be some compensation for the harshness, suspicion, and injustice which they are apt to indulge," Eliot feared that "the multiplicity of objects" would diminish the resources of each (pp. 150–153). Eliot urged Bostonians to give to established institutions—to consolidate and target their giving, much as they had their investment capital. In doing so, he was applying to the domain of charity themes that had traditionally been voiced about the partition of estates.

Eliot similarly appropriated the reasoning behind the Prudent Man Rule to the domain of organized charity in criticizing the tendency of some givers to limit and restrict "the uses to which funds may be applied, to such a degree, that, when the circumstances of society change even but slightly, the means provided for a previous state of things are no longer applicable to the corresponding wants of the present and succeeding times" (p. 156). Citing the example of the trusts "for the benefit of young married mechanics in the cities of Boston and Philadelphia" established under the will of Benjamin Franklin, Eliot pointed out that, only fifty years after the great man's death, it had become "almost impossible, to find persons of such a description, and in such situations. If Franklin's sagacity could not foresee for a score of years what was to occur in a class with whose interests, habits, and character he was entirely familiar," Eliot asked, "who shall presume to direct future generations? The only way in which a man can do permanent good with the money which he must leave behind him is to trust something to the discretion of those who would follow him," Eliot declared, echoing Justice Putnam's dictum that the only truly sound investment was in individuals who could conduct themselves "faithfully and exercise a sound discretion" (p. 157).

Eliot concluded his essay with a defense of the Brahmins against charges that their philanthropy and the institutions it supported were instruments of class domination. In Jacksonian America, where the monied were "jealously watched" and "constantly suspected," Eliot argued that riches alone did not enable the wealthy to oppress the masses (p. 158). Claiming that philanthropy and the institutions it supported represented not only giving by the wealthy, but also "mites of the generous poor," Eliot suggested that benevolence presented an even playing field in which all could support the causes and institutions in which they believed. Rather than being instruments of oppression, the sums given by the "generous rich" for an impressively wide variety of purposes suggested that their influence had "been exerted, in this country, only for beneficent purposes" (p. 158).

Eliot's pride in the Brahmin's generosity was undercut by the fear of democracy evident in his denunciation of the ingratitude and hostility of the masses. Thus, while able to muster facts and arguments to defend the civic-mindedness of his class, he was unable to articulate a positive rationale for the existence of great hereditary concentrations of wealth in a democratic society. The chief obstacle to his conceptualizing the role of wealth in a democracy lay in part in the weakness of his class's identity as a coherent group. As he portrays them, they are merely wealthy and meritorious, representing, as Oliver Wendell Holmes would put it a few years later, "a permanent fact of wealth with a variable human element" (Holmes, 1961). Only the possession of surplus wealth distinguished them from a broader civic community with which Eliot still strongly identified himself. Not until the Brahmins (as Holmes would dub them in 1859) fully came to terms with the full extent to which wealth made them different from everybody else, would they be able to clearly articulate their claims to leadership.

In 1860, on the eve of the Civil War, Eliot again surveyed the growth of Boston's charities (Eliot, 1860, pp 149–165). The tone of this essay is considerably different from his earlier one: As spokesman for the city's patricians, he had a far clearer and more confident sense of who they were as a group and the distinctive nature of their role as community leaders. The defensiveness of the 1845 essay was notably absent, perhaps because the influx of mostly Catholic immigrants and the rising political challenge they represented had led the battling Protestant factions to finally find common cause and to settle their long-standing differences (p. 151).

Eliot's 1860 analysis of Boston charity denoted fundamental shifts both in the Boston elite's view of itself and in its understanding of philanthropy. Most important, he described the elite and its philanthropic activity as having *national* implications: He evoked Boston as an example for other cities and their elites to follow. Whereas in his earlier essay he had been reluctant to prioritize philanthropic objectives, suggesting instead a synergy between all benevolent activities, by 1860, Eliot was willing to unambiguously assert that certain institutions—especially the complex of cultural and education institutions of which Harvard was the core—were more important and hence more worthy of support than others.

By the 1850s, Harvard already had become, as Henry Adams wrote, the Brahmins "ideal of social self-respect"—its degree a basic credential for class membership (Adams, 1931, p. 16). But as it transformed itself from being a provincial college to becoming the nation's leading university, it also served a broader public, helping Boston to "drain a large watershed of intellect" and helping the city's elite to recruit into its ranks the "promising young author and rising lawyer and large capitalist"—and "the prettiest girl" (Holmes, 1961/1859, pp. 119–120). In the 1860s, the work of Samuel Atkins Eliot's son, Harvard president Charles W. Eliot, would further extended Boston's "suction range," expanding both its cultural influence and helping to fuel the growing scale and scope of the elite's leading role in the creating a national economy.

But in being transformed by Brahmin wealth and imagination into institutions of national significance, Harvard and the constellation of cultural and scientific enterprises transcended their origins. Although Boston would be eclipsed by New York as the nation's financial center, the pattern it set for elite philanthropy would not only profoundly affect other aspiring metropolitan ruling classes but would also lead to the creation of a new national elite—based on educational and professional credentials. This "new middle class" of public-spirited experts, serving in corporations, in government, and in institutions of culture, health care, and social welfare, would lead the nation into the twentieth century.

The Bostonization of American Wealth, 1880–1990

Just as Greece conquered Rome, Boston's legal and institutional cultures would have an enormous impact on New York and other metropolitan centers. As New York's economic importance grew after the Civil War—and with it, private fortunes—the legal obstacles to putting private wealth to public purposes became more evident, making New York a lightning rod for those concerned about the impact of new wealth on American society.

Despite James Kent's pioneering efforts to establish an Americanized system of equity jurisprudence in New York in the first decades of the 19th century, Jeffersonian and Jacksonian resistance to the concentration of private wealth and, more important, the institutional deployment of concentrated private wealth, proved unusually effective. By 1800, the state had placed all eleemosynary entities—including churches—under the oversight of the Regents of the University of the States of New York, requiring regular reports of their activities and imposing on them a variety of limitations. By the 1820s, the legislature had passed a range of additional restrictions on the power of testators to leave funds to charities and on the ability of charities to receive such gifts and bequests.

In the 1880s, these restrictions were challenged in two celebrated cases involving bequests to eleemosynary institutions: the failure of the multi-million dollar Tilden Trust in 1887 and of the $1.5 million Fiske bequest to Cornell University the following year. Although the highly technical legal issues underlying the Tilden and Fiske cases differed in terms of their broad political implications, they had important similarities. In both, the body of laws intended to limit the wealth and power of private institutions, adopted by New York State during the Jacksonian era, permitted litigious relatives to defeat major charitable bequests.[14]

The Tilden case had centered on the general status of charitable trusts in states such as New York, which had annulled the Statute of Charitable Uses and, more particularly, the capacity of testators to bequeath property to charitable trusts not yet in being. The Fiske case centered on restrictions that New York had placed on the size of endowments that could be held by charitable corporations, which were limited to amounts specifically authorized by the legislature.

Samuel J. Tilden, one of New York's leading corporate lawyers and 1876 presidential candidate, gave serious thought to the problem of his wealth and felt that "a rich man is primarily a trustee of society" (Flick, 1939, pp. 510–518). His 10,000-word will, executed in 1884, provided generously for his relatives, giving them approximately $1,400,000—with the remainder, amounting to two-thirds of his estate, bequeathed for cultural and scientific purposes.

Particular care was taken to safeguard the fortune from speedy disintegration by setting up life trusts and making provision for second- and third-generation descendants.

With covert encouragement from upstate Democratic leader David Hill, who harbored deep suspicions about private philanthropy, Tilden's nephews, who needed money to prop up their tottering brokerage firm, challenged the will, claiming that its charitable provisions were too indefinite, because they gave the executors authority to use the residue of the estate for "such charitable, educational and scientific purposes" as they might deem "beneficial to the interests of mankind." Though lower courts ruled in favor of the bequest, repeated appeals—and a great deal of political string pulling—eventually sustained the "laughing heirs."[15]

The Fiske will case involved a bequest of the $1.5 million to Cornell University. Again, with encouragement from Democratic party leader Hill, the will was challenged by the testator's husband on grounds that the university's charter prohibited Cornell from taking any property beyond $3,000,000. After winding its way through the state courts, the case was appealed to the U.S. Supreme Court, which upheld New York's restrictions on institutional endowments.[16]

The failure of the Tilden Trust and the Fiske bequest set off a storm of protest and concern in reform circles—concern that was intensified by the death of Jay Gould in 1892. Despite having left one of the largest estates ever probated in the United States, Gould left no money for charitable purposes. Fearing that this combination of private selfishness and public hostility to philanthropy would lead the country either into a revolution or to rule by a plutocracy, reformers organized a national campaign to change New York's charities laws (American Millionaires, 1893, pp. 48–60; Stead, 1893, p. 37). The effort was supported politically by financier–philanthropists such as J. P. Morgan (who was also, not coincidentally, a major benefactor of Harvard) and led intellectually by such men as Harvard Law School dean James Barr Ames. "Melancholy the spectacle must always be," Ames intoned in an article in the *Harvard Law Review*,

> when covetous relatives seek to convert to their own use the fortune which a testator has plainly devoted to a great public benefaction. But society is powerless in a given case, so long as the forms of law are observed. When, however, charitable bequests have been repeatedly defeated, under cover of law, and that, too, although the beneficent purpose of the testator was unmistakably expressed in a will executed with all due formalities, and although the designated trustees were ready and anxious to perform the trust reposed in them, one cannot help wondering if there is not something wrong in a system of law which

permits this deplorable disappointment of the testator's will and the consequent loss to the community. The prominence of the testator, and the magnitude of the "Tilden Trust," which has recently miscarried, have aroused so general an interest that this seems a peculiarly fit time to consider the legal reasons for the failure of that and similar charitable bequests in New York. (1913, p. 285)

Ames's concern—shared by civic-minded New Yorkers and their Boston allies— was that without legal capacity to devote private wealth to public purposes, the vast new fortunes of the era would become the basis for a plutocracy, bringing with them not only the weakness and degeneracy associated with inherited wealth, but also open class warfare.

In the spring of 1893, with hardly a murmur in the press, New York's legislature, in two strokes, swept away nearly a century of hostility to private institutions—and in doing so cleared the path for the reformers' "mission to the millionaires." In an act passed in April, the legislature gave a blanket exemption to the property of religious, charitable, and educational corporations. A few weeks later, the Legislature passed the "Tilden Act," which broadly affirmed the validity of charitable trusts and answered the objections to such trusts that the judiciary had raised in the Tilden case. In order to prevent "laughing heirs" such as the Tilden nephews from taking title to properties left for charitable purposes, the legislature mandated that the state supreme court should take control of such properties and assigned to the state's attorney general the tasks of representing the interest of charitable beneficiaries and seeing to the enforcement of charitable trusts.

The impact of such legal reforms was dramatic. When the *Review of Reviews*, which had spearheaded the reform effort, surveyed the growth of charitable giving a decade later, it found compelling evidence for the growth of "a stalwart unselfishness, a willingness of favored ones to promote the welfare of the less favored, and particularly a growing tendency on the part of men and women of large means to personally administer a fair share of their estates to aid the educational, religious, and philanthropic activities of the country" (Hagar, 1904, pp. 464–465). It estimated that annual philanthropic giving had increased from $29 million in 1893 to $107 million in 1901. "Giving has become a business," the article concluded, pointing out that "many of the best-known givers have been obliged to surround themselves with barriers against professional solicitors" (p. 465).

Thus, in ways he could not have anticipated, Oliver Wendell Holmes's characterization of Boston as the "hub of the solar system" proved correct— at least insofar as the architecture of American institutional culture was concerned. The reform of New York's charities laws assured the dominance of elite-dependent private institutions in American culture—a configuration that was in every sense a product of Boston and its merchant family founders.

Dynastic Wealth

The industrial fortunes built up after the Civil War dwarfed the accumulations of those that preceded them. In earlier times, the rich had tended to collectivize and institutionalize the administration of both their fortunes and identities, using both testamentary and charitable endowment trusts to create close ties between themselves and complexes of privately funded and governed public cultural, educational, health, and welfare institutions, and the extent to which these institutions served demonstrable public purposes, such as caring for the poor and educating the impecunious, played an important part not only in defining their creators' collective identity and purpose, but also in persuading the public, which was inclined to see private wealth and power as inimical to democratic and egalitarian values, that elites were not a threat to the polity.

By the turn of the century, the wealthy were not only giving more, but they were also beginning to explore new ways of giving. Not only was the scale of their fortunes so immense as to defeat conventional ways of distributing charitable dollars, events since the publication of Carnegie's "Gospel of Wealth" in 1889 had underscored the need for an entirely new approach to giving — an approach directed at the *causes* of problems rather than the mere alleviation of distress. "Your fortune is rolling up, rolling up like an avalanche," Frederick Gates, John D. Rockefeller's philanthropic advisor is said to have shouted at him one day early in the century. "You must keep up with it! You must distribute it faster than it grows! If you do not, it will crush you and your children and your children's children" (quoted in Fosdick, 1952, p. 3).

The sheer size of the post–Civil War fortunes, as well as the national (and sometimes international) scope of the enterprises in which they were based, precluded their being easily integrated into any preexisting metropolitan elite structure. The metropolitan elites tended (and still tend) to be tradition oriented, defining themselves and their mission in terms of historic ties to the communities in which they were located, cementing ties to institutions in which they had heavily invested, and to which they looked not only for the collective socialization of their children, but also as mechanisms for recruiting and certifying new members, and the rewriting of history in order to secure for themselves and their client institutions the legitimacy conferred by tradition.

Fortune-founders of the Gilded Age such as Andrew Carnegie and John D. Rockefeller not only understood that the scale and scope of their fortunes made such an accommodation a practical impossibility, but also believed that they and their fortunes represented an entirely new historical force. Rather than seeking legitimacy in the past, they sought it in the future. Rather than rewriting history, they sought to reconstruct understanding of social and economic life, both to explain why "men of affairs" such as themselves should have come to control such vast resources and to legitimate that control as part of the natural scheme of things. In doing this, they did not entirely leave behind certain central themes of the older elite ideology: Like their predecessors, they justified themselves in terms of a role of service to the public. But they portrayed themselves as servants of Progress—midwives, as it were, of the new industrial order. Even their philanthropy, as Carnegie's 1889 "Gospel of Wealth" took pains to point out, would differ dramatically from traditional almsgiving: It would be scientifically targeted, rationally administered, and would aim to identify and eradicate the *causes* of poverty, dependency, and ignorance rather than merely treating (and, Carnegie argued, aggravating) its symptoms.

Although the founders of the great post–Civil War fortunes may have agreed on the unprecedented nature of their achievements and the challenges they posed, there was very really disagreement as to how to respond to these challenges. Several "men of affairs," notably Carnegie and E. H. Harriman, eschewed the notion of creating family dynasties. Carnegie gave most of his money away—primarily to grant-making foundations. Harriman gave modestly to charity and provided generously for his descendants but made no effort to formally institutionalize either the family fortune or the family's philanthropic interests.[17] Commodore Vanderbilt and John Jacob Astor similarly eschewed both grand charitable gestures and efforts to institutionalize their fortunes—with the result, as one family member put it recently, "there is no Vanderbilt fortune."[18]

The most fully developed model for the institutionalization of the great new fortunes was framed by John D. Rockefeller, who, in passing his wealth on to his descendants, pioneered the mechanisms that, while nominally allowing it to remain under the control of the family, placed it increasingly under the management of experts—lawyers, accountants, advisors, and consultants. Although a similar distinction between ownership and management had taken place in the older metropolitan elites, with the rise of family trustees and incorporated charities, in its earlier form the displacement of control had featured a collectivization of the resources of many families, whereas in the dynastic setting, it involved only the assets and activities of a single family, usually structured around a "family office" that coordinated the management of investments, philanthropy, and public relations.

It has been conventionally assumed that the perpetuation of dynastic families' sense of purpose, mission, and identity has been quite separate from the "hard" financial and legal complexes that manage their fortunes, and that the former have been fashioned interpersonally within the family itself, through such informal means as telling family stories and rituals, and displays of family togetherness, as well as through collected letters and memoirs produced by commissioned scribes. This view of dynastic wealth greatly oversimplifies the reality. Recent studies of dynastic families in twentieth-century America suggest that these "soft" functions may, in fact, may be far more thoroughly integrated into the formal processes of administering family fortunes than generally believed while, at the same time, formal administrative structures and processes may be, in a variety of ways, shaped by the peculiar emotional dynamics and configurations that define the interrelationships of individuals within the family.

This more complex, interactive, and multicentered model of dynastic structure and process is analogous to the view of corporate enterprise emerging from the work of contemporary organization theorists, who increasingly view business corporations as institutions whose primary purposes involve social reproduction of managers and the reducion of uncertainty rather than as rational, efficient, or innovative responses to market forces. In a similar way, the highly rationalized fiduciary functions of dynasties appear to interact with the nonrational dynamics of family life, moving away from purely economic imperatives and becoming mechanisms for the optimization of noneconomic goods. On the face of it, this would appear to be a prescription for decline, since, in theory, the less responsive an economic entity is to market forces, the less successful it is likely to be. What this overlooks, however, is the extent to which market forces may themselves be shaped by dynasties, both in the exercise of their considerable economic power and in their capacity to influence the public policies that frame the marketplace.

The study of dynasties and dynastic inheritance practices thus becomes an investigation of interfaces of public and private power—and of the ways in which public and private dimensions of family mission and identity inevitably overlap. Great fortunes have both a public and private character, mixing the management of great private wealth with stewardship of the philanthropic institutions that justified the families' existence in terms of public purpose.

Like the fiduciary management of their money, management of the collective identity of dynastic families has exceeded the capacity and competence of their own members. Both necessitate the involvement of expert outsiders. Although the first two generations of Rockefellers zealously guarded their privacy, commissioning hagiographic biographies and suppressing unfavorable ones, later generations began to define their collective mission—and the ever-growing accumulation of papers produced by family members, the family office, and institutions tied to the family—as having a public character. By the late 1950s, they had come to see their papers as "evidence for a large segment of American history during the past century" which illuminated "such varied developments as the growth of big business, scientific philanthropy, educational, medical, and religious change, and cultural awakening."[19]

By the 1970s, the Rockefellers came to understand that the papers could not only play a crucial private role in the family's continuing efforts to redefine its own mission and goals, but also an important public one in shaping the purposes of American philanthropy and the emerging nonprofit sector. John D. Rockefeller III, through his sponsorship of the Commission on Private Philanthropy and Public Needs (the Filer Commission) and the establishment of INDEPENDENT SECTOR, a national umbrella organization that promoted research and public awareness of philanthropy, was able to transform the identity of the rapidly growing universe of charitable tax-exempt enterprises into a coherent and cohesive cartel of benevolent organizations (Marcus and Hall, 1992, pp. 155-248; Hall, 1992, pp. 13-84). At the same time, through such things as a conference celebrating the sesquicentennial of the family founder's birth—a meeting that brought together family members and the leaders of the nonprofit sector—the family was able to merge its public and private identities.

Reprise

As Langbein reminds us, a new generation of fortunes has come into being in the post-World War II decades—the most impressive of them in the years since 1970. Their founders—Buffet, Gates, and others—face the same challenges that confronted the late eighteenth century Bostonians and the late nineteenth-century dynasts: the need to justify their wealth in terms of democratic values, the need to protect their fortunes from the folly and extravagance of their descendants, and the need to protect their descendants from the corruptions of wealth.

Langbein's suggestion that the new billionaires share a new ethos of inheritance seems largely correct: Few of those listed in the higher ranks of the Forbes 400 have either made major commitments to philanthropy (though many promise to do so); few have institutionalized their wealth in Rockefeller-style family offices; and none—with the sole exception of Ted Turner—have articulated any coherent convictions about the public responsibilities of wealth and those who hold it.[20] Although it is certainly true that most Americans have chosen (by preference or necessity) to invest in their children's education rather than to transfer to them farms, firms, or other tangible assets, it does not appear that the new wealth intends to follow this path.

The most perplexing aspect of the new money is, precisely, its lack of conviction and its lack of commitment to the future of families, communities, and institutions that comprise the charitable and cultural infrastructure of the country, or, indeed, to the future of capitalism. If there has been a revolution in wealth transmission, it has not, as Langbein would have us believe, involved a new ethos of inheritance. Rather, it is distinguished by its lack of an ethos, its lack of a vision of commitment to anything beyond maximizing returns on investment over the short term.

ACKNOWLEDGMENTS: The research on which this chapter is based was supported by grants from the AAFRC Trust for Philanthropy, the Aspen Institute's Nonprofit Sector Research Fund, the Lilly Endowment, Inc., and the Program on Non-Profit Organizations, Yale University.

Notes

1. Langbein did not break down the differences between the costs of public and private education, nor did he consider philanthropic giving in support of education, which in 1990 amounted to more than $12 billion. Doing so would doubtless further strengthen his hypothesis, since his study is concerned with wealth transmission among the upper and upper-middle classes — the propertied groups mostly likely to patronize private institutions and who, traditionally, have been their most significant source of donations and bequests.
2. General works covering post-Revolutionary legal developments and giving attention to interstate differences include Roscoe Pound, *The Formative Era of American Law* (1938); William E. Nelson, *Americanization of the Common Law* (1975); and Morton J. Horowitz, *The Transformation of American Law, 1780–1860* (1977). Work giving particular attention to the development of equity jurisdiction includes Edwin H. Woodruff, "Chancery in Massachusetts" (1889); Spencer Liverant and Walter H. Hitchler, "A History of Equity in Pennsylvania" (1933); William L. Curran, "The Struggle for Equity Jurisdiction in Massachusetts" (1951); Stanley N. Katz, "The Politics of Law in Colonial America: Controversies over Chancery Courts and Equity Law in the Eighteenth Century" (1971); John H. Langbein, "Chancellor Kent and the History of Legal Literature" (1993); and Austin Wakeman Scott, "Charitable Trusts in New York" (1951).
3. On Jefferson's attitude toward the Common Law, see his "Revisal of the Laws of Virginia" (in Koch, 1965, pp. 296–298). On the impact of Jeffersonian attitudes on charitable trusts, see E. S. Hirchler's "A Survey of Charitable Trusts in Virginia" (1939). A good account of the struggle between legal ideologies can be found in Howard S. Miller's *Legal Foundations of American Philanthropy* (1961).
4. Curran refers to Story's unpublished 1808 report to the legislature, which I have been unable to locate. Evidently Story's 1820 article, "Chancery Jurisdiction," published as an unsigned piece in the *North American Review* (1820, pp. 161ff.) is an expanded version of that report. The essay appears under Story's by-line in William W. Story, Ed., *Miscellaneous Writings of Joseph Story* (1851, pp. 148–179).
5. Perhaps the best study of the differences between the elites and institutional

cultures of Boston, New York, Philadelphia, and other cities is E. Digby Baltzell's *Puritan Boston and Quaker Philadelphia: Two Protestant Ethics and the Spirit of Class Authority and Leadership* (1979). See also P. D. Hall, "Cultures of Trusteeship in the United States" (1992, pp. 135–206). While they do no seek to make explicit comparisons between New York and other cities, the following studies shed important light on these issues: Thomas Bender, *New York Intellect: A History of Intellectual Life in New York City from 1750 to the Beginnings of Our Own Time* (1987); Thomas Bender, *Intellect and Public Life: Essays on the Social History of Academic Intellectuals in the United States* (1993); David C. Hammack, *Power and Society: Greater New York at the Turn of the Century* (New York, 1982); F. C. Jaher, *The Urban Establishment: Upper Strata in Boston, New York, Charleston, Chicago, and Los Angeles* (1982); and Sam Bass Warner, *The Private City: Philadelphia in Three Periods of Growth* (1968).

6. The best account of Kent's influence is John H. Langbein's "Chancellor Kent and the History of Legal Literature" (1993). On Jacksonian strictures on charitable giving and trustmaking, see James Barr Ames, "The Failure of the Tilden Trust" (1893) and Austin Wakeman Scott, "Charitable Trusts in New York" (1952). See also, John S. Whitehead's fine overview of legal issues affecting eleemosynary corporations, *The Separation of College and State: Columbia, Dartmouth, Harvard, and Yale, 1776-1876* (1973).

   A more recent study by Stanley N. Katz, Barry Sullivan, and C. Paul Beach, "Legal Change and Legal Autonomy: Charitable Trusts in New York, 1777-1893," argues that New York's hostility to charities was an artifact of the state's legal system and that strictures on charities were not as severe as earlier scholars had assumed.

7. See also Erwin N. Griswold's description of the impact of the unofficial status of equity in Pennsylvania on the development of testamentary trusts *Spendthrift Trusts under the New York Statutes and Elsewhere*, 1947, pp. 21-22):

   > In the early part of the [nineteenth] century there were no equity courts in Pennsylvania, and the law courts did not have equity powers. The result was that if a man had what elsewhere would have been regarded as an equitable right, there was little or no means of dealing with it in Pennsylvania. Creditors were therefore unable to reach the interest of the beneficiary, since there was no procedure at law for that purpose. In this state of the law, the courts became accustomed to interests owned by beneficiaries which could not be reached by creditors. When, in later years, the Pennsylvania courts gradually acquired equity powers, spendthrift trusts had become firmly established and an accepted part of the law.

8. Baltzell concisely, if crudely, posits the differences between Boston and other cities' capacities to produce leaders in the introduction of *Puritan Boston and Quaker Philadelphia*:

   > A clue to the relationship between hierarchy and leadership is suggested by [John] Gardner's list of Founding Fathers. *All* these men

were reared in Massachusetts or Virginia; *none* was reared in the colony of Pennsylvania, though Philadelphia was the largest city in the new nation and contained the wealthiest, most successful, gayest, and most brilliant elite in the land. Not only had Pennsylvanians little to do with taking the lead in our nation's founding, but the state has produced very few distinguished Americans throughout our history.... Thus, [the] list of 400 notable Americans in the *Encyclopedia of American History* shows that Massachusetts produced twice as many prominent individuals as did Virginia and more than three times as many as Pennsylvania. As might be expected, moreover, Virginia led in the proportion of men of power and authority (including presidents of the the United States); Massachusetts, providing a more balanced group of leaders, excelled in arts and letters; Pennsylvanians were more likely to be men of innovation and change, a large proportion of whom made their careers outside the state. Indeed, the sole president from Pennsylvania, James Buchanan, was one of the weakest in American history (1979, pp. 4-5).

9. A scholarly study of the "Boston Trustee" has yet to be written. Valuable light on the subject is shed by Donald Holbrook's *The Boston Trustee* (1937), by "Boston," *Fortune* (1933), by William J. Sheehan's "Unique to Boston Are the Famous 'Boston Trustees,'" (1934), and by the biographies of such notable trustees as Philip Dexter and William Minot in the Harvard classbooks.

Important insight into the growing power of trustees is provided by a stockholder protest by J. C. Ayer, *Some of the Uses and Abuses in the Management of Our Manufacturing Corporations* (1863). Although Ayer directed most of his barbs at the MHLI, they are equally applicable to private trustees, since the leading ones were also officers and directors of the company. Describing the power of trustees, Ayer wrote:

> By their position, with the affairs of the Corporation closed to all but themselves, they can buy stock when it has been prosperous, and sell out to the innocent public when it has been unfortunate.... Manufacturing stocks are holden in large proportion by women, widows, orphan children, charitable institutions, and retired old men, who are dependent on them for their support. The proxy vote of nearly all of these can always be gathered by the officers because they alone know who they are." (p. 16).

10. For an account of the separation of ownership and management in the administration of the financial affairs of wealthy families, see George M. Marcus and Peter Dobkin Hall, *Lives in Trust: The Fortunes of Dynastic Families in Late Twentieth Century America* (1992) and George M. Marcus (Ed.), *Elites: Ethnographic Issues* (1983).

11. Gray's sentiment was echoed a century later by Harvard law professor Erwin N. Griswold, who described spendthrift trusts as devices "designed to protect the fortunes of Pennsylvania manufacturers and Massachusetts shipping and textile

overlords from the depredations of their extravagant, and none too competent progeny" (1947, p. 31).

12. On Harvard's shift toward recruiting members of the elite as faculty, see Ronald Story (1981, pp. 57-88). Massachusetts General Hospital was no less closely tied to the merchants who governed and funded it: The hospital's first two staff physicians, both of whom served for more than 20 years, were James Jackson, son of merchant Jonathan Jackson and husband of Elizabeth Cabot, and John Collins Warren, whose father-in-law, merchant Jonathan Mason, was a cofounder and director of the Massachusetts Bank. Later appointments also drew from the pool of merchant sons, including Henry Ingersoll Bowditch, Samuel Cabot, Henry J. Bigelow, Algernon Coolidge, J. B. S. Jackson, Francis Minot, George W. Otis, George and Samuel Parkman, George C. Shattuck, Benjamin S. Shaw, D. H. Storer, and J. Mason Warren.

13. In the Amory, Cabot, Codman, Higginson, Jackson, Lawrence, Lee, Lowell, and Peabody families, of the cohort of sons born 1760-1779 (and coming to maturity in the years 1780-1799), less than 30 percent attended Harvard. For sons born after 1760, the proportion climbed steeply: 55 percent of the 1780-1799 cohort attended; 80 percent of the 1800-1819 and 1820-1839 cohorts attended. Initially, college education had been used as a way of steering sons into nonbusiness occupations. By the second quarter of the 19th century, higher education was being made available to all sons. One reason for this, it appears, is that Harvard came to be viewed as an arena for testing the competence of future leaders of business and the professions. See P. D. Hall, "Family Structure and Economic Organization: Massachusetts Merchants, 1700-1850" (1977, pp. 38-61).

14. It also appears that the motives underlying these litigations, though certainly self-serving, also had political elements. David B. Hill, a major figure in the anti-Tammany faction of New York's Democratic party, was involved in both cases. Unfortunately, neither the press of the period nor Hill's own papers illuminate whether his motives were self-serving or based on a principled opposition to private philanthropy.

15. Again, politics seems to have played a critical role in the decision. According to Tilden's biographer,

> This division of the Court of Appeals was composed of judges of the Supreme Court temporarily designated by Governor Hill to assist in clearing its clogged calendar. Angling for votes for the United States Senatorship, Hill promised Samuel J. Tilden, II, who was on his military staff, that he would "fix it" so the family and creditors would "succeed in what they wanted." Hence he arranged to have the case brought before the second division, on which sat two judges "who would positively vote against the validity of the Tilden will and one other who, he thought, might." The last named judge was Alton B. Parker, whose vote turned the decision "against the validity of the will." (Flick, 1939, pp. 515-516).

16. As in the Tilden case, politics seems to have played an important role. The litigation was initiated by Charles P. Bacon, a student at Cornell University who also served as a clerk in the law office of democratic notable David B. Hill (who

also played a key role in challenging the Tilden Trust). Hill acted as associate counsel to those seeking to break the will, although as Lieutenant-Governor he was one of the trustees of the university.

17. His widow, in fact, played a leading role in the 1914 hearings of the Walsh Commission, a congressional investigation of the impact of foundation philanthropy on American economic and political life. On this, see *Industrial Relations: Final Report and Testimony Submitted to Congress by the Commission on Industrial Relations* (1916). Mrs. Harriman also was a major supporter of William H. Allen, one of the Progressive Era's sharpest critics of foundations and the wealthy people who created and controlled them. She wrote the foreward to his critical study of philanthropic practices; see William H. Allen, *Modern Philanthropy: A Study in Efficient Appealing and Giving* (1912).

18. On this, see Arthur T. Vanderbilt II, *Fortune's Children: The Fall of the House of Vanderbilt* (1989) and Dominick Dunne, "American Dynasty: Twilight of the Vanderbilts" (1995). On the Astors, see Derek Wilson, *The Astors, 1763-1992* (1993).

19. Joseph Ernst, "The Rockefeller Archives," January 1955, RG-2, Family, JDR3rd General Files, Box 3, no folder, Rockefeller Archive Center.

20. Maureen Dowd, "Liberties; Ted's Excellent Idea," (1996). In this op-ed piece, Turner criticized his fellow billionaires for their stinginess and challenged them to follow Carnegie's example in giving generously during their lifetimes.

References

Adams, H. (1931). *The education of Henry Adams*. New York: Modern Library. (Originally published in 1918.)

Allen, W. H. (1912). *Modern philanthropy: A study in efficient appealing and giving*. New York: Dodd, Mead.

American millionaires and their public gifts. (1893). *The Review of Reviews, 7*, 37, 48-60.

Ames, J. B. (1913). The failure of the Tilden Trust. In J. B. Ames (Ed.), *Essays in legal history* (pp. 285-297). Cambridge, MA: Harvard University Press.

Ayer, J. C. (1863). *Some of the uses and abuses in the management of our manufacturing corporations*. Lowell, MA: C. M. Langley and Company.

Baltzell, E. D. (1979). *Puritan Boston and Quaker Philadelphia: Two Protestant ethics and the spirit of class authority and leadership*. New York: Free Press.

Bender, T. (1987). *New York intellect: A history of intellectual life in New York City from 1750 to the beginnings of our own time*. New York: Knopf.

Bender, T. (1993). *Intellect and public life: Essays on the social history of academic intellectuals in the United States*. Baltimore: Johns Hopkins University Press.

Berle, A. A., Jr., & Means, G. C. (1933). *The modern corporation and private property*. New York: Macmillan.

Boston. (1933). *Fortune, 8*(2): 2, 27-29, 32-36, 98-106.

Curran, W. L. (1951). The struggle for equity jurisdiction in Massachusetts. *Boston University Law Review, 31*, 269-296.

de Tocqueville, A. (1945). *Democracy in America* (Henry Reeve, trans.). New York: Vintage Books. (Original published in 1840)

Dowd, M. (1996). Liberties: Ted's excellent idea. *New York Times* (August 22), A25.

Dunne, D. (1995). American dynasty: Twilight of the Vanderbilts. *Vanity Fair, 58*(1): 188ff.

Eliot, S. A. (1845). Public and private charities of Boston. *North American Review, 56*, 135-159.

Eliot, S. A. (1860). Charities of Boston. *North American Review, 71*, 149-165.

Encyclopaedia Britannica. 1911. New York: Encyclopaedia Britannica Company, Vol. 9, 726-727.

Flick, A. C. (1939). *Samuel Jones Tilden: A study in political sagacity.* New York: Dodd, Mead.

Fosdick, R. (1952). *The story of the Rockefeller Foundation.* New York: Harper and Row.

Gray, J. C. (1882). *Restraints on the alienation of property.* Boston: Boston Book Company.

Griswold, E. N. (1947). *Spendthrift trusts under the New York statutes and elsewhere.* Albany: Matthew Bender.

Hagar, G. J. (1904). Magnitude of American benefactions. *The Review of Reviews, 29*, 464-465.

Hall, P. D. (1977). Family structure and economic organization: Massachusetts merchants, 1700-1850. In T. K. Hareven (Ed.), *Family and kin in urban communities, 1700-1930* (pp. 38-61). New York: New Viewpoints.

Hall, P. D. (1992). Cultures of trusteeship in the United States. In P. D. Hall (Ed.), *Inventing the nonprofit sector and other essays on philanthropy, voluntarism, and nonprofit organizations* (pp. 135-206). Baltimore: Johns Hopkins University Press.

Hammack, D. C. (1982). *Power and society: Greater New York at the turn of the century.* New York: Columbia University Press.

"The Gospel of Wealth." (1889/1900). In Andrew Carnegie, *The gospel of wealth and other timely essays.* New York: The Century Company, pp. 1-46.

Harvard College and Massachusetts General Hospital v. Francis Amory, Trustee. (1829). *Pickman's Reports, 9*, 446-465.

Higginson, T. W. (Ed.). (1866). *The Harvard memorial biographies.* Cambridge: Sever and Francis.

Hirchler, E. S. (1939). A survey of charitable trusts in Virginia, *Virginia Law Review, 25*, 109-116.

Holbrook, D. (1937). *The Boston trustee.* Boston: Marshall Jones.

Holmes, O. W. (1957). *Autocrat of the breakfast table.* New York: Sagamore Press. (Original published in 1854)

Holmes, O. W. (1961). *Elsie Venner: A romance of destiny.* New York: New American Library. (Original published in 1859)

Horowitz, M. J. (1977). *The transformation of American law, 1780-1860.* Cambridge, MA: Harvard University Press.

Industrial relations: Final report and testimony submitted to Congress by the Commission on Industrial Relations. (1916). 64th Congress, 1st Session, Document 415 (Washington, DC: Government Printing Office.

Jaher, F. C. (1982). *The urban establishment: Upper strata in Boston, New York, Charleston, Chicago, and Los Angeles.* Urbana: University of Illinois Press.

Katz, S. N. (1971). The politics of law in colonial America: Controversies over chancery courts and equity law in the eighteenth century. In D. Fleming & B. Bailyn (Eds.), *Law in American history* (pp. 257-288). Boston: Little, Brown.

Katz, S. N., Sullivan, B., & Beach, C. P. (1985). Legal change and legal autonomy: Charitable trusts in New York, 1777-1893. *Law and Society Review, 3*(1): 51-89.

Koch, A. (Ed.). (1965). *The American enlightenment.* New York: George Braziller.

Kolko, G. (1967). Brahmins and businessmen. In B. Moore & K. Wolfe (Eds.), *The Critical spirit: Essays in honor of Herbert Marcuse* (pp. 348-365). Boston: Beacon Press.

Langbein, J. H. (1988). The twentieth century revolution in wealth transmission. *Michigan Law Review, 84*, 723-750.

Langbein, J. H. (1993). Chancellor Kent and the history of legal literature. *Columbia Law Review, 93*, 547-610.

Liverant, S., & and Hitchler, W. H. (1933). A history of equity in Pennsylvania. *Dickinson Law Review*, *37*, 156-183.

Marcus, G. E. (Ed.). (1983). *Elites: Ethnographic issues*. Albuquerque: University of New Mexico Press.

Marcus, G. E., & Hall, P. D. (1992). *Lives in trust: The fortunes of dynastic families in late twentieth century America*. Boulder, CO: Westview Press.

Miller, H. S. (1961). *Legal foundations of American philanthropy*. Madison: State Historical Society of Wisconsin.

Nelson, W. E. (1975). *Americanization of the common law: The impact of legal change on Massachusetts society, 1760-1830*. Cambridge, MA: Harvard University Press.

Newhall, G. (1942). *Future interests and the rule against perpetuities in Massachusetts*. Boston: E. W. Hildreth.

Newmyer, K. (1985). *Supreme Court Justice Joseph Story: Statesman of the old republic*. Chapel Hill: University of North Carolina Press.

Nichols v. Eaton. (1875). *United States reports*, 716-722.

Nightingale v. Burrell. (1833). *Massachusetts Reports*, 22, 104ff.

Perry, J. W. (1872). *A treatise on the law of trusts and trustees*. Boston: Little, Brown.

Pound, R. (1938). *The formative era of American law*. Boston: Little, Brown.

Prescott v. Tarbell. 1 *Massachusetts Reports* (1804).

Scott, A. W. (1939). *The law of trusts*. Boston: Little, Brown.

Scott, A. W. (1951). Charitable trusts in New York. *New York University Law Review*, *26*(2), 251-275.

Sheehan, W. J. (1934). Unique to Boston are the famous "Boston trustees," *Boston Transcript* (July 21), 1.

Stead, W. T. (1893). Jay Gould: A character sketch. *The Review of Reviews*, 7, 37.

Story, J. (1820). Chancery jurisdiction. *North American Review*, *9*, 161-170.

Story, J. (1836). *Commentaries on equity jurisprudence as administered in England and America*. Boston: Hilliard, Gray.

Story, R. (1972). *Class development and cultural institutions in Boston, 1800-1870*. Ph.D. dissertation, State University of New York at Stony Brook.

Story, R. (1981). *Forging of an aristocracy: Harvard and the Boston upper class, 1800-1870*. Middletown, CT: Wesleyan University Press.

Story, W. W. (Ed.) (1851). *Life and letters of Joseph Story*. Boston: Charles C. Little and James Brown.

Vanderbilt, A. T., II. (1989). *Fortune's children: The fall of the house of Vanderbilt*. New York: William Morrow.

Warner, S. B. (1968). *The private city: Philadelphia in three periods of growth*. Philadelphia: University of Pennsylvania Press.

White, G. T. (1957). *History of the Massachusetts Hospital Life Insurance Company*. Cambridge, MA: Harvard University Press.

Whitehead, J. S. (1973). *The separation of college and state: Columbia, Dartmouth, Harvard, and Yale, 1776-1876*. New Haven: Yale University Press.

Wilson, D. (1993). *The Astors, 1763-1992*. London: Weidenfeld and Nicholson.

Woodruff, E. H. (1889). Chancery in Massachusetts, *Law Quarterly Review*, 5, 370-386.

8

Will Contests

Legacies of Aging and Social Change

JEFFREY P. ROSENFELD

If you want them to mourn, you had best leave them nothing.

—MARTIAL, A.D. 70

Give your heirs more to fight over.

—BARRON'S, APRIL 1996

Introduction

Disinheritance and will contests are deviant components of the inheritance system. Inheritance is predicated on social norms that maintain family and kinship structures. Within the nuclear family, for example, it is normative for wealth to pass first from spouse to spouse, and then from generation to generation. Disinheritance is an intentional departure from the norm of intergenerational continuity and is the deviant behavior of the benefactor.

A will contest is deviant behavior of beneficiaries. Just as the inheritance system is predicated on the benefactor's decisions, so does it rest on the assumption that beneficiaries will abide by those decisions. Will contests violate the social norm that inheritance should be a consensus-producing

JEFFREY P. ROSENFELD • Department of Sociology, Nassau Community College, Garden City, New York 11530.

Inheritance and Wealth in America, edited by Robert K. Miller, Jr., and Stephen J. McNamee. Plenum Press, New York, 1998.

173

event. They represent conflict between and among beneficiaries, and sometimes among those who argue that they should have been beneficiaries.

Disinheritance has become increasingly rare. A combination of social, legal, and financial changes have resulted in fewer cases where a benefactor disinherits a son or daughter. For example, wills have become increasingly standardized during the past 50 years. The legalistic boilerplate is not conducive to something as personal as disinheritance. More important, changes in estate, inheritance, and gift-tax law encourage sanctions during the benefactor's lifetime rather than after death. It is now easier to make gifts to some sons and/or daughters or to give them power of attorney during the parent's lifetime. As a result, disinheritance has become a statistically rare and economically insignificant feature of the inheritance system.

Will contests are socially and economically significant events, however. They can rupture and realign the social fabric of families and keep millions of dollars tied up in litigation for years. Statistically, they are rare events, occurring in fewer than 3 percent of probated estates. But will contests often involve large estates and can create decades of ill will in families.

This chapter reports on in-depth interviews with twenty-eight estate-litigators. Estate-litigators are attorneys who specialize in will contests. The interviews were conducted in 1995 and indicate that the incidence of will contests has remained about the same over the past 30 years, but that the social causation is changing. In 1975, for example, the majority of will contests occured in families where there had been divorce and remarriage. Sociologically speaking, estate litigation in 1975 reflected the ambiguity of power and status in reconstituted families more than any other social condition. In 1995, divorce/remarriage was still a frequent cause of estate litigation, but close behind is conflict over inheritance based on other causal factors. The three most significant of these are

- *Home Health Care:* Some aged decedents are naming a nurse or home-health aide as major beneficiary instead of family members.
- *The HIV Epidemic:* HIV-positive people living openly gay lifestyles are naming a lover or close friend as major beneficiary instead of family members.
- *New Roles for Older Americans*: Elderly people in unconventional relationships or lifestyles are naming friends, companions, or organizations as major beneficiary instead of family members.

In short, recent data on will contests indicate that they are legacies of social and demographic change. The decision to litigate over a decedent's estate plan is closely linked to the complexities of aging, chronic illness, and alternate lifestyles, which are becoming more common than ever before in the United States today.

New Roles, New Beneficiaries

Martial had heirs in mind when he wrote, "If you want them to mourn, you had best leave them nothing." But if he were writing today from Boston or Portland instead of Rome in A.D. 70, he would have to expand the list of mourners. Massive changes in family structure, coupled with new roles and lifestyles for older Americans, have broadened the ranks of people and organizations claiming a share of the decedent's estate.

More older Americans than ever before are becoming involved in church, civic, and social activity. In fact, a 1994 survey on this subject indicates that there has been a 7 percent increase in volunteerism and community service among older Americans over the past five years. The survey, which focused on giving and volunteering in the United States, found that the percentage of people aged seventy-five or older who said they had done some volunteer work during the past twelve months rose from 29 percent in 1988 to 36 percent in 1993 (Giving and volunteering in the United States, 1994, pp. 39–41). Such activities provide important psychic benefits to older Americans, including feelings of revitalization and connection to the larger community (Wolfe, 1994, p. 32). Older people are also involved in new family forms and functions, which are impacting on their trusts and estate plans as when, for example,

- An elderly person acts *in loco parentis* for a grandchild. As of 1991, an estimated 3.2 million grandchildren were living full-time with a grandparent rather than a mother or father (Creighton, 1991, p. 83).
- An older person becomes a stepgrandparent because a son or daughter has remarried.
- People sixty-five or older immerse themselves in close-knit peer groups. In many cases, meaningful involvements with peers become functional equivalents of family for older people, especially those who have lost contact with their children (Rosenfeld, 1980, 1991; Friedan, 1993). In fact, a recent survey of affluent older people (Neuberger and Berman, 1993, pp. 5–8) found that 11 percent of those sampled said they anticipated making bequests outside family as a result of their outside relationships.

Until recently, fewer than 2 percent of probated wills actually resulted in litigation. Irate or anxious family members might have threatened to contest a will. But prior to 1980, estate litigation was a rare event and one that reflected common faultlines of family life: divorce, remarriage, and sibling rivalry. How often does such legal action occur today? And what motivates it? Interviews with estate-litigators indicate that estate litigation reflects social and demographic changes reshaping marriage and family life across America.

Estate-Litigators: A Snowball Sample

Snowball sampling is a useful way of gathering data when little is known about a population or social process. A snowball sample is *purposive* and not random. In snowball sampling, the people who have been interviewed are encouraged to refer others to the interviewer; thus, sample size increases through referrals, much like the proverbial snowball rolling down a hill. Snowball sampling is appropriate for exploratory or preliminary research (Waitz, 1991) because it maximizes the inclusion of respondents with a particular set of characteristics.

In this case, the snowball sample was comprised of attorneys who specialize in estate litigation, who practice in large or midsized law firms, and who have been doing estate litigation for at least five years. The original sample was comprised of seventeen estate-litigators. They, in turn, referred eleven more.

The data consist of twenty-eight telephone interviews with estate-litigators in New York, Boston, Chicago, and Washington, D.C. The interview was semistructured in the sense that it always included a set of standard questions (see Appendix A for the semistructured interview schedule) but also permitted respondents to provide additional information if they wished to do so. The information they supplied is purely anecdotal, but it calls attention to the social and demographic contexts in which estate litigation occurs.

Social and Demographic Contexts of Estate Litigation

Social and demographic change are common threads running through most of the interviews. The twenty-eight estate-litigators who shared their opinions and experiences for this study repeatedly linked will contests with changes in family structure and the inability of families to control bequests to outsiders such as charities, friends, or organizations.

Most of the changes in family structure occurred when people had been divorced and remarried, or were step(grand)parents. Sociologically speaking, these are social relationships in which norms and reciprocities are as yet undefined. In other words, there is no simple or standard formula for bequeathing wealth to stepchildren or stepgrandchildren.

There are also situations where family members feel they cannot control bequests to outsiders, and they take legal action for that reason. For example, what is the appropriate legacy for a gay son's lover, or for the dedicated home-health aide who nursed a parent for years? Such bequests are socially uncharted in terms of norms, values, and reciprocities. This is why old age means more than new relationships. It also means new strains and conflicts.

TABLE 8.1. Social and Demographic Contexts
of Estate Litigation

Responses to the question, "What were the reasons for the five most
recent will contests in your caseload?"

Changes in family structure	42.8%	(*n* = 60)
Impact of divorce and remarriage	32.1%	(*n* = 45)
Impact of chronic illness and long-term care	15.0%	(*n* = 21)
New roles and lifestyles for elderly people	4.3%	(*n* = 6)
Homophobia/AIDS epidemic	3.5%	(*n* = 5)
Other	2.3%	(*n* = 3)
		N = 140

Table 8.1 summarizes the social/demographic context of estate litigation,
as reported by the twenty-eight respondents who were interviewed for this
study. All twenty-eight were asked to describe the reasons for the five most
recent will contests in their caseloads. Instead of focusing on legal issues such
as undue influence or testamentary capacity, the semistructured interview
probed for social and demographic information. This information is summarized by the frequency distribution in Table 8.1.

The largest single category can best be called (1) changes in family
structure (42.8 percent), because it refers to changes in status and power
among survivors, particularly siblings. Following this came (2) *impact of
divorce and remarriage* (32.1 percent), which referred to conflicts between
first and second spouses, or children and stepchildren. After this came (3) *impact of chronic illness and long-term care* (15.0 percent), which usually
pivoted on bequests to a nurse or home-health aide. Other categories included (4) *new roles and lifestyles for elderly people* (4.3 percent), and
(5) *homophobia/AIDS epidemic* (3.5 percent). These are summarized according to frequency, starting with the largest category.

Changes in Family Structure (42.8 Percent)

Virtually all lawyers interviewed for this study said they had recently
handled cases in which estate litigation followed realignments in family structure after an older person had died. Their descriptions of families that had
retained them were refreshingly free of sociological jargon but nevertheless
spoke to changes in power and status. "Many of my cases result from shifts in
power and control during probate," says a lawyer from an affluent suburb in
the greater New York area. "Siblings just go to war. They have no loyalty to
each other or to their family." An estate-litigator from Chicago adds, "There are

fewer sibling bonds." In fact, his heavy caseload consisted mostly of siblings either as proponents or contestants in will contests.

"It's not just kids from stepfamilies," concludes an estate-litigator from Washington, D.C. "It's siblings from the same family, which is something I would not have seen fifteen years ago." When asked what could explain the increase in sibling conflict, he said, "I suppose it's a breakdown in the family. Families are not so effective at controlling kids as they once were." If this is a problem in conjugal families where parents had never divorced, it is amplified in the reconstituted, or stepfamilies that are created when divorced or widowed people with children remarry.

One attorney practicing in Boston added that his caseload was skewed heavily toward litigation over men's estates. "It's the dad's," he said, "not the mom's." When asked why, he mentioned that men "are still entrepreneurial, even at eighty-five. They scheme more." In this context, it is worth mentioning the comment of an estate-litigator from Chicago, who recalls that a client once asked, "Can I deprive my spouse of her share?" (He went on to mention that a husband actually *can* deprive his wife of her spousal share, but only in a joint tenancy account.)

Another attorney, this one from a wealthy New York suburb, echoed the idea that estate litigation occurs more frequently after a father's death than after a mother's death. "Men are more apt to remarry. And I've [recently] handled cases where a man told one story to his kids from the first marriage, and another story to his second wife." A lawyer from Washington, D.C., mentioned that he is familiar with cases where a wife and a mistress took legal action over a decedent's estate, as well as other cases in which the first and the second spouse went to court. Men are also more likely to have children from second or third marriages, thus complicating probate even further when they die. Finally, men often die leaving more assets. For all of these reasons, men's estates are more conflict-prone.

The Impact of Divorce and Remarriage (32.1 Percent)

It is a familiar fact that divorce and remarriage have reshaped family life in the United States. At present, the United States may have the highest divorce rate in the world. In 1988, for example, there were twenty-one divorces per 1,000 married women aged fifteen or older. Along with divorce, remarriage has become a reality in American life. Sixty percent of women and 70 percent of men who divorce will eventually remarry (Eshleman, 1991, p. 511). Remarriage creates social units called step- or reconstituted families. The reconstituted family has already been identified in the sociological literature as a crucible of ambiguity, or what sociologist Andrew Cherlin (1978) has referred to as an "incomplete institution" that affects child care, parenting, and the relationship between remarried spouses. Inheritance of wealth has also been affected by the proliferation of this "incomplete institution."

Virtually all of the estate-litigators in the sample (94 percent) mentioned that a significant number of their clients came from reconstituted families. Typically, the contest involved the estate of an older man who had divorced and then remarried. This is "major" in my practice [in a wealthy New York suburb]," said one New York attorney. An estate-litigator from Boston mentioned that in many of the cases he handles, the litigation pits the decedent's children from a first marriage against the second wife. This was echoed by an estate-litigator from Chicago: "It's either the children versus the stepmother, or the children from [the decedent's] two marriages slugging it out," and takes the form of "a second marriage, a 'trophy wife' versus kids."

"Even when there is a QTIP [qualified terminal interest in property]", observes a Boston lawyer, "the kids [from the first marriage] are prone to grab the second wife's share." The QTIP arrangement can sometimes prevent this form of conflict by ensuring that the second spouse only gets a qualified interest in property and that remarriage of the spouse will not alter the decedent's bequest goals. Yet even the presence of a QTIP does not prevent estate litigation in some reconstituted families.

Three of the most important surveys of beneficiaries and their social behavior (Sussman, Cates, and Smith, 1970; Fellows, Simon, and Rau, 1978; Titus, Rosenblatt, and Anderson, 1979) were done during the 1970s. All three of the studies found that stepfamilies were litigation-prone during probate. Such families lacked the cohesion and social controls necessary to avoid legal intervention. That finding gains salience today, because an estimated 1,300 stepfamilies are being formed every day (Maglin and Schniedewind, 1989, p. 13). More than 6 million children live with the biological mother and a stepfather; 740,000 live with the biological father and a stepmother. In fact, divorce and remarriage have become so common that Larson (1992, p. 37) predicts more than half of Americans today are or will be in "step situations." An estimated 20 percent of U.S. grandparents are already stepgrandparents because of the divorcing and remarrying their children have done (Rosenfeld, 1992a). As Titus et al. (1979, p. 16) observed years ago, the "strain and structural ambiguity present in step relationships ... seems to be a source of conflict over inheritance."

The Impact of Chronic Illness and Long-Term Health Care (15.0 Percent)

It is well known that the U.S. population is aging. The 1990 census counted 31.1 million people aged sixty-five and older, or 12.5 percent of the population. This represents a 22 percent increase over the 1980 census figures

(Taeuber, 1992, p. v). As chronological age increases, so too does the probability of having multiple chronic illnesses. Many of these chronic conditions require assistance of some kind. For example, a Census Bureau study done in 1990 reports that 17.2 percent of men and 30.2 percent of women over the age of 75 needed some kind of assistance with everyday activities (as cited in Taeuber, 1992, pp. 3–13). An estimated 9–11 million elderly people require such assistance (Braus, 1994, p. 40).

This demographic fact has spawned a $21 billion home health-care industry in the United States. The percentage of elderly people living with an adult child actually declined from 7.5 percent in 1980 to 4.8 percent in 1991. Home health-care workers have stepped in to take up the slack. Some are also ending up as beneficiaries in the trusts and estate plans of the elderly people they care for.

The best publicized will contest in recent years, *Johnson v. Johnson*, pivoted around the decedent's decision to leave the bulk of his billion-dollar estate to the young woman who was first his nurse and then his wife (Margolick, 1993). Fifty-six percent of the estate-litigators in this snowball sample said they were familiar with cases in which families were litigating to overturn a bequest to a caregiver. "I now see more cases involving custodians," says an estate-litigator from the New York area. "The kids can't cope with a parent's illness. But they get riled over gifts to the caretaker when the parent dies." Another New York attorney adds, "There has been a huge rise in litigation over power of attorney now that there are so many more caretakers." His counterpart in Chicago observes that "much estate litigation now centers on caretaking issues … and we are seeing more elderly people who want to reciprocate for home health care with bequests to the caregiver."

Hanks and Sussman (1991) propose an informal arrangement they call the "inheritance contract" as a way of legitimizing the linkage between home health care and inheritance. They point to the fact that many older people already reciprocate for home health care by leaving a larger bequest for the son or, more typically, the daughter, who has provided the care. "Inheritance contracting" would be a way of minimizing conflict and legal action during probate by specifying the quid pro quo basis for inheritance while the elderly parent was still alive. Although inheritance contracting is quite unusual right now, it is consistent with new forms of communication on inheritance issues and may be more commonplace in years to come.

New Roles and Lifestyles for Elderly People (4.3 Percent)

Betty Friedan (1993, pp. 39, 385–386) observes that the elderly are almost always stereotyped as frail and chronically ill. Such catastrophic theories of aging emphasize the "plight" of the elderly and the "problem" of age but ignore the fact that many elderly people live vital and dynamic lives. This includes small but growing numbers of older people who enter into nontraditional roles and relationships.

Larsen (1991, pp. 32–33) reports, for example, that an estimated 5 percent of American families now consist of a grandparent raising a grandchild. Such "unplanned parenthood," as Larsen calls it, cuts across class and ethnic lines, affecting well-to-do households as well as poverty-stricken ones. Unplanned parenthood means assuming full-time responsibility for childcare at a point in life when the norm is to be finished with such obligations. Often, an older person assumes childcare responsibilities for offspring who are alcoholic, substance abusers, or otherwise incapable of caring for themselves. This commonly results in the formation of custodial and caretaker trusts so that these children will be taken care of in the event that something happens to the grandparent(s).

Apart from unconventional family roles, some older people are nurturing involvements with friends and lovers. There is also a small but significant movement toward cults and fundamentalist religious groups. Collins and Frantz, writing for the influential *Modern Maturity* magazine, warn, "No longer satisfied with recruiting wide-eyed and penniless youth, the cults have shifted their focus to older people," later adding that "it's the accumulation of wealth that brought America's older population into the sights of America's cults" (pp. 23–25). Indeed, as many as one million cult members are over the age of fifty.

Eleven percent of older people surveyed for a study of estate planning indicated that they had planned to make bequests outside the family (Rosenfeld, 1992b, p. 48). Such "distancers," as they are called, had developed outside involvements with friends, neighbors, or organizations and had planned to reciprocate in their trusts and estate plans.

Five percent of the attorneys in this snowball sample said they had recently handled cases in which older people had made bequests "to a neighbor or a best friend." An attorney in Washington, D.C., gives the following illustration: "*A* has a friend and disinherits relatives in giving it to the friend instead." And from an estate-litigator in the New York area, "Branches of the family fall into and out of favor as a decedent ages. This is when a friend or charity stands to inherit a lot of money—when the family falls out of favor." An additional 6 percent had handled cases in which an older person had established custodial or caretaker trusts for a grandchild under his or her care. One respondent had been involved in estate litigation over a large bequest to a fundamentalist religious group. The attorney, who practices in Chicago, was retained by the decedent's family to contest the bequest on grounds of undue influence and testamentary capacity.

Homophobia and the AIDS Epidemic (3.5 Percent)

The fifth most common cause of will contests is not related to aging but is socially significant in its own right. Homophobia and dread of HIV disease are responsible for a rise in litigation over the estates of gay men who die relatively young. American society is reeling from the AIDS epidemic. AIDS is now the leading killer of young people in the United States and has reshaped the sexual, social, and political behavior of millions of people. The family, as a social institution, has been particularly hard-hit by the AIDS epidemic. According to sociologist Rose Waitz (1991, p. 103), "Following diagnosis with a serious illness or other similar trauma, most persons will turn to their families for support. For persons with HIV disease, however, this coping strategy is fraught with dangers." Families often shun or isolate a son or daughter with AIDS (Waitz, 1991). The diagnosis can prompt homophobic feelings and actions, especially if the illness can be attributed to homosexual behavior rather than intravenous drug use. At least among the estate-litigators interviewed for this study, there has also been an increase in estate litigation following the death of a person with AIDS. Thirty-five percent of the attorneys in this snowball sample mentioned that they were seeing such an increase. "HIV disease is definitely a factor in estate litigation today" in the opinion of an attorney from the greater New York area.

Most persons dying of AIDS have already done some estate planning. "Actually, they gay community is more attuned to estate planning," says an estate-litigator who practices in Chicago. "Being diagnosed HIV positive is an automatic message to plan. And there is an ABA [American Bar Association] committee set up to provide assistance for persons with AIDS." And one attorney reminisces, "I've handled cases where the estate passed to three gay men, a serial inheritance" after the first and then the second one died. The AIDS victims whose wills are contested tend to have larger estates, and this after the dramatic cost of medical treatment. Yet lawyers also mentioned that estate litigation sometimes ocurred when the estate was of no value, and that it reflected conflict and ambivalence more than economic concerns.

In spite of all this estate planning, families are more apt to contest the will of a person with AIDS, especially when he or she names a lover as sole or major beneficiary. "The family is in denial. I've heard families accuse the lover of infecting their son," says one estate-litigator from Boston. An attorney in New York, saddened by the behavior he has seen, says, "Families go through a unique grieving process when a son dies of AIDS. Part of that process is denial. Estate litigation can be one way that this denial gets expressed."

Twelve percent of attorneys interviewed for this study said that they had recently handled cases in which estate litigation was motivated by homophobia, though not necessarily by fear of HIV disease. In one instance, a family contested a *per stirpes* distribution between two brothers because one of the brothers had opted for a gay lifestyle. The contesting sibling resented the fact that the father still loved and respected the brother who had adopted a lifestyle that he found unacceptable. In another case, there was hostility toward a son who was openly gay but had inherited more of his father's estate than either of his two siblings. "There was an agenda in this case," said the Boston lawyer who represented the proponent (i.e., the son). "The siblings couldn't handle the fact that my client was gay and still socially acceptable in the eyes of his father."

Other Perceptions (2.3 Percent)

Attorneys in the snowball sample said there were other issues fueling estate litigation. "Pollution," said a Boston lawyer, "is a new issue. I know of a case where there was a fuel tank on an industrial property. It polluted a nearby water supply and nobody wanted to be responsible for cleaning it up. So both sides contested to *avoid* being responsible." Another attorney from Boston said he had recently handled a case where "nobody wanted to take responsibility for a piece of real estate, not even the charitable organization that could have inherited it."

Will Contests: Frequency and Net Worth

The popular stereotype is that estate litigation is on the rise throughout the United States. There is no shortage of books, movies, and talk-show segments dealing with this theme. Even some lawyers and probate judges believe that there has been what one probate judge from Houston calls an "avalanche of estate litigation."

Incidence of Estate Litigation

Fifty-four percent of lawyers interviewed for this study believe that the incidence of estate litigation is increasing. The response of an attorney from Chicago, which describes estate litigation as an up-and-coming specialty for lawyers, typifies this viewpoint. As he puts it, "Estate litigation is a growth area for lawyers" because "there are more and more challenges to wills." Similarly, an attorney from Boston says, "We live in a litigious society, and will contests are on the rise just like other forms of litigation."

Lawyers who specialize in estate litigation are probably experiencing an increase in the number of cases that cross their desks every month. And this might explain why they assume there is an avalanche of will contests. After all, more people now die testate than ever before.

But although the absolute *number* of will contests may be rising, the *proportion* of probated wills that is contested has not increased. At least this is true in New York State, one of the few states that keeps annual records on probate, objections raised, and trials/hearings. In New York, it is possible to compare the percentage of contested wills in 1983 and 1993. Table 8.2 indicates that statewide, the absolute number of probates and will contests both increased between 1983 and 1993, but the *proportion* of will contests did not. Statistically speaking, there has not been an increase in estate litigation New York between 1983 and 1993.

Size of Estates Involved in Will Contests

Most lawyers interviewed for this study assume that estate litigation is a maneuver of the very rich. "Estate litigation gets interesting when there are *really* valuable assets ... and that's because the people with those assets *really* know about lawyers," says an estate-litigator from New York City. The implication is that estate litigation requires access to legal expertise and enough funds to pay for the best. This is echoed in the comments of a lawyer from Washington, D.C.: "Larger estates? Yes! Money has a lot to do with it, *or* the feeling that a fiduciary was not fit or competent to act." Eighty-six percent of lawyers in this snowball sample ($N = 28$) believe that estate litigation typically involved large—often the largest—estates.

Interestingly, the remainder insist that estate litigation sometimes occurs when there is not much wealth at stake. A Boston lawyer reminisces that she has had clients who litigated over dishes and a car, "really minimal assets." When asked why this had happened, she said, "They felt that they had been wronged and wanted their day in court." This is consistent with Schoenblum's (1987, p. 615) finding that "smaller estates generate at least as much, if not more, controversy than larger estates." Data on the dollar-value and estate litigation are available for selected counties in New York State for Judicial Year

TABLE 8.2. Hearings and Objections
as a Percentage of Probates
in New York State, 1983 and 1993

	Probates	Hearings and objections	%
1983	39,309	4,032	10.2
1993	44,647	4,407	9.9

TABLE 8.3. Objections and Hearings as a Percentage of Probates
in Selected New York Counties, 1993, by Value of Estate

	County					
	New York		Nassau		Monroe	
Value of estate	Probates	% Contested	Probates	% Contested	Probates	% Contested
Less than $10K	66	—	62	—	88	—
$10K under $20K	127	2.2	98	1.0	117	0.8
$20K under $50K	232	—	198	1.5	358	0.2
$50K under $100K	288	.1	239	—	246	0.8
$100K under $250K	474	1.7	635	0.6	451	0.4
$250K under $500K	444	2.9	812	1.1	497	0.6
$500K or more	948	2.6	817	1.1	620	1.1

1993. This information appears in Table 8.3, which indicates that smaller estates generate about as much litigation as larger estates, which is consistent with data from Davidson County, Tennessee (Schoenblum, 1987, pp. 612–614). It would appear that cost is a major consideration but by no means the only one determining estate litigation. Perceptions of equity, communication patterns, and family structure also play a part, especially in reconstituted or stepfamilies.

Motivation for Will Contests

The decision to contest a will is often but not always based on financial concerns. There are cases in which a will contest pivots on what Schoenblum (1987, p. 616) calls "nonpecuniary impulses on the part of the contestant." Beneficiaries may take legal action out of anger or hostility toward other people mentioned in the decedent's will, or feelings that the inheritance was not equitable.

Titus et al. (1979) were among the first social researchers to elaborate on this theme. They note that estate litigation, far from being a calculated struggle for money, can sometimes be a struggle for status and power in families. After interviewing family members who were embroiled in will contests, they conclude that estate litigation can sometimes be the last in a string of disputes among conflict-habituated siblings. "In that sense," they conclude, "it resembles the 'last straw' reported in breakups in other close relationships" (p.

240). Even when siblings do get along with each other, they may become embroiled in conflict over property with sentimental or emotional value—the family bible, or the set of dishes mentioned earlier—when they perceive that it is not being distributed equitably.

As noted earlier, estate litigation increasingly involves people from non-traditional families: either the stepfamilies formed when an older person remarries, or the ones resulting from remarriage by divorced sons or daughters of an older person (Rosenfeld, 1992a, p. 173). Such reconstituted families are often plagued by "inadequate communication between survivors," especially between siblings and steprelations (Titus et al., 1979, pp. 15-16). This is because sibling bonds had broken down, or because of the "structural ambiguity" of relationships in stepfamilies. Table 8.4 indicates attorneys' responses to the following question: "Who were the parties to your five most recent will contests?" Attorneys were told to focus *only on contestants*, which is to say, the person(s) contesting a decedent's will. Thirty-four percent of contestants were stepparents or children. Phrased in a slightly different way, 38 percent of all families involved in estate litigation were reconstituted families, at least in this analysis of the five most recent cases.

Traditional forms of social control are less effective in stepfamilies, perhaps because roles and obligations of people in such relationships have yet to be defined. The "structural ambiguity" (Titus et al., 1979, pp. 19-21) of stepfamilies helps explain why stepchildren and/or second spouses are more apt to litigate, namely, they have less of a stake in the continuity of the family as a social unit.

TABLE 8.4. "The Contestants in Your
Five Most Recent Will Contests"

(Check as many as apply) Relationship to the decedent	N	%
Children	113	42.1
Stepchildren	79	29.2
Spouse (#1)	25	9.1
Spouse (#2)	11	4.1
Siblings	21	7.6
Cousins	5	2.3
Uncles/aunts	4	2.2
Other family	7	2.6
Other	2	.8
	267	100
Total number of cases:	140	
Total number of stepfamilies:	53	

Reconstituted families are a familiar and sometimes expected source of conflict during probate. Less familiar are the legal maneuverings of nonprofit organizations. Nonprofit organizations now display a willingness to litigate when decedents renege on the promise to make a charitable bequest. As Fabrikant and White (1995, p. 13) observe, "[Some] people give their money away, then take it back." Those who stood to inherit that money must then go to court to collect. John Murawski, writing in *The Chronicle of Philanthropy* (1995, p. 1), observes that a growing number of nonprofit organizations actually feel they have an *obligation* to litigate "if that is what it takes to collect on a pledge." Murawski then discusses a variety of cases in which charities have decided to sue donors or their estates when an expected bequest did not materialize. This illustrates the sociological point that the level and intensity of conflict will increase when the norms of reciprocity (Gouldner, 1960; Moller, 1990) that knit a group together are eroded or restructured. Deviant behavior, in the form of will contests, is one response to these changes in social structure. It might occur more frequently if not for powerful social controls associated with the inheritance of wealth, which are discussed in the following section.

Social Controls on Inheritance of Wealth: Judicial, Economic, and Social

That estate litigation occurs at all is significant given the deviant status of will contests in probate court and family life. The fact that it often involves people in stepfamilies, or those individuals or organizations who feel they had been promised something while the decedent was still alive, makes the behavior more comprehensible.

Beneficiaries are under enormous pressure *not* to litigate over trusts and estate plans. Probate courts throughout the United States typically favor the proponent in will contests and not the contestants. In addition, there is the economic reality that will contests are expensive. Between one-fourth and one-third of an estate can be eaten up by legal costs when parties contest a will. Finally, it is not socially acceptable to raise objections during probate. Powerful social norms work to maintain consensus, or at the very least, to prevent legal action when a decedent's will is probated. From judicial, economic, and social perspectives, then, estate litigation is deviant behavior.

Judicial Attitudes: Proponents' Claims Upheld

Probate courts throughout the United States are inclined to construe a decedent's will as the true expression of intent unless proven otherwise.

Moller (1990) observes that courts typically turn to the general morality of the transaction and tend to assume that the decedent's will reciprocates for important relationships in his or her life unless proven otherwise. "Better than 99 percent of will contests are unsuccessful," warns Bove (1993) in an article in *Worth* magazine. In fact, there are jurisdictions in which contestants can end up paying the legal fees for both sides if the probate court rules that their claim is without merit. This must be taken as serious judicial warning not to enter estate litigation frivolously.

Legal scholar Jeffrey Schoenblum (1987) documents the judicial tendency to uphold a decedent's will against challenges by contestants. Based on an analysis of the 7,638 wills filed in Davidson County, Tennessee, between 1976 and 1984, he found that estate litigation was usually decided in favor of proponents and *not* contestants. "There is a more favorable orientation toward proponents in cases decided by a judge" (p. 627).

Economic Reality: The High Cost of Litigating

Most heirs, no matter how disgruntled, are intimidated by the cost of litigation and do not contest wills for that reason. Estate litigation is usually expensive enough to make contestants think twice before taking their complaints to probate court. An attorney whose practice pivots on estate litigation warns that "some fights absolutely destroy the value of the estate. Property is degraded. Income and value go down." Another estate-litigator, this one from Atlanta, adds that "the cost of litigation is enormous. I know of a $1,000,000 joint tenancy account which accrued $400,000 in costs" as a result of litigation. He went on to say that "each side could easily generate $400,000 in costs during a large [estate] litigation case." These sentiments were echoed by an attorney employed by the New York (City) Surrogate's Court, who maintains that "will contests are so expensive that it doesn't make sense to litigate." The time, energy, and expense of litigation do dissuade most people from raising legal objections. Those who are not dissuaded by the expense are often prevented by social pressures from family and kin.

Socially Unacceptable Behavior

Apart from having a reputation as risky litigation, will contests are socially unacceptable. Social pressures and sanctions against litigious survivors also play a part in explaining the low incidence of will contests. Ever since Martial wrote his epigram in A.D. 70, it has been known that people can be unhappy with what they inherit. However, most families exert social controls on disgruntled beneficiaries. They are informally pressured to get over their disappointment and to focus instead on the social continuity of their family.

The literature on bereavement indicates, for example, that heirs and beneficiaries in close-knit families often resolve their differences out of a desire to
"move on" with their lives and preserve the social structure of their families
(Doka, 1992).

Toward an Even Less Litigious Future:
New Forms of Communication in Families

It is clear that estate litigation occurs more frequently in families where
social structure is ambiguous, or where lines of communication have broken
down. In response, families are now developing strategies to communicate
about the inheritance of wealth, which may impact on estate litigation rates in
years to come.

A small but growing number of will-writers now divulges trust and estate
plans while still alive. Some actually do so on videotape, so that there can be
no question about their intent or testamentary capacity. In recent years, estate
planners have been encouraging clients to share information about their
trusts and estate plans with beneficiaries while they are still alive. Many
families are indeed discussing—if only for tax or legal reasons—what would
have been kept strictly secret a few decades ago. Even *Fortune Magazine* has
advised its readers (Kirkland, 1986, p. 23): "Forget about locking your will
away like some nineteenth-century miser. Bring the family finances into the
daylight, so the children will know what they are getting and where it will
come from."

More recently, the investment firm of Neuberger & Berman (1993) has
surveyed wealth holders on attitudes about inheritance. Wealth holders were
asked, "Do I let my heirs know my intentions beforehand—or tell them
nothing and let them be surprised after my funeral?" The majority of wealth
holders sampled answered in the affirmative, that they do want to let their
heirs know in advance (1993, p. 9). One consequence could be a decline in
family conflict as more heirs are emotionally prepared for what they will
inherit. At very least, these heirs will be forewarned. And forewarned in
probate, as in so many other social situations, is forearmed.

ENDNOTE.   A total of 66 wills, or less than 1 percent of the 7,638 wills in
Schoenblum's sample, had been contested. In short, vindictive wills are
"permissible" as long as they meet standard requirements in terms of form,
execution, and testamentary capacity of the will-writer. The bias in favor of
proponents is familiar to most trust and estate lawyers (Bove, 1993, p. 96).

Presumably, they advise their clients that the odds of winning a will contest are quite low. Surely, they warn that estate litigation is expensive.

Appendix: Interview Schedule for Estate Litigators

1. Name: _____
2. Number of partners in your law firm: _____
3. Are you a partner? If so, how long have you been a partner? _____
4. How long have you been an estate-litigator? _____
5. What is (are) the most common causes of estate litigation in the cases you handled this year? (Probe causes. Look for social/demographic factors.)
6. It has been said that estate litigation is nothing but a battle for money, and that it is not about power or control in families. Do you agree that estate litigation is only a battle for money? Explain.
7. Think for a moment about your five most recent cases. Sociologically speaking, who were the parties contesting the decedents' estates in those five most recent cases? In other words, what was their relationship to the decedent?
8. Would your answer to this question have been different five years ago? Why, or why not? Is it that inheritance or tax codes have changed, or have there been changes in family life/structure that would explain your answer?
9. How about five years from now? Who will be contesting in the year 2000?
10. Can you refer me to any other estate-litigators who might be interested in helping me with this research project?

References

Bove, Jr., A. A. (1993, October). How to break a will. *Worth*, *2*(8): 96–99.

Braus, P. (1994, March). When mom needs help. *American Demographics*, pp. 38–47.

Caseload activity in Surrogates' Courts statewide, 1973, 1983, and 1993. State of New York Unified Court System. Office of Court Administration.

Cherlin, A. (1978). Remarriage as an incomplete institution. *American Journal of Sociology*, *84*, 634–650.

Collins, C., & Frantz, D. (1994, June). Let us prey: Cults have scored with youth, now they're after you. *Modern Maturity*, pp. 23 –30.

Creighton, L. L. (1991, December 16). Silent saviors. *U.S. News & World Report*, pp. 83–88.

Doka, K. J. (1992). The monkey's paw: The role of inheritance in the resolution of grief. *Death Studies*, *16*, 45–58.

Eshleman, J. R. (1991). *The family* (6th ed.). Boston: Allyn & Bacon.

Fabrikant, G., & White, S. (1995, April 30). Noblesse oblige ... with strings. *New York Times*, Sec. 3, p. 1 et seq.

Fellows, M. L., Simon, R. J., & Rau, W. (1978). Public attitudes about distribution at death and intestate succession laws in the United States. *American Bar Foundation Research Journal, 2*, 321-388.

Friedan, B. (1993). *Fountain of age*. New York: Simon & Schuster.

Giving and volunteering in the United States: Findings from a national survey. (1994). *Independent Sector* Washington, D.C.

Gouldner, A. (1960). The norm of reciprocity: A preliminary statement. *American Sociological Review, 25*, 161-179.

Hanks, R., & Sussman, M. B. (1991). *Inheritance contracting: Implications for theory and policy*. Paper presented at annual meetings of National Council on Family Relations.

Kirkland, R. I., Jr. (1986). Should you leave it all to the children?" *Fortune Magazine, 114*, 18-26.

Larsen, D. (1991). Grandparent: Redefining the role. *Modern Maturity*, December 1990/January 1991, pp. 31-38.

Larson, G. (1992, July). Understanding stepfamilies. *American Demographics*, pp. 35-42.

Maglin, N. B., & Schniedewind, N. (Eds.). (1989). *Women and stepfamilies*. Philadelphia: Temple University Press.

Margolick, D. (1993). *Undue influence: The battle for the Johnson & Johnson fortune*. New York: Morrow.

Moller, S. L. (1990). Undue influence and the norm of reciprocity. *Idaho Law Review, 26*, 275-308.

Murawski, J. (1995, March 9). Charities' lawsuit dilemma. *Chronicle of Philanthropy*, pp. 1-7 et seq.

Neuberger & Berman. (1993). Inheritance: The problems and the promise. A survey on attitudes about inheritance. Stamford, CT. The Gediman Research Group.

Rosenfeld, J. P. (1980). *Legacy of aging: Inheritance and disinheritance in social perspective*. Norwood, NJ: ABLEX.

Rosenfeld, J. P. (1991). The heir and the spare: Evasiveness, role-complexity and patterns of inheritance. In J. Blau and N. Goodman (Eds.), *Social roles and social institutions: Essays in honor of Rose Laub Coser* (pp. 71-90). Denver, CO: Westview Press.

Rosenfeld, J. P. (1992a). Step grandparents: New clients, new concerns. *Tax Management, Estates, Gifts and Trusts Journal, 17*, 173-178.

Rosenfeld, J. P. (1992b, July). Old age, new heirs. *American Demographics*, pp. 66-74.

Schoenblum, J. A. (1987). Will contests: An empirical study. *Real Property Probate and Trust Journal, 22*, 608-660.

Sussman, M. B., Cates, J. N., and Smith, D. T. (1970). *The family and inheritance*. New York: Russell Sage Foundation.

Titus, S., Rosenblatt, P., & Anderson, R. (1978). Family conflict over inheritance of property. *Family Coordinator, 28*, 237-246.

Taeuber, C. (1992). *Sixty-five plus in America*. U.S. Bureau of the Census, Current Population Reports, Special Studies, P23-178RV. Washington, DC: U.S. Government Printing Office.

Waitz, R. (1991). *Life with AIDS*. New Brunswick, NJ: Rutgers University Press.

Wolfe, D. B. (1994, March). Targeting the mature mind. *American Demographics*, pp. 32-37.

9

Inheritance and Stratification

STEPHEN J. MCNAMEE AND ROBERT K. MILLER, JR.

The individual chapters of this volume have examined various aspects of estate inheritance from historical, legal, and social perspectives. In this concluding chapter, we will return to a more general discussion of the impact of estate inheritance on stratification outcomes.

We will first discuss the impact of inheritance on stratification outcomes and then review how the major stratification theories have treated the inheritance factor. Next, we will propose a modification of conflict theory that more explicitly takes the inheritance factor into account. We will then summarize the major trends in inheritance patterns and discuss both future areas of research and the policy implications associated with these trends.

Inheritance and Stratification Outcomes

Inheritance has important economic, political, and cultural consequences for individuals and society. As we have observed in Chapter 1, inheritance provides individuals from privileged backgrounds a combination of advantages that includes prestigious cultural capital, economic help at critical junctures in the life course, insulation against downward mobility in the event of personal setbacks, as well as lump-sum estates upon the death of family members. Those who benefit from inheritances in these various forms are

STEPHEN J. MCNAMEE AND ROBERT K. MILLER, JR. • Department of Sociology and Anthropology, University of North Carolina at Wilmington, Wilmington, North Carolina 28403-3297.

Inheritance and Wealth in America, edited by Robert K. Miller, Jr., and Stephen J. McNamee. Plenum Press, New York, 1998.

afforded a higher standard of living and enhanced opportunities to accrue additional wealth. This applies not just to the top 1 percent of Americans, who own an estimated 37.2% of the total available net worth of wealth in America (Wolff, 1995a, p. 67), but in varying degrees to all those from relatively privileged backgrounds. Even minor initial advantages of wealth may be amplified during the life course and over generations. In this way, inheritance produces a cumulative economic advantage, reinforcing and extending existing wealth inequality across generations.

Inheritance is also related to the distribution of power in society. In other words, inheritance not only affects "who gets what" but also "who decides." To the extent that economic resources can be converted into political power, it follows that economic advantages of inheritance should also have political consequences. Political advantages permit those in power to create social arrangements most likely to sustain and expand existing bases of power and privilege, including mechanisms that permit transfer of privilege across generations. In the case of dynastic wealth, economic and political power converge. As modern forms of representative democracy have developed, the political effects of inheritance have become less direct. Although there are some celebrated cases in America of direct political participation by members of familial political dynasties (e.g., Roosevelt, Kennedy, Rockefeller), most political influence in the modern era is exerted through indirect means such as campaign financing, lobbying, and the private funding of policy institutes (Domhoff, 1990; Dye, 1995; Useem, 1984) and philanthropic organizations (Marcus and Hall, 1992). Although there is some movement in and out of these elite policy circles, inertial forces tend largely to sustain sources of influence over time. Inherited wealth thus provides a mechanism for continuity of concentrated political influence.

Ideologically, the challenge to those who inherit great fortunes is to convince those who stand to inherit little or nothing that inheritance itself is right and just. On the one hand, the acquisition of wealth through fraud, theft, or exploitation is widely viewed as illegitimate. On the other hand, wealth acquired by merit, luck, marriage, inheritance, or some combination of these is seen as acceptable. Of these, individual achievement based on merit is viewed as the most acceptable way to acquire wealth. American cultural folklore is replete with stories of rugged individuals of exceptional talent and fierce determination who overcame great obstacles to achieve success.

Other means of acquiring wealth, although tolerated, pose a more difficult challenge of legitimation in a highly competitive and meritocratic culture. While merit hard-liners might insist that individuals "make their own luck" (which, of course, is then not really luck at all), luck is seen by most as simply fortuitous. Indeed, there is something democratic about luck that resonates well with Americans. Luck is random; anyone can be a potential recipient. A lottery winner, for instance, can instantly go from rags to riches and fulfill the American Dream without discriminating against anyone else or personally taking advantage of anyone else in the process.

Acquiring wealth through marriage also poses a potential challenge to the dominant ideology of merit. We suspect that most Americans are not opposed to wealth through marriage as long as the prospect of money is incidental and not the essential "motive" for marriage. As long as the essential criterion of love is present, wealth through marriage may even have an element of meritocracy attached to it; those clever enough, charming enough, or attractive enough to marry beyond their station could be seen as achieving wealth through merit. Anthropological evidence in this regard suggests that in all cultures, women tend to be attracted to men of wealth, power, and status, whereas men tend to be attracted to women of youth and beauty (Fisher, 1992). This type of mobility, then, is somewhat more available to women then men (Chase, 1975). The Cinderella story, although statistically rare, neverthe-less holds great romantic appeal for Americans.

In the case of inheritance, we suspect that the primary means of justifica-tion defines the right of individuals to dispose of their wealth as they choose as a component of larger property rights and combines it with the almost universal desire of parents to do the most they can for their children. In this latter context, the "inclusive fitness-maximizing" theory of inheritance (Ham-ilton, 1964; Smith, Kish, and Crawford, 1987) suggests that there may be a biological imperative for inheritance. According to this theory, beneficiaries are favored according to their relatedness and reproductive value. Apart from any biological imperative, the desire to "protect" sunk costs in child-rearing "investments" may also stimulate parental motivation for attempting to maxi-mize the futures of children. Economic investment in the future of children might also be seen as "insurance" for parents who might depend on adult children for support in later years (Rosenfeld, 1990). Finally, parents might realize vicarious prestige through the successes of their children, which in turn may be seen as validation of their own genetic endowments and/or child-rearing abilities.

Despite these individual-level justifications, inheritance ultimately con-flicts with equality of opportunity at the societal level and may therefore be a source of a certain degree of generalized cognitive dissonance. Although Americans embrace the ideology of merit, their lived experiences tell them that "it takes money to make money" (economic inheritance), "it's not what you know, but who you know" (social capital), "it's just as easy to fall in love with a rich person as a poor one" (marriage), and success is a matter of "being at the right place at the right time" (luck).

Although inconsistent with the dominant ideology of meritocracy and equality of opportunity, inheritance of wealth ironically carries prestige value

196 STEPHEN J. MCNAMEE AND ROBERT K. MILLER, JR.

of its own, particularly if the path of inheritance is of long standing. Studies of the American upper class (Baltzell, 1958, 1964; Domhoff, 1970; Mills, 1956; Warner and Lunt, 1941) have consistently observed sharp prestige differences within the upper class between "old money" and "new money." Old money confers higher status and provides advantages in cultural capital accumulation. In this regard, the justification for wealth resides in the past, with wealth of the longest duration providing the highest social standing. Because inheritance must be justified on nonmerit terms, it is possible in this context to make prestige distinctions along other criteria, including the size, duration, and use (e.g., philanthropy) of estates.

Inheritance and Stratification Theory

For the most part, stratification theory in sociology has ignored or downplayed the inheritance factor (McNamee and Miller, 1989). Functionalist theory has consistently emphasized merit over inheritance as the major mechanism for the distribution of valued resources in modern industrial societies. Emile Durkheim (1964), the father of modern structural functionalism, viewed inheritance as dysfunctional, because it created inequalities unrelated to merit or contribution to society as a whole. Although familial inheritance was prevalent during the agrarian period, Durkheim predicted that as societies became more urbanized and industrialized, property would increasingly be transferred to voluntary and intermediate organizations (e.g., worker organizations, hospitals, and other charitable institutions) rather than to individual heirs. Current research on inheritance (Engler-Bowles and Kart, 1983; Judge, 1995; Rossi and Rossi, 1990; Schwartz, 1996) shows, however, that beyond surviving spouses, there continues to be a strong tendency for children and other immediate family members to be preferred beneficiaries of estates compared to distant relatives, unrelated individuals, or charitable institutions.

Following in the Durkheimian tradition, Davis and Moore (1945) later formalized a functional theory of stratification that emphasized the importance of merit-based rewards. In this theory, merit-based inequality creates a system of incentives that supposedly ensures that the most competent individuals in society will perform the most demanding and critical tasks. The resulting degree of inequality is considered necessary, efficient, and equitable. It is necessary to motivate people to cooperate in joint economic production. It is efficient because it results in an optimum match between the collective tasks that need to get done and the pool of individuals available to perform them. It is equitable because individuals get out of the system what they put into it; that is, individuals are rewarded in proportion to their contribution to society as a whole. Inheritance, however, is not accommodated within this theory. In this version of functionalist theory, inheritance is dysfunctional because it does not encourage individual achievement or contribute to an efficient division of labor in society. In strictly economic terms, inheritance is a form of getting something for nothing. Indeed, in a digressive footnote, Davis and Moore refer to the inherited wealth simply as "functionless ownership."

Although meritocracy contributes to the efficiency of society, Talcott Parsons (1940, 1953, 1970), in his general functional theory, recognized the value of inheritance in sustaining tradition and promoting the solidarity of familial systems. Like Durkheim, Parsons sees that achievement factors are rapidly replacing ascriptive factors in the assignment of statuses in modern society. Parsons notes, however, that this change comes at the expense of both tradition and familial solidarity. Sussman, Cates, and Smith (1970) present a similar functionalist-exchange analysis of inheritance and family systems. They point out that in addition to maintaining continuity and stability of family systems, inheritance further provides a means of social service and reciprocity across generations. In this sense, inheritance is viewed as a reward for demonstrations of familial loyalty, including the caring for aging parents in their declining years.

Marxian and neoconflict theorists have had surprisingly little to say about the inheritance factor. Marx's writings focus on ownership of the means of economic production, rather than inheritance per se. Although Marx and Engels (1948) call for the abolition of estate inheritance in the *Manifesto of the Communist Party* (third principle), they do not directly incorporate inheritance into their overall theory. In a separate analysis of family systems, Engels (1972) addressed the issue more directly. There, he noted that inheritance contributed to both oppressive state structures (designed to uphold property rights of those who stood to inherit property) and to the oppression of women (who generally inherited little or nothing), but a systematic treatment of inheritance was not forthcoming. Neo-Marxian theories have tended to emphasize changes in the social relations of production emergent in advanced capitalist societies, including monopoly capital (Baron and Sweezy, 1966), authority relations (Dahrendorf, 1959), and contradictions of capital accumulation (O'Connor, 1973) but have generally neglected the inheritance factor itself.

Max Weber's (1966) multidimensional theory of stratification could accommodate inheritance but does not directly do so. Weber defines *class* as blocked opportunities for mobility. Inheritance could be seen in this model as an impediment to mobility. Noting the disintegration of tradition and the decline of familial partnerships and estates, Weber instead shifted the focus of his stratification theory away from inheritance to the "capacities" that individuals bring to the market. Class divisions solidify to the extent that opportunities to acquire market capacities are blocked across generations. Implicitly, the ability to acquire market capacities is, in this context, at least partly a function of inheritance. Two contemporary theories organized around Weber's concept of mobility closure lend themselves to accommodating the inheritance factor—Anthony Giddens's (1984) theory of structuration and Frank Parkin's (1979) exclusion and usurpation theory. Giddens, for instance, suggests that market capacities include the ownership of property (upper class), the possession of educational and technical qualifications (middle class), and the possession of manual labor skills (working class). Class divisions are crystallized through the process of "class structuration" to the extent that opportunities to acquire these market capacities are blocked over time, again, presumably, at least partially through the effects of differential inheritance.

Parkin more directly incorporates the inheritance factor in his exclusion-usurpation theory, although he underestimates its effects. He defines exclusion and usurpation as reciprocal modes of mobility closure. *Exclusion* refers to the efforts of privileged groups to monopolize control of resources and access to them; *usurpation* refers to the efforts of excluded groups to acquire access to resources denied them. Exclusion may be based on a number of factors such as property, position, educational credentials, citizenship, race, ethnicity, gender, religion, or any other social division in which one group controls advantages over the other.

Parkin downplays the inheritance factor by suggesting that the ideology of meritocracy has undermined the ability of the capitalist class to reproduce itself. Parkin provides no evidence, however, as to how the ideology of meritocracy in itself has prevented or even curtailed the practice of inheritance. Parkin further suggests that the capitalist class is split among landed, industrial, and financial segments, and can therefore not easily defend against usurpation along so many fronts. This contention, however, overlooks two important trends. First, the overall trend has been toward increasing rather than decreasing market and aggregate concentration of capital (Blumberg, 1975; Fusfeld, 1982; U.S. Senate, 1978). Second, although there are different sectors of capital wealth, wealth holders in mature stages of capital accumulation typically diversify their holdings across these sectors (Avery and Elliehausen, 1986). Diversification of individual holdings reduces the risk of capital accumulation and, indeed, increases rather than decreases the chances that familial concentrations of wealth can be transferred unscathed across generations.

To our knowledge, symbolic interactionists have not directly examined the issue of inheritance. Nevertheless, there is a fairly extensive symbolic interactionist literature on the life cycle and sociology of death, especially as the latter relates to the grieving process (Glaser and Strauss, 1965, 1968;

Sudnow, 1967). Whereas functional theory focuses on the utility of inheritance and conflict theory focuses on the impact of inheritance on class reproduction, a symbolic interactionist treatment on inheritance might focus on the symbolic meanings and emotional significance of inheritance. Bequests of family heirlooms and other items of sentimental value, for instance, might operate as mechanisms that not only represent but also maintain familial attachments and generational identity. This aspect of inheritance, however, has not been systematically examined.

Overall, stratification theory and research have focused mostly on individual occupational attainment and income inequality. Relatively little attention has been paid to wealth inequality and the transfer of assets across generations. Three recent studies present notable exceptions. Using the Survey of Consumer Finances and the Bureau of Census Survey of Income and Program Participation, Oliver and Shapiro (1995) demonstrate the persistence of advantage in asset accumulation across generations. Blacks, in particular, are at a considerable disadvantage in asset accumulation compared to whites. Oliver and Shapiro (p. 86), for instance, report that although the median income of black households in 1988 was 62 percent of whites, the median net worth of black households was only 8 percent of whites. Simply put, occupational and income attainment do not translate into comparable gains in the accumulation of wealth. The issue of wealth and inheritance is also being directly examined as part of a national Health and Retirement Survey sponsored by the Institute on Aging. Preliminary findings from this study included rather extensive analysis of wealth transfers and inheritance patterns published in a special edition of *The Journal of Human Resources* (Burkhauser and Gertler, 1995). The studies included in this edition confirm the extent and significance of wealth transfers across generations, both in the form of bulk estates and *inter vivos* gifts given at critical junctures in the life course. Finally, the Internal Revenue Service has compiled an impressive data set on estate taxation (Rosenfeld and McCubbin, 1989) that formed in part the basis for the analysis of one of the few books published on the topic (Clignet, 1992).

Toward a Theory of Inheritance

Elsewhere (McNamee and Miller, 1989), we proposed an extension of conflict theory that would directly incorporate the inheritance factor. Our original argument adapted the first three tenets of conflict theory, as summarized by Turner and Starnes (1976), and added a fourth tenet that took inheritance into account. Since then, we have come to believe that "scarcity theory," summarized by Sanderson (1995), better explains the *origin* of stratification, and have therefore revised our theory accordingly. Our revised theory may be outlined as follows:

1. Population pressures produce resource scarcity that leads some groups to claim individual ownership of the means of economic production in society.
2. The ensuing struggle for control over resources inevitably results in economic inequality in the form of differential control of economic surplus.
3. To decrease reliance on force and coercion, and concomitantly to increase the portion of economic surplus that can be devoted to securing further wealth, the privileged seek, through establishment of normative-legal systems and the use of ideology, to mitigate the inherent conflicts of interests between themselves and the less privileged.
4. Accumulated surplus is transferred intergenerationally through the process of inheritance, thereby tending to perpetuate existing inequalities across generations.

The first tenet identifies the beginning of structured inequality with the growing scarcity of productive resources generated by population pressure, which in turn leads to conflict over the use and control of productive resources. The second tenet specifies that conflicts, which emerge over the acquisition and control of resources, produce groups of winners and losers, that is, differential control of surplus. The former use their economic advantage of resource ownership and control to intensify production that is expropriated as "economic surplus." The third tenet identifies the process of justification of privilege. It is not enough merely to possess wealth; the few who get the most must convince everyone else that their claim to wealth is legitimate. The greater the wealth disparity, the greater the need for justification. Successful legitimation reduces conflict; unsuccessful or unconvincing claims of legitimation increase the potential for conflict. The fourth tenet specifies the mechanism of transfer of privilege across generations.

Inheritance establishes the process by which existing inequalities are perpetuated. To the extent that inheritance occurs, the class system is reproduced. Unlike caste or slave systems of stratification, class systems of stratification are not reproduced completely. There is some movement in and out of class categories. In this way, inheritance and meritocracy coexist. Both factors operate in determining who gets what and how much. For the most part, however, meritocracy is superimposed on inheritance rather than the other way around. In other words, whatever effects produced by merit or luck or current life circumstances come *after* whatever effects are produced by the advantages (or disadvantages) of initial class placement at birth.

Based on our review of the literature, we are now in a position to offer a

specific set of theoretical propositions regarding inheritance. These propositions are not intended to be exhaustive or conclusive but are offered as an
initial way to frame the issues related to inheritance and as a guide to future
research.

Inter Vivos *Gifts*

- As life expectancy increases, *inter vivos* giving increases.
- The greater the amount of familial wealth, the greater the probability
  of *inter vivos* transfers.
- As forms of wealth become more fungible and easily partible (changing from family firms and farms to financial assets such as stocks,
  bonds, bank deposits, mutual funds shares, insurance contracts and
  the like), intergenerational wealth transfers shift from testamentary to
  inter vivos transfers.
- The greater the differences among earning potential of heirs, the
  greater the probability that *inter vivos* gifts will be divided unequally,
  with larger shares going to those with the least income potential.

Intestate

- The greater the accumulation of wealth, the less likely that individuals
  will die intestate.
- The greater the number of children, the less likely than individuals will
  die intestate.
- As age increases, the probability of individuals dying intestate decreases.
- As education increases, the probability of individuals dying intestate
  decreases.
- There is an inverse relation between a population's acceptance of
  provisions of intestate law and the proportion writing wills.

Family

- Excluding surviving spouses, biological kin are more likely to be
  named as beneficiaries of estates than nonbiological kin.
- As the nearest surviving biological kin become more distantly related,
  the likelihood of extrafamilial bequests increases.
- As the size of the estate increases, the probability of extrafamilial
  bequests increases.
- As family forms become more complex, there is greater probability of
  extrafamilial bequests.

- As the number of children increases, the size of individual estates decreases.
- As the number of children decreases, the probability of extrafamilial bequests increases.
- As the rate of divorce and remarriage increases, the incidence of will contests increases.
- As the incidence of divorce and remarriage increases, there is a greater probability of disinheritance of biological children of first marriages.
- As bequests are made outside the immediate family, the probability of will contests increases.
- There is no relationship between the size of estates and the probability of estate litigation.
- As life expectancy increases, generation-skipping trusts increase.
- The more liquid the form of wealth assets at the time of death, the more equally those assets will be distributed among heirs.
- The greater the differences among earning potential of heirs, the greater the probability that estates will be divided unequally, with larger shares going to those with the least income potential.
- The greater the amount of inheritable wealth, the greater the perceived degree of familial obligation of prospective heirs to prospective testators.

Class

- As socioeconomic status increases, the likelihood of receiving *inter vivos* gifts increases.
- As socioeconomic status increases, the likelihood of receiving bequests increases.
- The greater the extent to which familial wealth is transferred across generations, the more closely existing class divisions of society are reproduced.
- The greater the amount of inheritance received, the greater the wealth and life chances of heirs.
- The larger the amount of inheritance, the greater the ratio of inherited wealth to total familial wealth.
- As forms of wealth become more easily partible, beneficiaries' shares become more equal.
- Bequests made for altruistic purposes are more wealth equalizing than bequests made for the purpose of exchange.
- The greater the extent to which wealth is distributed across generations through inheritance, the more unequal the distribution of power in society.

- As the political power of the economically privileged increases, the proportion of all privately held wealth that is transferred across generations increases.
- As the political power of the economically privileged increases, the costs of transferring wealth across generations decreases.
- The greater the extent to which wealth is distributed across generations through inheritance, the greater the prestige value of the wealth received.

Race and Ethnicity

- The longer the duration of ethnic inequality, the greater the degree of wealth inequality among ethnic groups is sustained through inheritance.
- As ethnic groups become more assimilated, the greater the probability that inheritance patterns will reflect those of the dominant group.
- The higher the socioeconomic status of ethnic groups, the greater the probability that inheritance patterns will reflect those of the dominant group.
- The greater the ethnic residential segregation, the less the probability that inheritance patterns will reflect those of the dominant group.
- The greater the ethnic occupational segregation, the less the probability that inheritance patterns will reflect those of the dominant group.
- The higher the frequency of ethnically exogamic marriages, the greater the probability that inheritance patterns will reflect those of the dominant group.

Gender

- The greater the degree of gender inequality in society as a whole, the greater the probability that male heirs will be favored to female heirs.
- The rights of women to hold, control, inherit, and alienate property is an inverse function of the degree of patriarchy in society.
- The greater the strategic economic importance of women, the more equally inheritances will be divided between male and female heirs.
- As marriage becomes defined as an equal economic partnership, widows will gain priority in inheritance over children.
- Males more often prefer wives to children in naming beneficiaries of wills, whereas females will more often prefer children to husbands in naming beneficiaries of wills.

The State

- As societies modernize, the rights of devise become elaborated and more legally formalized.
- The greater the degree to which the state subsidizes retirements, the less the total amount of wealth transferred at the time of death.
- The greater the value of an estate, the greater the effort expended in avoiding estate taxation.
- The extent of taxation of estates is inversely related to the degree of public acceptance of claims of legitimate bases of ownership of wealth.
- *Inter vivos* transfer rights are more fully protected by the state as components of property rights than are testamentary rights.
- Testamentary rights are more fully protected by the state than inheritance rights.
- The form of intergenerational transfers (*inter vivos* gifts vs. testamentary) is a function of the net tax burden of each, with the greater proportion being transferred in the form that entails the least net tax burden.
- Federal estate taxes have a larger equalizing impact on the distribution of wealth in society as a whole to the extent that wealth is accrued through inheritance rather than through self-accumulation.

Trends and the Future of Inheritance

Colonial America was comprised of mostly family farms and small businesses. Even as late as 1820, 72 percent of the labor force was employed on farms (U.S. Bureau of the Census, 1975). In this context, children learned what occupational skills they would need as adults primarily from their parents. Because children worked and contributed to the family income, they could be considered economic assets, and birthrates were relatively high. If the father died before the mother, property was left to children, and the surviving spouse was given a "life interest" or "maintenance" income. In other words, unless otherwise stipulated in a legal will, property devolved through "blood lines" (Hill, 1995). Small family farms and small businesses could not be easily or continually subdivided and remain sustainable (principle of impartibility). To avoid rapid dissolution of assets, the running of the family business was often passed on to the eldest surviving male child, who either inherited everything (primogeniture) or would buy out remaining shares of the estate from other siblings.

Since then, dramatic changes have occurred that have drastically altered patterns of inheritance. First, the composition of the labor force has changed. Farming has become mechanized and commercialized, leading to the rapid decline of the small family farm; by 1993, less than 3 percent of the labor force was employed in farming occupations (U.S. Bureau of the Census, 1994). With the shift from agricultural production to manufacturing production, displaced farm labor flocked from rural areas to expanding urban factories. By the 1930s, the industrial sector had already begun to decline as total portion of the labor force, while the tertiary service sector began an expansion that continues into the present. Inheritable property is now much less likely to take the tangible form of discrete farms or businesses and is more likely to be partible and fungible. Personal assets such as houses, furniture, cars, and the like are typically sold and the proceeds distributed among heirs. The remaining value of estates more typically takes the form of financial assets such as savings and investments. Because there is no diminution of per unit value in financial assets, equal transfer of assets to multiple heirs is easier.

Second, birthrates in the twentieth century have fallen sharply, from 32.3 per 1000 in the population in 1900 (U.S. Bureau of the Census, 1975) to 15.7 per 1000 in the population in 1993 (U.S. Bureau of the Census, 1995). Holding constant the absolute size of estates, this means that accumulated assets are less subject to subdivision among multiple heirs, allowing for more significant and substantial wealth transfers across generations. It also means that there is potentially less downward mobility within family units, because the size of the shares is larger and there is less chance that a child within the family unit would be excluded from inheritance by gender or birth order.

Third, there has been a recent rapid increase in the educational attainment of the adult population as a whole, from a mean of 8.6 years of school completed in 1940 to 12.7 mean years of education completed in 1991 (U.S. Bureau of the Census, 1994). As Langbein (1991) has argued, for most Americans, education has come to be seen as a form of human capital investment (Becker, 1964; Schultz, 1971) and has largely replaced tangible assets as the primary means by which advantage is passed on between generations. Instead of learning economic skills from parents, formal educational institutions have come to allocate occupational opportunity, sorting children by a combination of merit and nonmerit (class) criteria. Sociologists agree on education's importance in job placement and earnings, but they disagree sharply over the reasons for this. It is because education provides important technical skills, knowledge, and human capital, as the functionalists claim? Is it because it provides docile workers who have accepted capitalist authority relations, as Marxists have argued? Is it because educational credentials have come to provide a convenient device to raise occupational status and a basis of social closure by restricting job access to individuals of certain backgrounds, as Weberian's claim? Or is it some combination of these? Whatever the explanation for the education–earnings connection, the connection itself is clear enough so that parents, anxious to secure their children's future, seek to provide the "best" educational opportunities possible. Because access to educational opportunities is stratified, so is the ability of parents to provide this access (Bowles and Gintis 1976; Collins, 1971, 1979; Squires, 1977). As costs of education increase as credentials inflation continues, and as federal funding for education has declined, the "tracking" of educational outcomes by social class is likely to become even more pronounced.

Fourth, life expectancy in the twentieth century has steadily risen from 47.3 years in 1900 (U.S. Bureau of Census, 1975) to 75.8 by 1990 (U.S. Bureau of Census, 1995). This results in the bulk of estate inheritances being transferred to children at much later stages of the life cycle. If parents live into their late seventies, then "children" are not likely to become recipients of their parents' estates until they themselves are beyond middle age and most typically in their fifties or sixties—too late to have significant impact on occupational careers. This fifty-year cycle of generations combined with the tax advantages of divesting of estates prior to death, has led to an increase in *inter vivos* transfers. In some cases, the new demographic reality has created a situation in which generation-skipping trusts have become more commonplace. These are trusts established by grandparents on behalf of grandchildren. Generation-skipping trusts are more likely to occur if parents are confident that the future of their own children has already been secured. This practice has the potential of the increasing the incidence of dynastic or multigenerational continuity of privilege within families.

Fifth, there has been a dramatic post–World War II increase in the divorce rate, from 2.6 per 1000 in the population in 1950 to 4.6 per 1000 in the population in 1994 (U.S. Bureau of Census, 1995). The increased divorce rate has immensely complicated inheritance patterns. As individuals divorce and remarry, reconstituted or blended families emerge. This dilutes the impact of inheritance (Hao, 1996) and increases the likelihood of will contests as different segments of fragmented families lay claim to inheritable property (Rosenfeld, 1982).

Finally, several post–World War II economic trends also are likely to have dramatic impact on future inheritance practices. The cohort of Americans born before the Depression is very significant in this regard. This cohort, which reached its income earnings peak in the post–World War II period of prosperity, has also received unprecedented government support in the form of New Deal Programs, the GI Bill, mortgage guarantees, and the Great Society Era expansion of benefits to the elderly. Reared in an age of frugality, earning incomes during a period of rapid expansion and prosperity, and having purchased homes that have greatly appreciated in value, this generation is expected to disperse accumulated assets in excess of $10 trillion between 1990 and 2040 (Shapiro, 1994). Assuming that most of these accumulated assets will not be expended in retirement or on medical bills, a substantial portion of these assets will be subject to divestiture through inheritance in the next several decades. How these assests become distributed is likely to have significant impact on succeeding generations.

The rapid "deindustrialization" of the American economy has shifted economic opportunity in America in distinct ways. As industrial production has shut down or shifted overseas, a base of economic stability and avenue of upward social mobility has been cut off for working-class Americans. Secure, high-wage, skilled industrial jobs in the "core" segment of the economy have been replaced by more precarious and less-well-paid employment in the service sector (Bluestone and Harrison, 1982). The service sector itself became split between high-tech jobs requiring more advanced education and the low-wage service people and information-processing segments. The 1980s were dominated by a new political climate favorable to the interests of investors but hostile to those of ordinary wage earners. Large segments of the economy were deregulated, encouraging a frenzy of mergers, buyouts, takeovers, and acquisitions (Stearns and Allan, 1996). During this period, investment income increased while real wage income decreased. The net result of these trends has been a steady bifurcation of the class structure in which the rich have become richer and the poor have become poorer (Braun, 1991; Danziger and Gottschalk, 1995; Frank and Cook, 1995; Wolff, 1995b).

Given other trends previously discussed, if economic resources become more concentrated, this trend is likely to have important consequences for the class structure. Although a portion of the middle class has broken into the ranks of the economically privileged, an even larger part of the working class and underclass have fallen further behind. Under these conditions, the "fault line" between the "haves" and the "have nots" could become sharper and more pronounced, which in turn may create deeper class tensions within society as a whole.

Policy Implications

The role of government in inheritance is both direct and indirect. The direct role of government is taxation—federal estate taxes on the transfer of property at death and state taxes of inheritances. The issue of taxation of estates has been debated at length (Bracewell-Milnes, 1989; Davies and Kuhn, 1991; Chester, 1982; McCaffery, 1994; Ryan, 1994; Thurow, 1976). The crux of the arguments for confiscatory taxation of estates is that the unchecked accumulation of wealth across generations increases social inequality to an unacceptable level. According to this position, inheritance of wealth destroys both the work ethic for heirs and equality of opportunity for the population as a whole. The case in favor of estate taxation argues that the right to inherit is a civil right granted by the state, which has the power to both regulate and tax estates. In this sense, the state may be considered a coheir to claims of private property that have been sanctioned and protected by the state.

The case against estate taxation, on the other hand, posits that confiscatory estate taxes discourage work, savings, and investment while encouraging spending. The argument is that the prospect of such a tax at death discourages the long-term accumulation of capital. An incentive for spending is created if whatever fortune accumulated is, at death, subject to heavy and progressive taxation. According to this viewpoint, incentive to spend and disincentive to save and invest hurt the poor in two ways. First, it robs the economy of significant sums for investment that are necessary to create additional wealth, jobs, and large-scale investment in societal development (supply-side economics). Second, the incentive to spend leads to conspicuous forms of consumption that in turn exacerbate class differences and lead to feelings of relative deprivation among the less fortunate. Advocates of this position tend to view inheritance as a natural rather than civil right, which should not be limited or abridged by the state.

Estate tax is only one way of taxing wealth. Some who oppose tax on estates favor other forms of wealth taxation. Tax on wealth, for instance, can be based on its possession (an assets tax), its use (consumption tax), or its exchange from donor to donee (transfer tax). Such taxes can further be either flat or progressive to varying degrees. Ultimately, the decision to tax wealth in whatever form is political. These decisions are therefore subject to the same factors that affect the outcome of other policy decisions, including differential access to resources and the policy-making process.

Federal and state government could decide to impose confiscatory taxes on estates as a means of generating government revenue or to redistribute wealth through government policy, or both. As estate taxation in the United States is currently constituted, however, the government's role in wealth redistribution is, in practice, already minimal (Johnson and Eller, Chapter 4). Revenues generated by estate taxation are small. Exclusions are generous, and individuals can avoid heavy tax burdens associated with intergenerational transfers through *inter vivos* giving and careful estate planning.

James O'Connor (1973) has argued that government serves two contradictory functions relative to capital. On the one hand, government protects private claims of ownership and seeks to assist individuals in capital accumulation. On the other hand, government also seeks to legitimize the system of capital itself. The legitimation function includes economic regulation in the interest of the long-term sustainability of capital as well as providing buffers against the worst excesses of capital accumulation in the form of various safety-net programs. O'Connor argues that as the state is successful in promoting the accumulation of capital, it creates greater pressures and costs for legitimation. Giving tax breaks to the rich, for instance, allows the rich to accumulate more capital. As the rich accumulate more capital, the gap between the rich and the poor widens, which in turn creates greater need to justify the fairness of the system as a whole. O'Connor argues that these functions of capital are in contradiction to one another and that a "fiscal crisis of the state" results when the state tries to perform both functions simultaneously.

Current state policy with regard to estate taxation, however, may be seen as avoiding this contradiction. Economist Lester Thurow (1976, p. 33), for instance, suggests that "the most obvious purpose of high nominal rates and low effective rates is to use the high nominal rates as a smokescreen to hide the transfer of wealth from generation to generation. The public is led to believe that stiff inheritance taxes exist when they do not in fact exist." On the other hand, political proposals to impose stiff inheritance taxes have met with little public support as exemplified in the 1972 presidential campaign, in which George McGovern proposed sharply increasing federal estate tax on inheritances of over $500,000. The usual explanation for lack of public support of such proposals is the so-called "lottery hypothesis." At an individual level, Americans may embrace the right of testamentary freedom on the grounds that if they were to somehow either come into great inheritance or be in a position to bequeath large sums to future generations, that they would want the freedom to do so, with minimal or no governmental interference. At a systems level, however, it is unclear how much inequality, sustained across generations through inheritance, can be tolerated within the limits of prevailing norms of meritocracy and distributive justice.

Government's role in inheritance practices can also be indirect. Government policy in other arenas can impact on testamentary behavior. To the extent that government can provide for individuals in retirement through non-means-tested programs such as Social Security and Medicare, individuals might be less inclined to "stockpile" resources as a hedge against illness or unexpectedly long periods of retirement (Langbein, 1991). This may encourage greater consumption of wealth prior to death and/or increase the tendency to dispose of wealth prior to death through *inter vivos* gifts. The "aging" of the American population may place increasing pressure on younger generations to provide support of older ones, in essence reversing the direction of intergenerational transfers. On the other hand, if such entitlement programs are cut back or eliminated, then the poor, who have no safety net of accumulated assets, would be the most likely to suffer.

One way to offset the effects of inequality through inheritance is for the state to decommodify critical resources, in essence, providing collective access to essential resources and services regardless of the ability to pay. This strategy reflects the "fair share" policy model advocated by William Ryan (1981). Ryan contrasts "fair share" ideology with the dominant "fair play" ideology. "Fair play" strives to provide unencumbered opportunities for individual success, whereas "fair share" strives to assure the right of equal access to essential resources. Fair share policies, for instance, would provide access to quality health care, housing, and educational opportunities, regardless of the ability to pay. Policy reforms proposed by Oliver and Shapiro (1995) could also be considered a fair share approach. They note that the primary source of existing economic inequality is in financial assets (wealth) rather than earned income. They advocate government policies designed to offset this form of wealth inequality by providing opportunity for asset accumulation to disadvantaged segments of the population. The government, for instance, could provide tax breaks to first home owners, stimulus packages to encourage self-employment and the establishment of small businesses, and state-sponsored educational opportunities. These asset-stimulation policies would be combined with increased taxation of existing wealth holdings in the form of increased capital gains and estate taxation.

When most Americans think of how to go about achieving the fair play goal of equality of opportunity, they think about eliminating sources of discrimination against individuals based on race, gender, sexual orientation, religious beliefs, or any other collective criteria irrelevant to individual educational and occupational achievement. What the fair play ideology overlooks is that even if such discrimination were eliminated, equality of opportunity would not be realized. Genuine equality of opportunity is not possible to the extent that inheritance of wealth constitutes an important nonmerit factor in determining who gets what and how much. Unequal inheritances not only create unequal starting points but also provide further advantages that accumulate over the life course in the forms of differential provisions of cultural capital and receipt of *inter vivos* gifts at crucial junctions of the life course.

In the final analysis, laws of succession to property are formalizations of customs, themselves based upon structures of power and privilege. Government policy on inheritance should be interpreted in this context. Current evidence suggests that American inheritance practices, including the formal-legal role of the state, have a strikingly high level of legitimacy; that is, Americans seem to endorse current inheritance policy that allows wealth to be transmitted across generations relatively undiminished by taxation. At the same time, Americans continue to subscribe to meritocratic ideology, seemingly unaware of the contradiction these beliefs represent. Under these conditions, a combination of *noblesse oblige* among the wealthy and governmental policies that minimize the redistribution of wealth will continue to provide only minimum "fair shares" to those who have the least and who stand to inherit little or nothing. Barring fundamental ideological change, the best practical advice for getting ahead in America remains as it has always been— choose your parents *very* carefully.

References

Avery, R. B., & Elliehausen, G. E. (1986). Financial characteristics of high income families. *Federal Reserve Bulletin, 72*, 163–177.

Baltzell, E. D. (1958). *Philadelphia gentlemen: The making of a national upper class*. New York: Free Press.

Baltzell, E. D. (1964). *The Protestant establishment: Aristocracy and caste in America*. New York: Random House.

Baron, P., & Sweezy, P. (1966). *Monopoly capital*. New York: Monthly Review Press.

Becker, G. (1964). *Human capital*. New York: Columbia University Press.

Bluestone, B., & Harrison, B. (1982). *The deindustrialization of America*. New York: Basic Books.

Blumberg, P. I. (1975). *The megacorporation in American society: The scope of corporate power*. Englewood Cliffs, NJ: Prentice-Hall.

Bowles, S., & Gintis, H. (1976). *Schooling in capitalist America*. New York: Basic Books.

Bracewell-Milnes, B. (1989). *The wealth of giving: Everyone in his inheritance*. London: Institute of Economic Affairs.

Braun, D. (1991). *The rich get richer: The rise of income inequality in the United States and the world*. Chicago: Nelson Hall.

Burkhauser, R. V., & Gertler, P. J. (Eds.). (1995). The health and retirement study: Data quality and early results. *Journal of Human Resources, 30*, S1–S318.

Chase, I. (1975). A comparison of men's and women's intergenerational mobility in the United States. *American Sociological Review, 40*, 483–505.

Chester, R. (1982). *Inheritance, wealth and society*. Bloomington: Indiana University Press.

Clignet, R. (1992). *Death, deeds, and descendants: Inheritance in modern America*. New York: Aldine de Gruyter.

Collins, R. (1971). Functional and conflict theories of educational stratification. *American Sociological Review, 36*, 1002–1019.

Collins, R. (1979). *The credential society*. New York: Academic Press.

Dahrendorf, R. (1959). *Class and class conflict in industrial society*. Stanford, CA: Stanford University Press.

Danziger, S., & Gottschalk, P. (1995). *America unequal*. Cambridge, MA: Harvard University Press.

Davis, J. B., & Kuhn, P. J. (1991). A dynamic model of redistribution, inheritance, and inequality. *Canadian Journal of Economics, 24*, 324–344.

Davis, K., & Moore, W. E. (1945). Some principles of stratification. *American Sociological Review, 10*, 242–249.

Domhoff, G. (1970). *The higher circles*. New York: Random House.

Domhoff, G. (1990). *The power elite and the state: How policy is made in America*. New York: Aldine de Gruyter.

Durkheim, E. (1964). *The division of labor in society*. New York: Free Press.

Dye, T. R. (1995). *Who's running America?: The Clinton years*. Englewood Cliffs, NJ: Prentice-Hall.

Engler-Bowles, C., & Kart, C. S. (1983). Intergenerational relations and testamentary patterns. *Gerontologist, 23*, 167–173.

Engels, F. (1972). *The origins of family, private property and the state*. New York: International Publishers.

Fisher, H. (1992). *Anatomy of love: The natural history of monogamy, adultery, and divorce*. New York: Norton.

Frank, R., & Cook, P. J. (1995). *The winner-take-all society: Why the few at the top get so much more than the rest of us*. New York: Penguin Books.

Fusfeld, D. R. (1982). *Economics: Principles of political economy*. Glenview, IL: Scott, Foresman.

Giddens, A. (1973). *The class structure of the advanced societies*. London: Harper & Row.

Glaser, B., & Strauss, A. (1965). *Awareness of dying*. London: Weidenfeld & Nicolson.

Glaser, B., & Strauss, A. (1968). *A time for dying*. Chicago: Aldine de Gruyter.

Hamilton, W. D. (1964). The genetical evolution of social behaviour. *Journal of Theoretical Biology, 7*, 1–52.

Hao, L. (1996). Family structure, private transfers, and the economic well-being of families with children. *Social Forces, 75*, 269–292.

Hill, G. (1995). Inheritance law in an aging society. *Journal of Aging and Social Policy, 7*, 57–83.

Judge, D. S. (1995). American legacies and the variable life histories of women and men. *Human Nature, 6*, 291–323.

Langbein, J. H. (1991). The inheritance revolution. *The Public Interest, 102*, 15–31.

Marcus, G. M., & Hall, P. (1992). *Lives in trust: The fortunes of dynastic families in late twentieth century America*. Boulder, CO: Westview Press.

Marx, K., & Engels, F. (1948). *Manifesto of the communist party*. New York: International Publishers.

McCaffery, E. (1994). The political liberal case against estate tax. *Philosophy and Public Affairs, 23*, 281–312.

McCubbin, J., & Rosenfeld, J. P. (1989, March). Introducing an IRS data base for estate tax research. *Trusts and Estates*, pp. 62–69.

McNamee, S. J., & Miller, R. K., Jr. (1989). Estate inheritance: A sociological lacuna. *Sociological Inquiry, 38*, 7–29.

Mills, C. W. (1956). *The power elite*. New York: Oxford University Press.

O'Connor, J. (1973). *The fiscal crisis of the state*. New York: St. Martin's Press.

Oliver, M. L., & Shapiro, T. M. (1995). *Black wealth/white wealth: A new perspective on racial inequality*. New York: Routledge.

Parkin, F. (1979). *Marxism and class theory: A bourgeois critique*. New York: Columbia University Press.

Parsons, T. (1940). An analytical approach to the theory of stratification. *American Journal of Sociology, 45*, 841–862.

Parsons, T. (1953). A revised analytic approach to the theory of stratification. In R. Bendix & S. Lipset (Eds.), *Class, status, and power* (pp. 92–128). New York: Free Press.

Parsons, T. (1970). Equality and inequality in modern society or social stratification revisited. *Sociological Inquiry, 40*, 13–72.

Rosenfeld, J. P. (1982). Disinheritance and will contests. *Marriage and Family Review, 5*, 75–86.

Rosenfeld, J. P. (1990, July/August). To heir is human. *Probate and Property*, pp. 21–25.

Rossi, A., & Rossi, P. (1990). *Of human bonding: Parent-child relations across the life course*. New York: Aldine de Gruyter.

Ryan, P. (1994). Inheritance: Symbols and illusions. In A. Glyn & D. Miliband (Eds.), *Paying for inequality* (pp. 181–204). London: IPPR/Rivers Oram Press.

Ryan, W. (1981). *Equality*. New York: Random House.

Sanderson, S. K. (1995). *Macrosociology*. New York: HarperCollins.

Schultz, T. W. (1971). *Investment in human capital*. New York: Free Press.

Schwartz, T. P. (1996). Durkheim's prediction about the declining importance of the family and inheritance: Evidence from the wills of Providence, 1775-1985. *Sociological Quarterly*, *26*, 503-519.

Shapiro, H. D. (1994). The coming inheritance bonanza. *Institutional Investor*, *28*, 143-148.

Smith, M. S., Kish, B. J., & Crawford, C. B. (1987). Inheritance of wealth as human kin investment. *Ethology and Sociobiology*, *8*, 171-182.

Squires, G. (1977). Education, jobs, and inequality: Functional and conflict models of social stratification. *Social Problems*, *24*, 436-450.

Stearns, L. B., & Allan, K. D. (1996). Economic behavior in institutional environments: The corporate merger wave of the 1980s. *American Sociological Review*, *61*, 699-718.

Sudnow, D. (1967). *Passing on: The social organization of dying*. Englewood Cliffs, NJ: Prentice-Hall.

Sussman, M. B., Cates, J., & Smith, D. (1970). *The family and inheritance*. New York: Russell Sage Foundation.

Thurow, L. (1976, April 11). Tax wealth, not income. *New York Times Magazine*, pp. 32-33, 102-107.

Turner, J. H., Starnes, C. E. (1976). *Inequality: Privilege and poverty in America*. Pacific Palisades, CA: Goodyear Press.

U.S. Bureau of the Census. (1975). *Historical statistics, colonial times to 1970*. Washington, DC: U.S. Government Printing Office.

U.S. Bureau of the Census. (1994). *Statistical abstracts of the United States*. Washington, DC: U.S. Government Printing Office.

U.S. Bureau of the Census. (1995). *Statistical abstracts of the United States*. Washington, DC: U.S. Government Printing Office.

U.S. Senate. (1978). *Voting rights in the major corporations*. Washington, DC: U.S. Government Printing Office.

Useem, M. (1984). *The inner circle: Large corporations and the rise of business political activity in the U.S. and U.K.* New York: Oxford University Press.

Warner, W. L., & Lunt, P. S. (1941). *The social life of a modern community*. New Haven, CT: Yale University Press.

Weber, M. (1966). *Economy and society*. Berkeley: University of California Press.

Wolff, E. N. (1995a). *Top heavy: The increasing inequality of wealth in America and what can be done about it*. New York: New Press.

Wolff, E. N. (1995b). The rich get increasingly richer: Latest data on household wealth during the 1980s. In R. E. Ratcliff, M. L. Oliver, & T. M. Shapiro (Eds.), *Research in politics and society* (pp. 33-68). Greenwich, CT: JAI Press.

Index